Health and Care in Neoliberal Times

This book argues that neoliberal changes in health and social care go beyond resource allocations, priority setting and privatisation, and manifest in an invidious erosion of the quality of our social relationships, including relationships between care provider and care recipient.

Critically examining the concept of culture and why shifts in what is considered "acceptable practice" happen, the book explores the conduct of conduct. It draws together what we know about neoliberalism's impact on the economy and public services with research around governmentality and social change. Looking at breakdowns in the quality of care in the NHS and social care across a range of settings it holds that macro influences, such as austerity and marketisation, cannot explain everything and many of the damaging things that go on in care breakdowns occur in micro-interactions between care provider and care recipient. Analysing the interactions between the calculations of political centres, the strength of professional identities, the effectiveness of oversight and supervision and the biographies of protagonists, Neil Small problematises the focus on culture, and culture change, in our response to care failures and examines what a different approach to care might involve.

Exploring the interaction of politics, economics and social change and their impact on health care and the wider welfare state, this is an important contribution for students and researchers in health and social care, sociology, political science and management studies.

Neil Small is Professor Emeritus of Health Research at the University of Bradford, UK and is a Fellow of the Academy of Social Sciences.

Routledge Studies in the Sociology of Health and Illness

For more information about this series, please visit: https://www.routledge.com/Routledge-Studies-in-the-Sociology-of-Health-and-Illness/book-series/RSSHI

Health and Care in
Neoliberal Times

Neil Small

Routledge
Taylor & Francis Group

LONDON AND NEW YORK

First published 2023
by Routledge
4 Park Square, Milton Park, Abingdon, Oxon OX14 4RN

and by Routledge
605 Third Avenue, New York, NY 10158

Routledge is an imprint of the Taylor & Francis Group, an informa business

© 2023 **Neil Small**

British Library Cataloguing-in-Publication Data
A catalogue record for this book is available from the British Library

Library of Congress Cataloging-in-Publication Data
A catalog record has been requested for this book

ISBN: 978-1-032-36514-5 (hbk)
ISBN: 978-1-032-43401-8 (pbk)
ISBN: 978-1-003-33240-4 (ebk)

DOI: 10.4324/9781003332404

Typeset in Goudy
by codeMantra

Contents

1   Introduction

Neoliberalism has been in place for a generation. It alters the parameters and priorities of the state and it promotes the merits of a particular sort of economically successful individual. Living under a system that privileges the market and valorises the pursuit of money is bad for the public's health. It's also bad for healthcare, the values that accompany neoliberalism infiltrate the encounter between care provider and care recipient. Changes go beyond resource allocations, priority setting and privatisation. They are also manifest in an invidious erosion of the quality of our social relationships, including those relationships between care provider and care recipient. Our most vulnerable citizens are those most harmed.

In recent years when institutional failings are brought to light there is a ubiquitous, and rarely problematised, response: a damaged culture and the creation of a new culture have been at the heart of the diagnosis of what went wrong and the prescription for putting things right. Can culture be blamed, and can it be shaped in the way these responses imply? Blaming breakdowns in culture for care failures and promoting culture change as the root to reform diverts focus from discussion of levels of resource and of how priorities are set, and it sidesteps the idea of failure being linked to mistakes by individuals or by organisations. You can't dismiss or discipline a culture.

There is a body of work that interrogates neoliberalism's impact on the economy and on public services. Its focus is on structural change and on social inequality. There is also considerable scholarship looking at governmentality, including the way social change is manifest in a revised relationship between power, expertise and the self. Both approaches to neoliberalism are needed if we are to understand its macro and micro sequelae.

Breakdowns in care

Box 1.1 offers a short description of breakdowns in care at Mid Staffordshire NHS Foundation Trust Hospital, in End-of-Life Care across the NHS and in maternity care in Shrewsbury and Telford Hospital NHS Trust. These are three examples from a series of failures in the NHS and elsewhere that came to public attention between 2012 and 2022. These breakdowns can be explained in part by staff shortages consequent on a sustained period of austerity in NHS funding. Perhaps

DOI: 10.4324/9781003332404-1

Box 1.1 Three health care failures: 2013–22

Failures were not just to do with the resources available or with the structures of care. There were also problems in the personal interactions between care providers and care recipients. In each case, official reports identified a flawed culture of care and argued that cultural change was needed to achieve meaningful reform.

Mid-Staffordshire NHS Foundation Trust

The Francis Report (Francis 2013) revealed that between January 2005 and March 2009 up to 1200 patients were believed to have died prematurely because of poor care at the Mid-Staffordshire NHS Foundation Trust. In addition to these deaths, the report documented activities at this trust that caused the suffering of hundreds of people under its care. Details included cases of patients left crying out for help because they did not get pain relief; of food and drinks being left out of reach of hungry and thirsty immobile patients; of patients being so thirsty they had to drink water from vases; patients left lying in their own faeces; patients given the wrong medication; of receptionists in the Accident and Emergency Department deciding which patients would be treated; of inexperienced doctors in charge of critically ill patients; of nurses who were not trained in the use of vital equipment and of a trust management who ignored patients' complaints.

The Francis report was damming, the NHS had put, "corporate self-interest ahead of patients with failings from the top to the bottom of the system" (Francis 2013). A part of that corporate self-interest was manifest in a preoccupation with meeting performance targets.[1] Francis blamed Mid-Staffordshire's "scandalous decline in standards" on an "insidious negative culture involving a tolerance of poor standards and a disengagement from managerial and leadership responsibilities" (Francis 2010). In addition, there was an ineffective trust board, problem in meeting national access targets and in achieving financial balance goals and the shifts in focus that accompanied seeking Foundation Trust status (Francis 2013).[2] (See Bailey 2012.)

End-of-Life Care and the Liverpool Care Pathway (LCP)

The LCP was a pathway to guide hospitals in end-of-life care provision, it was widely used across the NHS. Informed by concerns from families of dying people that its implementation created serious harm its use was scrutinised in the Neuberger Report (Neuberger et al. 2013, see also Neuberger 2016) and the essence of the criticisms were, in large part, upheld in a report from the Royal College of Physicians (2014). There had been an elevation of the financial interests of the hospital above the needs of dying patients and their families. These troubling assumptions are given more heft by the proximity in time, and similarities in the details of what had been happening in Mid-Staffordshire including what was seen by many as a callous withholding of food and water and a lack of communication with patients and their families.

Shrewsbury and Telford NHS Trust

The preliminary Ockenden Review (2020 see also Ockenden 2019) was on 250 cases from a list of 1862 investigated at this trust. The report revealed concerns about the deaths of hundreds of babies, about abnormally high maternal deaths, about a "deeply worrying lack of kindness and compassion", and it reported a catalogue of incompetence, neglect and cruelty:

- Bereaved families treated with a lack of kindness and respect (including deceased babies being given the wrong name or being referred to as "it").
- Women struggling in labour were mocked as "lazy" and were blamed for babies' deaths.
- Lack of transparency, honesty and communication with families when things went wrong – for example parents being told they were the only ones affected and that lessons would be learnt. There is considerable evidence that lessons were not learnt.
- Many specific clinical failings were highlighted – foetal heartbeats not properly monitored: oxytocin, a drug used to increase the frequency and intensity of contractions, was injudiciously used in cases where babies died or developed serious disabilities.
- Women were not directed towards consultant-led care when risk factors emerged in their pregnancy and many were inappropriately persuaded to attempt a vaginal birth.

things were so bad in Mid Staffordshire because this was a hospital trust where the Francis Inquiry tells us there were three nurses in charge of 40 people on two wards (Francis 2013). But Box 1.1 illustrates that they can also be linked to a shift towards marketisation in health care with a resulting priority to meet financial targets even at the cost of a reduced focus on quality of care. However, these macro influences do not explain everything. Many of the damaging, even cruel, things that went on in care breakdowns occurred in the close interactions between care providers and care recipients. While there may be some cruel people working in care settings it is more likely that there has been a widespread shift in what is considered acceptable practice.

Examining this possibility, and the reasons why shifts might have taken place, requires engaging with debates about governmentality, the conduct of conduct. The calculations of political centres do impact on micro-locales where conduct is shaped, in hospital wards and care homes for example (Rose 1999). That impact is mediated by other factors, including the strength of professional identities, the effectiveness of oversight and supervision and the biographies of protagonists, but over time top-down orthodoxies accumulate considerable social power.

System and lifeworld

Linking a concern with the politics of resource allocation, with the organisational dynamics of service delivery, and with a consideration of changes in our sociality necessitates a complex approach. Bauman describes a process he calls "sociological hermeneutics":

> The meaning of social institutions and collectively pursued patterns of conduct is sought through considering them as members of such sets of strategies as are, in a sense, pre-selected and made realistic (available for choosing and possible to deploy) in given social figurations. In this instance, sociological hermeneutics demands that the continuous and changing aspects of life strategies alike be traced back to the social figurations they serve (in a dialectical process of reciprocal determination) – and forward, to the patterns of daily life in which they find expression.
>
> (Bauman 1992: 10–11)

For Bauman, then, social hermeneutics includes scrutiny of how shifts in the system within which we live enter the private domain, into our personalities and into the everyday choices we make. Some choices are manifestations of the sorts of shared values that we develop over time within our families and communities. Husserl called these understandings part of the "life world", "that barely noticed social, historical and physical context in which all our activities take place, and which we generally take for granted". Within this life world is the impact of our being embodied – we move around and sense things in our bodies and in our physical world without having to "think" about it. This process is called the "proprioception" – the perspective of the self. Husserl says that when I encounter another person, I recognise them implicitly as beings who have "their personal surrounding world, oriented around their living bodies". "Body, life-world, proprioception and social context are all integrated into the texture of worldly being" (Husserl 1970: see Bakewell 2016: 30).

But we can lose our proprioception, or our capacity to appreciate others proprioception. If this happens, we might, for example, see the sick as not quite living bodies, or as just a body and not a self. We lose it if the system world colonises the life world. This colonisation has been linked with modernity by Habermas, and we will look at this in detail in Chapters 2 and 6. I will argue that this colonisation has been accelerated under neoliberalism. I will also approach the same process by considering the sorts of moral position we take towards others. That moral position sometimes draws on the immediate reactions we have – moral gut reactions, things Nagel has called "ordinary morality". These are the sorts of things that give us lines we must not cross (Nagel 2021: 3). How we treat the vulnerable prompts these sorts of moral gut reactions. But they exist in an interaction with consequentialist decision making, a sense that we can make moral decisions by balancing cost and benefit and by considering the route to promote the greatest good for the greatest number, that is by considering the wider consequences of the choices we make.[3] As with the colonisation of the lifeworld by system world concerns proponents of particular political and economic agendas can elevate consequentialist thinking and increase the possibility that an individual's ordinary morality might be overridden. Both system world encroachments on lifeworld domains and the balance between consequentialism and ordinary morality impact on our perceptions of the possible and the desirable in the choices we as individuals make.

Economic man (sic)

Foucault has explored the route between the public world and personal choice, a route shaped by "regimes of truth" that are mobilised by the state to craft the self and to deflect, diminish and defeat oppositional discourses. To respond to this, we should always ask the question, "how do we know what we know?" In order to do this, you have to do two things, first view official statements through a sceptical lens and second seek out dissenting accounts and alternative discourses.[4] But there are cautionary notes to make here. In Chapter 2, I will discuss populism and its attacks on experts – scepticism is not the same as a blanket dismissal of official positions, and not all alternative discourses are welcome.

A whole generation has grown up, been educated, and joined the workforce steeped in a paradoxical idea that, as Foucault puts it, the government sees its role as limiting itself in its imposing on society (the small state idea) but at the same time impacting on society as, "a target for permanent governmental intervention to produce, multiply, and guarantee the freedoms required by economic liberalism" (Foucault 2008). For Foucault, the consequence of this project is the creation of a new man, homo oecconomicus (economic man).[5] In and through this figure neoliberalism has eliminated, "the open question of how to craft the self or what paths to travel in life" (Brown 2015: 41). The self, and one's path in life, is dedicated to being a successful economic man.

At the same time, government is bound by particular forms of knowledge. An evaluation of what can and should be done is shaped by a conception of truth as something verified by the market: "One must govern with economics, one must govern alongside economics, one must govern by listening to the economists" (Foucault 2008: 286). To this effect governments stimulate and steer, they seek to operate through regulatory practice but also through social and cultural milieus (see Lasslett 2015). These milieus allow an ascendancy of "mischievous forces of disorder" which devalue and weaken the fabric of the everyday,[6] the "ordinary" assumptions that shape our understanding of the right thing to do. These ordinary understandings are eroded or ignored when there is not a residual institutional wisdom or practice supporting them (Le Guin 2015).

Foucault is concerned to make it clear that his regimes of truth are not a search for origins, such a search rests on an erroneous essentialism. He offers, as an alternative, a recognition of "accident and succession" (Foucault 1977: 142), and space for power to be contested.

This warning to not search for origins appears to put Foucault at odds with another strong intellectual tradition, the Marxist tradition. Some of that tradition is drawn on by critical theorists, albeit critically, and I will explore the differences between Foucault and Habermas below (and will also take on the rather more challenging task of seeking to reconcile them into one hybrid approach in my concluding chapter). At this point, as I focus on introducing my argument, it will suffice to quote Marx's most well know summary on consciousness and being: "The mode of production of material life[7] conditions the social, political, and intellectual life process in general. It is not the consciousness of men that determines their being, but on the contrary, their social being that determines their consciousness" (Marx 1859). But in 1884 Engels argued that the economic sphere was determinate in the last instance – a position that leaves space to debate the relative autonomy of ideology and politics from economic conditions, to consider the space for manoeuvre and for mobilisation (see Engels 1884).

Changing times

Although a long time in its germination, this book has been written in 2021 and 2022 during the Covid-19 pandemic. The response to Covid-19 prompted considerable extra spending and a much more interventionist state. Changing the role of the state in the provision of health and social care means a shift from neoliberal orthodoxies. But I will argue in Chapter 5 that we can characterise Covid-19 as a neoliberal epidemic. The arrival of an issue of concern in healthcare has the potential to reveal much about the society that now must respond to it. Covid-19 does just that, as did responses to HIV-AIDS in the early years of neoliberalism, and as do all major epidemics/pandemics, Albert Camus in *The Plague* said, "The pestilence is at once blight and revelation" (Camus 1947).[8]

Further, there is already some evidence that any shift from neoliberalism in terms of public spending and the engagement of the state is ending, as the pandemic shifts from the centre of political and public attention.[9] President Biden's Chief medical adviser Anthony Fauci said, in July 2022, that we are probably exiting in the emergency phase of Covid 19, as it becomes another disease in public health to manage among the many that make people ill. At about the same time a poll in the US found that for the first time in two years the majority of Americans didn't see Covid-19 as a major threat (quoted in Sridar 2022). In what follows I will argue that Covid is an interlude, how it was manifest and the pattern of its impacts replicating existing divisions, and that neoliberalism has been paused not superseded. It is a conceit of every age that it is experiencing a time of unprecedented changes and that both the speed and profundity of change make it difficult to understand our own place in the world or intervene in that process of change. (There is even a term for this, chronocentrism.)[10] It is a conceit that risks suspending critical judgment and stifling opposition to established hierarchies.

A cautionary note

Underlying my approach is a hypothesis that something called neoliberalism, active since the early 1980s, has changed structures, priorities, attitudes and behaviour both within society and, in the last three of these areas, in individuals. The attitudes that praise competition in our economic activity and the devaluation of the social, over-time, colonise our everyday encounters and we begin to see relationships as instrumental and worth as economic. The result is an erosion of our social contract and collateral damage to our most vulnerable.

But this hypothesis comes with some serious caveats. First, is neoliberalism sufficiently different from what went before to support the weight I put on it? Perhaps the culprit is one that has been around for longer, are modernity and capitalism more plausible candidates? Or can we look even further back to an approach to reason, an understanding emerging from the Enlightenment that privileged a narrow understanding of science and that then infused our economics and our politics.[11,12]

In her exploration of *The Origins of Totalitarianism* (1951, reprinted 2017) Hannah Arendt explored many different factors including: the destruction of social bonds; the presentation of a powerful story and its colonisation of the individual's mind to further the belief that there was only one way to think; a split between the body and the social such that some people could be cast out from the social, a precursor to being able to treat them inhumanely. Most importantly she was presenting a picture where one would not make the mistake of saying "this happened because that happened" but where you would recognise the many factors that had to come together to create the perfect storm that became totalitarianism. (You also need to be wary not to scratch what E.P. Thompson called "that old sociological itch", the "overanxious tendency to derive from particular evidence generalizations and typologies which are then translated to inappropriate contexts" (Thompson 1976: 387).)

Second, how far can we be confident that changes in society, at this historical juncture and predicated on a shift to neoliberalism, can shape social practices in the intimate encounters that are at the heart of our response to the vulnerable. Perhaps the sorts of changes engendered by neoliberalism don't change these encounters, or even our sociality, much at all because these are separate realms in which we exercise our agency, informed by our ethical judgement. Sociologists use the term "autopoiesis" to describe those situations where certain things remain stable even though change is constantly happening around them (see Thompson 2017: 130).

Third, is the neoliberal ascendancy a transitory phenomenon? Hegemonic constructions come and go, either subsumed by something new or consumed by their own contradictions.[13] Will this one be succeeded (is it being succeeded) by a new populism or by a new progressive alliance and what are the implication of each of these options for the social contract and, specifically for the welfare state?[14] Any conclusions have to be tentative and the evidence for making them based on an emerging picture that scholars and commentators have not had time to reflect on, or to bolster with the wisdom of hindsight. In what follows I draw on contemporary accounts including those in the media – I am engaging with still emerging phenomenon and with the subjective impacts these are having. Contemporary views, even those arrived at quickly, help shape that subjectivity. My choice of sources is, of course, and by necessity in a vast media landscape, selective. Hilary Mantel in her Reith Lecture (27 June 2017 BBC Radio 4) answered a question from the audience on writing history and the historian's art in the context of debates about post-truth society: you must ask, she said,

> Who is telling me this, can I trust them, why are they telling me, why do they want me to believe? … you interrogate your sources of news, your sources of information in that way… you mobilise your intelligence…. all effective narrative depends on selection… if you try to tell the reader everything it means you have not done [your] work … selection is not a grubby or compromised art it's an essential part of making sense of a narrative for the reader….If someone did not seize the authority to make a selection there would be no history, there would be no knowledge. There would only be information.

A note on style

The cast of authors I accumulate in what follows are exploring difficult issues (sometimes in difficult ways), and they often do not agree with each other. Meanings here are often elusive and are contested, but this resonates with my understanding of the link between policy, structure change, professional practice and personal subjectivity – those meanings and what links them are just at the edge of our grasp. I feel a little presumptuous in doing so but I would adhere to Merleau-Ponty's characterisation that, "The philosopher is marked by the distinguishing trait that he possesses *inseparably* the taste for evidence and the feeling for ambiguity" (1945) A constant movement is required between these two – a kind of rocking motion "which leads back without ceasing from knowledge to ignorance, from ignorance to knowledge" (Bakewell 2016: 241).[15,16]

Derrida, never knowingly easy, is in this matter succinct, "If life were simple word would have got around" (see Salmon 2020). He borrows from Levi-Strauss to characterise what he does in his writing:

> The *bricoleur*, says Levi-Strauss, is someone who uses 'the means at hand, ' that is, the instruments he finds at his disposition around him, those which are already there, which had not been especially conceived with an eye to the operation for which they are to be used and to which one tries by trial and error to adapt them, not hesitating to change them whenever it appears

necessary, or to try several of them at once, even if their form and their origin are heterogenous.

(Derrida 1966)

My style then is to engage with facts and ideas in a way that does not seek to separate them. In a much-cited "Letter to the New Left" (published in 1960) C. Wright Mills opposed those people who refuse,

> to relate isolated facts and fragmentary comment with the changing institutions of society [this] makes it impossible to understand the structural realities which these facts might reveal: the longer-run trends of which they might be tokens. In brief, fact and idea are isolated, so the real questions are not even raised, analysis of the meanings of fact not even begun.
> (Wright Mills 1960).[17]

Separating facts and ideas leads to a situation were, "reasoning collapses into reasonableness". Mine is a reasoned argument but not, I hope, a bloodless reasonable one, I'm clear there are wrongs to be called into account and to be put right. I'm sure we can combine facts and ideas in such a way as to interrogate why things happen and what we can do to put them right. Another leading sociologist, Howard Becker, would have us ask those who study social problems, "Whose side are we on?" (1967).

> We take sides as our personal and political commitments dictate, use our theoretical and technical resources to avoid the distortions that might introduce into our work, limit our conclusions carefully, recognise the hierarchy of credibility for what it is, and field as best we can the accusations and doubts that will surely be our fate.
> (247)

Sartre thought there was a connection between description and liberation – a person who can exactly describe what they experience can also exert some control over these events. For him, this was the connection between writing and freedom. He said that if you were fence sitting because you feared making an error then you are definitely making one (see Bakewell 2016: 259).[18]

Chapter summaries

This chapter has set the scene for what follows. Since the early 1980s, we have been living with a dominant ideology of neoliberalism. It tells us of the imperative for markets and stresses a different kind of relationship between state and individual. Neoliberalism has impacted on the structures and scope of the welfare state and of the NHS. A generation of workers in the UK have only known neoliberalism, how might its attitudes about individualism and concomitantly about the social contract have impacted on the way they undertake their jobs?

Part I – Underlying ideas

Chapter 2

What is new about neoliberalism? How different is it from liberalism before the "neo"? Is neoliberalism being superseded by populism?

Part II – The impacts of neoliberalism

Chapter 3

What new thinking in economics is associated with neoliberalism? This chapter looks at markets and at privatisation, and considers how the pursuit of profits changes priorities and attitudes.

Chapter 4

In this chapter changes in the nature of the professions that contribute to the NHS and changes in the organisations they work within are considered. Are these neoliberal changes and can they be linked to the promotion of new priorities?

Chapter 5

How can a political and economic philosophy make someone sick? This chapter explores factors that impact on population health and also at specific conditions that can be seen as "neoliberal epidemics".

Chapter 6

How far can neoliberalism be linked with peoples' attitudes and actions. How might key aspects of our sociality and our subjectivity be changed.

Part III – Culture as diagnosis and as prescription

Chapter 7

What is culture? This ubiquitous word is used without consideration of the complexities of the term and without critique as to its appropriateness. This chapter examines the myriad ways culture has been defined and then considers examples of where culture change has been attempted in the NHS.

Chapter 8

A series of concepts that are critical to care provision, that infuse practice and that can be seen as components of the broader culture in which care is enacted are considered. These concepts include compassion, suffering, dignity and trust. While these concepts are lifeworld concerns, over time, they can be shaped by the imperatives of the political and economic system.

Part IV – Conclusions

Chapter 9

Is our capacity to be sensitive to the needs of others or our indifference (at best) and our neglect and cruelty (at worst) the sort of thing that we can link with changes in social structures and intellectual beliefs? Is neoliberalism the culprit and is reforming culture the cure? Can we improve care of the vulnerable without a change in underlying systems of belief?

Notes

1 A specific example of this was provided by another hospital, Colchester General, where staff were pressurised by their managers to change data about waiting times for cancer patients to meet targets. Bernard Jenkins MP captured the significance of this in illuminating the underlying clash between a particular approach to NHS management and what the NHS is for: "The whole point about the leadership in our public services is that it can't be just about targets….We mustn't replace values with targets, targets are not values. Targets do not tell you what is the right thing to do" (BBC Radio 4 Today Programme 6 Nov 2013).

2 The elevation of financial and organisational status needs is linked with neoliberalism throughout this work – but they also link with an argument that short term sacrifice is needed to cement long-term progress, it might be argued that getting the finance right and taking some time to restructure the hospital in ways that better equip it to compete in the health marketplace will be in the long-term interests of patients. But, most starkly in end-of-life care, "in the long-term we are all dead" and by promoting a utilitarian position we are infringing on the Kantian imperative not to treat people as means in pursuit of ends external to them (explored elsewhere in this work).

3 This is a position we generally identify as utilitarianism.

4 An excellent example of someone doing this is Phil Scraton's work *Hillsborough: The Truth* (on the deaths of 96 – now 97 – Liverpool football supporters at Hillsborough football ground in 1989) (Scraton, 2016). In Chapter 9, I will look at Foucault's position on the normative – he is not trying to tell us what to think and is not making judgements on what are welcome alternative discourses.

5 Wendy Brown examines the gender assumptions of the term homo oeconomicus (Brown 2015: 99–107) – a necessary addition to the debate especially in the context of a large female workforce in health and social care and the extent of unrecognised care in the domestic sphere. She presents femina domestica even as she underlines the danger of a terminology that marginalised women to "occupy their old place as unacknowledged props and supplements to masculinist liberal subjects" (Brown 2015: 105).

6 These forces of disorder manifest across history and are explored in, amongst other things, the visual arts: Goya's 1799 engraving "The Sleep of Reason Produces Monsters", capturing a febrile time in Spain between the French Revolution and Napoleon's invasion in 1808 (Le Guin 2015). In a speech to constituents in 1922 Winston Churchill said,

> What a disappointment the twentieth century has been. How terrible and melancholy is the long series of disastrous events, which have darkened its first twenty years. We have seen in every country a dissolution, a weakening of bonds, a challenge to those principles, a decay of faith, an abridgement of hope, on which the structure and ultimate existence of civilised society depends.
>
> (quoted in Davis 2012: 454)

7 Mode of production is the constitutive characteristic of a society or a social formulation based on the socio-economic system predominate within it, e.g. capitalism, or neoliberalism. Mode of production is defined in terms of the interaction of relations and forces of production – the system of ownership of the means of production. This forms the foundation (base) of all social systems and social, economic, ideological, political relations are derived from this.

8 Snowden's (2020) book on epidemics from the Black Death to the present argues that epidemic disease has shaped nations and civilisations as starkly as has economics, politics or war. The history of epidemics, across that time frame, also reveals the shortcomings of leaders in responding to them.

9 The pandemic was replaced as the centre of public attention in 2022 by concerns about price rises, particularly in energy and by the twin concerns of inflation and the possibilities of recession. UK Government responses drew on established neoliberal tenets, the chance for change – if ever it existed – rapidly disappearing from the stage.

10 This sort of perception is easily found if one looks at, say, the early 1600s, or the years around the French Revolution, or the advent of the twentieth century. Many people identify a contemporary "cyber/information age" as just such a historical moment. But such a conceit mistakes a prevalent confusion, Manuel Castells (2009), who knows a great deal about all things cyber, said we are living in a state of "informed bewilderment" (and many of us would delete the word informed in describing our own position), and that it is easy to mistake this for profundity or even historical significance. We may have unprecedented access to digital data even if we are unsure about what to do with it, and it's certainly impressive that from the phone in our pocket we can shop from around the world or watch the latest movie, but is this sort of change the equal of say the first 50 years of the twentieth century – just by way of example: in the UK life expectancy increased by six months in each of the first 25 years of the century and three months for each of the next 25; maternal and infant mortality dropped to the extent that a mother could safely anticipate that she would survive the birth, and so would her baby; there was widespread urbanisation building on the industrialisation that had begun in the previous century; two World Wars, the Russian Revolution, the loss of Empire, the birth of the Welfare State…. Social geographer Danny Dorling convincingly argues that the rate of change across the world is slowing down in his succinctly titled book *Slow Down* (Dorling 2020).

11 Einstein provides rich insights into the shortcomings of a narrow approach to the scientific method: he talks of the importance of intuition, the free creativity of the mind, "intuition, the feeling about how the universe should be is more important than the results of any given experiment". "One arrives at a concept after free association, dreaming, wondering. You know you are right and you wait confidently for experiment to bear you out" (quotes from Bernstein 1973). Bernstein also quotes Keynes on Newton – "The proofs, for what they are worth, were…dressed up afterwards – they were not the instrument of discovery" (in Bernstein 1973: 138). Einstein (and perhaps even Newton) seem closer to the Romantics than to our "certain about everything" legislators. Wordsworth for example, warns against our search for certainties bound up in reason (and in our science). "Science appears but what in truth she is/ Not as our glory and our absolute boast, / But as a succedaneum and a prop/ To our infirmity". It is a "false secondary power by which / In weakness we create distinctions, then/ Deem that our puny boundaries are things/ Which we perceive, and not which we have made" (Wordsworth 1805 Book II from line 219). I will return to consider certainty and doubt in Chapter 9.

12 But we do need to appreciate that the Enlightenment was not a monolith, there was both a mainstream and a radical enlightenment – the Enlightenment of Locke, Hume and Kant with its respect for order and a radical enlightenment, Spinoza and Diderot for example, who were uncompromising in the defence of equality even when this challenged powerful core interests, for example of those profiting from racism and colonialism – theirs are the sorts of critique that Hobsbawn could point to when he said of the Enlightenment, "All progressive rationalist and humanist ideologies are implicit in it and indeed come out of it" (see Israel 2011).

13 Marx and the historical dialectic or Vico and the turning wheel of history offer explanations about which I will elaborate later (see Berlin 1960 on Vico). The different ways the term "revolution" is used is relevant her, historically in England revolution was seen as the turning of a circle, only in a more modern manifestation is it seen as a break or a rupture.

14 The old progressive alliance, the pre-welfare state one, was between the Liberal and the Labour Parties (personified in the varied contribution to the establishment of the

Welfare State and NHS by Beverage and Bevan). But now a new progressive alliance may be more likely to emerge from bringing together labour with a range of issue-based groups; women's movement, anti-racist alliances, green, environmental groups, anti-capitalist, local issue based and so on. One theoretical implication is that neoliberalism is not best understood as the ill-conceived child of postmodernism (something I will consider in Chapter 2), rather that postmodern politics may offer a route towards a new social contract (see my Concluding chapter).

15 The psychologist Steven Pinker describes his work in exploring war and peace across history as theoretically eclectic but based in data. He advises; be humble, be surprised and keep your eye on the prize (see Pinker 2012). Or, more bluntly, you may hope that, as economist Amartya Sen does, that it's better to be vaguely right than precisely wrong (Sen 1987).

16 Another possibility is offered by Keates "negative capability"; here you trust to plunge, without irritability or insistence, into the dark, even when you are not sure you will find a way out at all.

17 In a book about scientific ideas, specifically in physics, Close described how things we don't understand have been quarantined within the discipline and theories have been developed out of the things we do know, without any reference to those missing areas (Close 2017). Fourth-century BC Chinese Philosopher Zhuang Zhou said, "To learn without thinking is labour in vain, to think without learning is desolation".

18 Bakewell also cites Iris Murdoch's encouragement to writers to return to the real writers' task which is to explore how we can be free and behave well in a complicated world amidst the rich density of life (Bakewell 2016: 291).

References

Arendt, H. 1951. (reprinted 2017) *The Origins of Totalitarianism*. London, Penguin Books.

Bailey, J. 2012. *From Ward to Whitehall*. Stafford, Cure the NHS.

Bakewell, S. 2016. *At the Existentialist Café*. New York, Other Press.

Bauman, Z. 1992. *Mortality, Immortality and Other Life Strategies*. Cambridge, Polity Press.

Becker, H.S. 1967. Whose side are we on? *Social Problems*, 14(3), Winter, 239–247.

Berlin, I. 1960. The philosophical ideas of Giambattista Vico. In, Acton, H. (Ed) *Art and Ideas in Eighteenth-Century Italy*. Rome, Edizioni Di Storia E Letterature, 156–244.

Bernstein, J. 1973. *Einstein*. London, Fontana.

Brown, W. 2015. *Undoing the Demos: Neoliberalism's Stealth Revolution*. Brooklyn, NY, Zone Books.

Camus, A. 1947. *The Plague*. London, Hamish Hamilton.

Castells, M. 2009. (2nd Ed) *The Rise of the Network Society*. Chichester, West Sussex, Wiley-Blackwell.

Close, F. 2017. *Theories of Everything*. London, Profile Books.

Davis, W. 2012. *Into the Silence*. London, Vintage.

Derrida, J. 1966. Structure, Sign and Play in the Discourse of the Human Sciences (lecture) published in Derrida, J. 1980. *Writing and Difference*. Chicago, IL, University of Chicago Press.

Dorling, D. (with McClure, K.) 2020. *Slowdown: The End of the Great Acceleration and Why It's Good for the Planet, the Economy and our Lives*. New Haven, CT and London, Yale University Press.

Engels, F. 2010 [1884]. *The Origin of the Family, Private Property and the State*. London, Penguin Classics.

Foucault, M. 1977. *Discipline and Punish: The Birth of the Prison*. London, Allan Lane, Penguin Press.

Foucault, M. 2008. *The Birth of Biopolitics: Lectures at the College de France, 1978–1979*. New York, Palgrave Macmillan.

Francis, R. (chair) 2010. Independent Inquiry into Care Provided by Mid Staffordshire NHS Foundation Trust: January 2005 – March 2009: Volume 1. The Stationary Office.

Francis, R. (chair) 2013. *Report of the Mid Staffordshire NHS Foundation Trust Public Inquiry*. London, The Stationary Office. HC 898-111.

Husserl, E. 1970. *The Crisis of the European Sciences and Transcendental Phenomenology*. Ed Biemel, W.; tr, Carr, D., Evanston, IL, Northwestern University Press.

Israel, J. 2011. *A Revolution of the Mind: Radical Enlightenment and the Intellectual Origins of Modern Democracy*. Princeton, NJ, Princeton University Press.

Lasslett, K. 2015. The state at the heart of capitalism: Marxist theory and Foucault's lectures on governmentality. *Critical Sociology*, 41(4–5), 641–658.

Le Guin, U. 2015. "The sleep of reason produces Monsters" (review of Salman Rushdie's book "Two Years, Eight Months and Twenty Eight Days"). *The Guardian*, 5 Sept 2015.

Mantel, H. 2017. *Reith Lecture*, 27 June, BBC Radio 4.

Marx, K. 1859. *Preface to a Contribution to the Critique of Political Economy*. In, Marx, K., Engels, F. (Eds) Selected Works 1968. Lawrence and Wishart, 181–185.

Nagel, T. 2021. Types of Intuition. *London Review of Books*, 3 June, 3–8.

Neuberger, J.R.B. 2016. The Liverpool care pathway: What went right and what went wrong. *British Journal of Hospital Medicine*, 77, 172–174.

Neuberger, J., Aaronovitch, D., Hameed, K., Bonser, T., Harries, R., Charlesworth-Smith, D., Jackson, E., Cox, D., Waller, S. 2013. *More Care, Less Pathway: A Review of the Liverpool Care Pathway*. London, Independent Review of the Liverpool Care Pathway.

Ockenden, D. 2019. The Ockenden Review. http://www.donnaockenden.com/the-ockenden-review-sath

Ockenden Review. 2020. *Emerging Findings and Recommendations from the Independent Review of Maternity Services at Shrewsbury and Telford Hospital NHS Trust*, House of Commons, HC1081.

Pinker, S. 2012. *The Better Angels of Our Nature: A History of Violence and Humanity*. London, Penguin.

Rose, N. 1999. (2nd Ed). *Governing the Soul: The Shaping of the Private Self*. London, Free Association.

Royal College of Physicians. 2014. *National Care of the Dying Audit for Hospitals*. England, London, RCP.

Salmon, P. 2020. *An Event Perhaps. A Biography of Jacques Derrida*. Verso.

Scraton, P. 2016. *Hillsborough. The Truth*. Edinburgh and London, Mainstream Publishing.

Sen, A. 1987. *The Standard of Living: The Tanner Lectures*. Clare Hall, Cambridge, Cambridge University Press.

Snowden, F. 2020. *Epidemics and Society: From the Black Death to the Present*. New Haven and London, Yale University Press.

Thompson, E.P. 1976. On history, sociology and historical relevance. *British Journal of Sociology*, 27(3), 387–402.

Thompson, N. 2017. Existentialism. In, Thompson, N., Cox, G.R. (Eds) *Handbook of the Sociology of Death, Grief and Bereavement*. London, Routledge, 128–140.

Wordsworth, W. 1805 [1995]. *The Prelude*. London, Penguin.

Wright Mills, C. 1960. Letter to the new left. *New Left Review* I/5, September–October.

Part I
Underlying ideas

2 The nature of change

Introduction

In the UK, the election of Margaret Thatcher's Conservative government in 1979 led to an ascendance of an economic and political approach then described as "monetarism", "free market economics" or a "social market economy" (Gamble 1979). The impetus for the spread of these ideas was greatly added to by the election of Ronald Reagan as US President in 1981. Indeed, Reagans' pronouncement in his 1981 inaugural address that, "Government is not the solution to our problem, government is the problem" offered a rhetorical clarion call for the rolling back of the state that followed on both sides of the Atlantic (Sassoon 2006). This merging of free market economics and, not just suspicion, hostility to state activity constituted the kernel of the project now being embarked on, somewhat ironically at the behest of these two new governments (see Wood 2019). This was the neoliberal project.

The latter part of the twentieth century and the early years of the twenty-first century have been the neoliberal years across a large part of the West.[1] Collins (1998) identifies generational periods of around 35 years as crucial in the history of thought, it's a period that approximates to an individual's creative work and, he argues, "a more or less minimal unit for structural change in an intellectual attention span" (Collins 1998: xix). The idea of "generations" is also prominent in popular discourse, we conceptualise the relationship between people and the passage of historical time in this way – the "War-Generation", the "baby-boomers", the "Millennials".[2] We should also identify a neoliberal generation and this book offers a summation of a key aspect of this time; the way neoliberalism is manifest in health and care, including its impact on the NHS.

The neoliberal generation

The idea shaping this chapter and, indeed, my overall argument, is that neoliberalism has set in train a distinct shift in the relationship between the individual and the state. That shift, while having some antecedents, began in the Thatcher years. A summary by novelist Kazuo Ishiguro (2016) is more succinct than many have managed.

DOI: 10.4324/9781003332404-3

The years between 1981 to 1985 were years of crucial, often fractious and bitter transition in Britain. The governments of Margaret Thatcher had brought an end to the post-war political consensus about the welfare state and the desirability of a "mixed" economy (in which key assets and industries are owned publicly as well as privately). There was an overt and strident programme to transform the country from one based on manufacturing and heavy industries, with large, organised workforces, into a predominantly service-based economy with a fragmented, flexible, non-unionised labour pool. It was the era of the miners' strike, the Wapping dispute, CND marches, the Falklands war, IRA terrorism, an economic theory – "monetarism" – that characterised deep cuts to public services as the necessary medicine to heal a sick economy.

(Ishiguro 2016)

Playwright David Edgar explores, autobiographically, the same period. He tells how his life divides into two parts, up to the end of the 1970s both political parties were trying to improve and enhance a post-war consensus that had developed the welfare state and the NHS. From the Thatcher years that consensus breaks, now one party is concerned to dismantle the idea of collective welfare provision and any dispute within that party is about how to do this and how fast it should be done (Edgar 2017).

The break in consensus can lead to a separation of cultural traditions from contemporary practices. This separation can leave people adrift as they seek to negotiate the expectations they have of others, and the ways they believe they should act themselves, without the familiar public signposts they could use to navigate by. Without noticing, and certainly without actively consenting, a new assumed normative arises[3] and, even though this new way of being can be significantly different to the ways it is replacing, its ascendancy is a stealthy unmarked one. John Berger's sense of setting out on a journey and, when you arrive at your destination, finding it is different from what you anticipated, captures this paradox:

Every day people follow signs pointing to some place which is not their home but a chosen destination. Road signs, airport embarkment signs, terminal signs. Some are making their journey for pleasure, others on business, many out of loss or despair. On arrival they come to realize they are not in the place indicated by the signs they followed. Where they now find themselves has the correct latitude, longitude, local time, currency, yet it does not have the specific gravity of the destination they chose.

(Berger 2007: 113–114)

Before neoliberalism all was not well

In 1920, R H Tawney's book *The Acquisitive Society* offered a critique of what he saw as profits before people politics. There was a retreat of ethics from economics (or economists from ethics) and the ethics being left behind were ones that had preserved communities and limited exploitation by affirming a shared and essential humanity. But materialism, which he was attacking, sees all aspects of life subjected to economics – humans become just tools of accountancy rather than the ends of ethical consideration and social duties are subsumed by "individual rights".

A hundred years later, Sacks (2020) identifies a change in our moral sense and in our sense of fellow feeling as emanating from the 1960s. He describes how a moral sense that makes you want to work to better the lives of others has been starved of oxygen for a long time. A preoccupation with "me" has replaced an idea of, "we the people" in what it means to be British. That shift, he argues, emerged in three waves: a social revolution in the 1960s that turned morality into "whatever works for you"[4]; a greed culture in the 1980s whose promotion of self-interest took shape under the umbrella of Reaganomics and Thatcherism; and a degradation of "the public square" engendered by a rise of social media with the disassociation from the personal and a coarsening of public discourse that has accompanied it. He sees social media as prompting a shame culture, something that replaces a more traditional Christian guilt culture. The latter makes possible a search for forgiveness, the former does not. There is no forgiveness in a shame culture and the result is that you do not face up to your own wrongdoings, you just keep denying them[5] (Sacks 2020). I will look at the theories of what has been called "moral decline sociology" in Chapter 6, this will expand on Sacks' critique of the 1960s and the impact of a "greed is good" mentality. I will also consider the impact of social media on the cultural glue of a shared civility (something Elias termed *The Civilising Process* (2000)) and on its facilitation of moral distancing via the capacity to re-cast the individual as an atomised abstraction (an over reliance on figures and protocols are other examples of ways this is done).[6] Finally, the reluctance to deny wrongdoing, part of shame culture, is explored in considering responses to revelations of things having gone wrong. The idea that one "did the right thing" and resigned when serious faults were identified that were your responsibility has almost disappeared, if a person resigns now it is characteristically after a period of denial followed by outside pressure that proves too uncomfortable to resist.

In the US, Putnam and Romney (2020) think the changes I have linked with the election of Ronald Reagan began earlier and that the Reagan reforms were a "lagging indicator" – a rise in income inequality and a decline in civic engagement preceded his election. They use an I-We-I curve to capture social mood, the "We" was already in decline as early as the 1960s. Individual fulfilment either through stripping away controls or pursuing personal liberation (the right and left agendas) comes at a cost in terms of one's social capital. They argue that one can see common patterns of change in the US over a 125-year period, putting that change into a graph produces a "hump-like" pattern, a growing swell over half a century of greater social trust, equality, bi-partisanship and civic "do-gooding" peaking around the 1960s followed by a marked and steady decline. It is an analysis that might find favour with Sachs but appears at odds with subsequent "arc of history" optimism expressed by President Obama.[7] Putnam's focus on social capital and civic engagement offers a different way of understanding the shifts that are captured by a narrower focus on economic policy. I will return to this when I consider trust in Chapter 8.

I am going to be saying a lot in what follows about ethics and morality. To be clear I am identifying ethics as being concerned with all the values that are instantiated in a person's life and morality as a narrower domain of moral obligation; what is right and wrong, what is forbidden and what is permitted. But I am persuaded by Bauman's characterisation of the way ethics encroaches on morality via the encouragement of normative regulation, and that its encroachment is achieved by "power-assisted heteronomy" (Bauman 1993: 3). This puts the relationship between morality and ethics into the same analytic domain as my exploration of the colonisation of the lifeworld by the system (see Chapter 6).

As well as these changes in our moral sense there is also a debate about the amount of state intervention in the economy. This debate considers absolute levels of funding and the patterns of that funding's allocation. Much of this has been a debate about the pre-neoliberalism policies of Keynesianism. Before Keynes, the idea was that governments set the legal framework, controlled the currency and allowed economic agents to pursue their goals within this framework. Keynes argued that the state could, and should, manipulate the level of aggregate demand so that economic activity was stimulated, and prosperity ensued. The aim was to make, "great art and beautiful evenings available to all citizens – a democratisation of fine living" (Keynes 1936). It was not to fetishize money, money is something illusory – a fiction, a floating signifier. In contrast neoliberalism set markets free, unleashed speculation, and fostered a globalisation that treats people as "disembodied profit maximisers" (see Carter 2020). In this scenario, the economy is controlled by a nomadic elite who determine the life of the settled majority with government simply "keeping the roads free for nomadic traffic and phasing out the remaining check-points" (Bauman 2000).

The achievements of individuals, including their financial rewards, were always dependent on the collective operation of society. You may need to reward people to fully mobilise their talents but any reward above that needed to bring them into play in the economy is tantamount to a sort of rent,[8] a figure that a person claims because of their advantageous position in society rather than because of any contribution they are making to that society, or to the economy. This attitude to reward was the justification for progressive taxation by which society would reclaim what society had created from those who wished to unduly profit.

But capital never sleeps, it seeks to keep remaking the world in its own image, and Keynesianism and progressive taxation were attacked by those who insisted that protection of capital is the overriding long-term goal of policy making. This position, argued by monetarists and operationalised by neoliberals, assumes that "anyone can make it" and that we should live amidst "free competition".[9] So those vulnerable and helpless in the face of economic forces are ignored – their "failures" are depicted as their fault, and this sleight of hand allows the exploiter to sidestep any sense of shame that they are benefiting whilst others suffer.

The NHS before neoliberalism

To criticise the underpinnings of the NHS is to address a shibboleth in post-war society. The easy resort to its being "the best thing about the UK" or the UK's "example to the rest of the world" is the normal default position. If the NHS is criticised, it's in the details of specific actions, not the founding basis. Occasionally, if the parochial lens we consider the NHS through slips, we see health systems, organised in different ways in other countries doing better than the NHS in terms of health outcomes, less inequality and higher life expectancy. "But the welfare state [including the NHS] was never the historical monolith that nostalgic social democrats boast of or that neoliberals caricature, it was always a hybrid and precarious achievement" (Vernon 2007: 15–16) (see Box 2.1). A focus on suffering and an absence of routes for public (and patient) input means it is a service responding to social change and not intervening "upstream" to prevent the Beveridge evils ever occurring.[10]

The NHS's focus has been on "output legitimacy", that is on the visible services it provides, and not "input legitimacy" which would look to how it is governed. Input legitimacy gives any service "ballast" to survive storms and setbacks.[11] Without it, long waiting lists for hospital care, challenges in getting a timely appointment with a GP, suffering not being alleviated - indeed being exacerbated by shortcomings in the system and in the care provided, and other output failings damage faith in the NHS. Damaging faith can prompt shifts to private services or it can lead disadvantaged groups to feel even more disadvantaged. The absence of input legitimacy leaves the NHS more vulnerable than it would be if it could demonstrate its being informed by an effective public voice. Further, without it a prevailing paternalism in the NHS is vulnerable to changes in the dominant ideology, it can slip from "looking after" to "domineering" or "dismissing" the concerns of others.

I will return to a consideration of the standing of the NHS in my conclusions chapter and will use Nietzsche's entreaty that we must have the strength to break up the past to make a theory that can inform a political project that can win ground in the future (see Wright 1985: 140).

Monetarism and markets

Some of the practices evident in this new monetarist approach were not that new in the UK, they had precedents in the preceding Labour administration[12] led by James Callaghan. That government cut social welfare spending at the behest of the International Monetary Fund to whom the government had turned for financial support in 1975. But if that was a move undertaken reluctantly, and under duress, the Thatcher administrations were enthusiastic and ideologically committed as they re-privatised parts of the welfare state, imposed higher charges on some areas of its service, restricted the availability of social security benefits and weakened the organised working class, including those delivering social welfare services (Gough 1980).

Box 2.1 Legacy aspects of the welfare state that limit its effectiveness today

1 Responding to need not reducing inequality.

    The Welfare State, as it evolved in Britain, was primarily about responding to need, in this it shows its liberal roots. It was not solely an invention of the 1945–51 Attlee Labour government, even though it was the drive and vision of that government that enacted it. Much of the shape of the post-war welfare state was a picking up and extension of the Liberal social reforms of the pre-1914 Lloyd George government, of legislation enacted between the wars and the synthesising actions proposed in the Beverage Report of 1942 (Edgerton 2018). It was not primarily about justice, nor was it an attack on inequality, "Its starting point was the relief of suffering, after which it took modest steps towards the prevention of suffering". Beverage's five giants, which his reforms were designed to overcome, were want, disease, ignorance, squalor and idleness, "These are all forms of deprivation … the central preoccupation … was poverty not inequality".

2 Absence of a popular voice – a democratic deficit.

    The history of the development of the welfare state was one that saw considerable input from the intellectual and political elite and social reformers but not a great deal of popular pressure for these reforms "the welfare state was something done to the British people much more than it was something done *by* them" (Collini 2017: 8).

    By the early 1980s the welfare state "was both corporatist in character (public discussion and political negotiation simulated in thoroughly institutionalised forms), and caught in the contradiction of its commodifying pact with private capital" (Wright 1985: 206: see Offe 1984).

The sorts of changes pursued with vigour by the Thatcher government were underpinned by the analysis and rhetorical positions occupied by political economists and philosophers including Friedman, Hayek and Nozick (Taylor–Gooby 1981). Friedman argued that freedom is enhanced by voluntary cooperation in the institutions of a free market and that this should be supported by a minimal state. Hayek saw the "hidden hand of the market" as the best way to preserve individual freedom, state intervention was immoral in that it interfered with this freedom and was also counterproductive, a position also propounded by Nozick who argued for a minimal state on the grounds that any infringement on the market is contrary to the rights of the individual. This sort of assertion of a conception of society that places the individual at centre stage and denies the importance, or relevance, of social structure provides the bedrock justification for the deregulation of finance and the cuts in services that have continued to characterise

---

Box 2.2 Rentier capitalism

This is a form of capitalism where market and political power allow privileged individuals and businesses to extract rewards over and above those required to induce the desired supply of goods, services, land or labour.

Main effects: (1) Damage to the real (non-financial sector) economy where goods and services are generated: fast-growing financial sectors become a drag on growth and improved productivity, there is "a diversion of talented human resources in unproductive, useless directions" "…the financial sector's ability to create credit and money finances its own activities, incomes and (often illusory) profits" (Wolf 2019).

(2) Enhanced inequality as finance awards itself excessive "rent". In the UK, the ratio of average chief executive pay to average workers' pay rose from 48 to one in 1998 to 129 to one in 2016 (in the US, the same ratio went from 42 to one in 1980 to 347 to one in 2017).

The result: What "we increasingly seem to have…. is an unstable rentier capitalism, weakened competition, feeble productivity growth, high inequality and, not coincidentally, an increasingly degraded democracy" (Wolf 2019).

---

debates up to the present day. They also help us understand what underpinned Margaret Thatcher's assertion that "there is no such thing as society" (talking to *Women's Own* Magazine Oct 31st, 1987).

At the same time, the entrepreneur is valorised. Ayn Rand, a more recent cheerleader for ultra-individualism, sees capitalism driven by heroic entrepreneurs challenging incumbents in a wild but socially advantageous process of creative destruction. They are the drivers of human progress (quoted in Greenspan and Wooldridge 2018) – a claim untroubled by either the positive experience of public intervention easing the errant behaviour of capitalist economies – the New Deal in the US for example – or the manifest damage done by seeking the integration of the whole economy via the steering medium of money and by the unbridled excess of finance capital, the banking crash of 2007–08 being a recent example (see Box 2.2).[13]

Liberalism (before the neo)

Baggini (2008) has argued that the British are not classic liberals, they did not adopt the core themes of Nineteenth Century liberalism. The classic post-Enlightenment conception of liberalism saw a universal human nature and the universality of basic rights. The British, Baggini thinks, are better described as communitarians; they believe that there are no rights without responsibilities and

Box 2.3 Before and after the "neo" prefix

Liberalism

Liberal has a philosophical and a political meaning, but it is also used to mean generous, open-minded, having a general sense of freedom and, with a more pejorative slant, a sense of being unrestrained or exhibiting a lack of vigour and characterised by weak and sentimental belief. One could have liberal opinions (open-minded to some, unorthodox to others) and pursue the liberal arts (as distinct from the mechanical arts) (see Williams 1983: 178). Philosophically, it is associated with individualism, toleration and the defence of liberty and with the writings of, amongst others, John Locke, John Stuart Mill and Alexis de Tocqueville. Fawcett (2015) offers a description that combines freedom, equality and order; liberalism is, "a search for an ethically acceptable order of human progress among civic equals without recourse to undue power".

There is also a history of liberal politics (and liberals in politics), Keynes and Beveridge for example or Lloyd George, in the US Franklin Delano Roosevelt and, in domestic policy at least, Lyndon Baines Johnson.

John Rawls in *A Theory of Justice* (1971) sought to reconcile political liberalism, the rule of law and formal rights, and social liberalism with its interest in equality, inclusion and social justice. (I will explore the relevance of his arguments further in Chapter 9).

Liberal is also used as a pejorative term. From the left, it is seen as individualist and lacking a sense of the social. Macpherson (1962) classified liberalism as a theory of "possessive individualism", in which a person is conceived as the sole proprietor of his or her skills, owing nothing to society for them. What follows is a belief that these skills (and those of others) are a commodity to be bought and sold on the open market. The next step is that society is seen as constructed around consumption and its' selfish pursuit is equated with a core aspect of "human nature". Macpherson believed that this culture of possessive individualism prevented individuals from developing their powers of rationality, moral judgment, contemplation and even friendship and love. These were what he termed the "truly human powers". Macpherson defined freedom as being able to develop one's fullest human potential. This is freedom "to" in contrast to an idea of freedom "from" (Macpherson 1973: 145). (In the US, liberal is used pejoratively to associate a person with a belief in an interventionist state, in "big government". The wish to advance a "Freedom from" approach is at the heart of criticisms of "liberal" from the right.)

Neoliberalism

As we have seen the belief that one owed nothing to society for one's skills and that freedom was negative, an absence of constraints on a person's choice, was present in classical liberalism. But these ideas were taken on by F. A. Hayek (1960) and Milton Friedman (1962) and given a new emphasis. Politicians, most notably Ronald Reagan and Margaret Thatcher, joined their political agenda with this philosophical reworking of liberalism to forge a new sort of neoliberalism, a liberalism redefined from the right.

The contrast between the two sorts of definitions about the role of government that represent liberalism and neoliberalism, can be captured by quotes from two US presidents F.D. Roosevelt and George W. Bush. In 1935, in the aftermath of the Great Depression, Roosevelt identified excessive market freedoms as being at the root of the economic and social problems of the 1930s. Americans, he said, must, "forswear that conception of the acquisition of wealth which, through excessive profits, creates undue private power". He went on to assert that "necessitous men are not free men" and that,

> The primary obligation of the state and its civil society was to use its powers and allocate its resources to eradicate poverty and hunger and to assure security of livelihood, security against the major vicissitudes of life, and the security of decent homes.

The liberalism of Roosevelt's New Deal of the 1930s focussed not on individual need, but on the collective good. It "inaugurated a liberalism filled with confidence, hope, pride, and a spirit of self-sacrifice" (Lilla 2018). In the US, initiatives such as *The War on Poverty* between 1965 and 1980 combined an income support policy and programmes to improve opportunity. It was a policy that, by the 1980s, resulted in a situation where, "the structural causes of poverty were not much altered although the relief of poverty was extended" (Haveman 1987).

Into the new millennium, and President George W Bush articulates a neoliberalism that is the antithesis of this conception of the state;

> The only way to confront our problems is for the state to cease to regulate private enterprise, for the state to withdraw from social provision, and for the state to foster the universalization of market freedoms and of market ethics.
>
> (both Presidents quoted in Harvey 2005: 184)

Three aspects of this new "neoliberalism" can be identified (from Steger and Roy 2010: 11–15).

- An ideology championed by global elites that has saturated the political and public discourse with an idealised image of a globalised free-market economy.
- An approach to governance, that emphasises ideas of competitiveness, decentralisation and the merits of self-interest. This sees a shift from the idea of the public good, "the transformation of bureaucratic mentalities

into entrepreneurial identities" (Steger and Roy 2010: 12). It is this aspect of neoliberalism that has spawned the "new public management" approach – with its customers or clients and its "entrepreneurial spirit" (see Osbourne and Gaebler 1992) (explored in Chapter 4).

- A set of public policies: deregulation of the economy/liberalisation of trade and industry/privatisation of state-owned enterprises. These policies are characteristically accompanied by tax cuts for businesses and high-income earners, reduction of social services and welfare payments and anti-trade union measures.

Additionally, and importantly as we look to the NHS and the care sectors to consider the impact of neoliberalism, there is a change in the focus of neoliberalism. A concern with the power of corporate monopolies and their ability to restrict new entrepreneurs in the early and mid-Twentieth Century morphed into a concern with the potential for the state itself to become a corporate monopoly (exemplified for the neoliberals by the New Deal and the Welfare State and by the growth of state taxation, in particular income tax). What followed was a belief that the state should be divested of powers and that marketisation, including the marketisation of health and care services, should become the state's main business. It is this sort of shift that opens the door to a change in the relationship between society and government and the encouragement of a new sort of individual – economic man. This is close to the possessive individualism Macpherson linked to liberalism before the "neo".

What is the difference between neoliberal and neoconservative? The latter is the same as the former in terms of economic policies with an added focus on "Family values", tough law enforcement and a strong military. (I will discuss below how neoconservative links with populism.)

But, while there has been the neoliberal ascendancy, the other liberalism has not gone away. President Obama equated liberalism with radical change made through practical measures. His liberalism is radical, he argues, because it involves making change happen and then making the change last. To do this you need to assure those who oppose you that, "while they may have lost the fight, they haven't lost their dignity, their autonomy, or their chance to adapt to the change without fearing the loss of all their agency". Obama recognises that it is a frustration that, "you can't alter the world with the wave of a rhetorical wand". Rather democratic societies work like ocean liners, "you turn the wheel slowly, and the big ship pivots", just a degree here and there, but in ten years, "Suddenly you are in a very different place than we are now". Why not turn the wheel more drastically? He answers, "If I turn fifty degrees, the whole ship turns over" (Gopnick 2016: 23–24).

that political morality emphasises particularities of time and place. But another potent theme in Nineteenth Century liberalism was a debate about the role of the state, and that does resonant with the Thatcher reforms and with neoliberalism. There was a vehement opposition to state intervention, even in areas that later became part of a widely accepted consensus as constituting minimal acceptable requirements for the public good. These liberals did not want public health innovations, protection for the health and safety of workers or the provision of elementary education (Zevin 2019). Box 2.3 captures some of the distinctiveness of neoliberalism by comparing it with liberalism before the "neo".

The unsteady triumph of neoliberalism

The first few years of neoliberalism heralded a period characterised by a "short-sighted triumphalism of western elites" (Habermas 2017: 26). One justification of this triumphalism was found in Fukuyama's "End of History/Post-history" argument, originating in a speech and then an article in a neoconservative magazine in 1989, and developed in a book in 1992 (Fukuyama 1989: 1992). Fukuyama's argument was seized upon as something of a catchphrase, belying the nuanced and complex Hegelian point he was making.[14] This catchphrase "end of history" was based on the belief that a harmony of market economy and democracy could, and had, been reached. A new consensus was evident, social democrats accepted neoliberalism as they pursued, "competition for the middle ground" to secure a democratic mandate (Clinton, Blair, Schroder in respectively the US, UK and Germany) and the rights' enthusiasm for neoliberalism lay in its stripping regulation and oversight from market economies. This was an aspect of neoliberalism Habermas called, "feral financial capitalism" (Habermas 2017: 26). Even when there appeared to be a resurgence of social democracy in Europe and in North America, in the last years of the century centre-left parties were in power in many Western countries, there was a focus on economistic policies not inconsistent with neoliberalism. In the UK, this was characterised by the idea of a "third-way", typified by the governments of Tony Blair, it was an approach widely discussed in Europe, North America, Latin America and captured in Giddens "*The Third Way*" book, subtitled "*The Renewal of Social Democracy*" (Giddens 1998). Mudge (2018) cites critics who termed this "the left gone right".

Neoliberalism can, for a time, peddle its "neoliberal myth that countries' competitiveness and economic performance depend on low taxes and deregulated markets" (Pettersson 2017: 7) especially when this is allied to a concerted mobilisation to unravel the social contract and to reduce alternative voices, particularly via attacks on trade union strength. But even the rhetorical claim of the importance of guaranteeing a relatively fair distribution of wealth that was part of the raison d'etre of post-war institutions was disappearing in a world where the return on capital was outpacing the level of growth. The accumulation of assets by the already rich challenges the idea of fairness and justice that are fundamental building blocks of western democracies (Piketty 2014). Piketty (2020) says we have created "inequality regimes" through a combination of the efforts of capitalists – creating a hyper capitalism which manifests concentrations of wealth not seen for 100 years – and the absence of an energetic progressive agenda to counter these excesses. But, as neoliberalism strips the cloak of democratic legitimacy away, it becomes vulnerable. A substantial part of the population is cut off from any financial benefits and disenfranchised by the spectrum of political views on offer. That is, the vulnerability is both economic, the 2008 crash illustrates this - the average real wage in the US had been stagnant for 40 years – and political, here it is the rise of popularism that provides evidence of this vulnerability.[15] Further, the "end of history" triumphalism could not survive the rise of the totalitarian socialism of China, of Islamic Fundamentalism, of the Arab Spring, of the trauma of the Twin Towers attack, of the financial crash or of a new global pandemic.

Neoliberalism doesn't enhance democracy.[16] Parties who once believed their job was to make capitalism work for voters now believed their job was to make voters fit for capitalism. Nor does neoliberalism work for the economy: "Liberalising markets did not lead to economic nirvana; instead, the orgy of speculation led to the financial crisis of 2008. The record shows that the managed capitalism of the cold war delivered better results than the unmanaged capitalism since" (Elliott 2018). The price of neoliberalism was and is, "the economic and socio-cultural hanging out to dry of ever greater parts of the populace" and a toleration of long-standing and growing social inequalities. "The US is today more unequal than in the last 100 years and one would have to go all the way back to the middle of the 19th century to find a more unequal UK" (Muniz 2017: 12). "Democracy has become more venomous – and at the same time more toothless" (Rawnsley 2018a: 46).

But there are some less pessimistic voices; Runciman (2018) uses an appealing image, he argues there is a stability at the heart of the mature democracies – they might have mid-life crises, Donald Trump is the US's "motorbike", but they can stave off the worst that can happen even when they are proving unable to tackle underlying fundamental problems. De Tocqueville, after visiting the young democracy of America, and writing about it in 1835, with an even more appealing image said, "More fires get started in a democracy, but more fires get put out too".

It is also the case that, as my heading suggests, neoliberalism's triumph is unsteady. Within the overall arc of its influence, dating from the 1980s, there have been periods when policy emphasis reflected a much more focussed attempt to address both poverty and to fund the NHS more generously. The Labour Party's social programmes between 1997 and 2010 lifted a million children and a million pensioners out of what was defined as poverty, and spending on the NHS rose at an average of 7% a year (Toynbee and Walker 2011). There have also been periods during neoliberal times that seem more akin to populism, and I will consider this below. I will also address if neoliberalism is over. Hennessy (2022) said that British history will be divided into BC and AC, before and after Covid.[17] He considers that the way the state has extended its perception as to its duty of care during the pandemic is the crucial signifier of this change and this shift required a move from neoliberalism at least in terms of government spending. But Hennessy may be premature in his judgement, perhaps Covid was an interlude and not a break. Or perhaps the impact of Covid-19 will be to accelerate changes already underway and not fundamentally change direction. For example, there may be a lasting acceleration of existing changes in work – working from home, on-line working – these fit well with a neoliberal approach, they fracture the workforce allowing more short-terms and zero-hours contracts, enhancing the power of employers and eroding worker solidarities.[18] (In Chapter 5, I will argue that Covid-19 is a neoliberal epidemic.)

By 2022, Fukuyama had returned to his consideration of liberalism, now concerned to defend it in a world where he identifies an assault on political rights and civil liberties. He argues that liberal democracy has delivered on many fronts but as it has advanced it has left many constituencies behind. He sees neoliberalism as a distortion of liberalism which has a much larger remit than simple economic efficiency and he is now concerned to argue for the importance of appreciating the social capital that attains from redistribution and a narrowing of inequalities.

Returning to the pessimists, in an exploration of *How Democracies Die* Levitsky and Ziblatt (2019) argue that they do not typically succumb during catastrophic events (like the seizure of power by the military), rather they die after a gradual weakening of crucial institutions such as the judiciary and the press, democracy is as strong as its institutions. But it's not just institutions that are gradually weakened, so too is the very idea of pluralism, the populists appeal is that "We are the people". It is an authoritarian ploy, or the triumph of "a fantasy of a coherent popular",[19] to speak for the people and to dismiss opponents as enemies of the people (Müller 2017, 2017a). It may be that it is this attitude to other people that is the real threat to democracy. Nussbaum (2018) argues persuasively for the importance of emotion. At the heart of the crisis of politics in America, she argues, is fear and its attendant emotions of anger, disgust and envy. All these undermine democracy by wounding love and hope, love here meaning treating others as fellow human beings. Hope is a practical thing, when we think and act in a hopeful way we get more hopeful outcomes.

Neoliberalism (or populism) is not unique in its capacity to engender fear – there have been many occasions even in recent history when it has felt that society was breaking down and that fear was pervasive – the Vietnam War and its impact on social solidarities in the US and the Cold War with its emphasis on the external enemy are examples. But neoliberalism and populism can distort our sense of fellow feeling in such a way that we identify our neighbours as being threats to what we hope for. It is damaging to our politics and distorts our emotions (Nussbaum 2001). This is a conclusion that resonates with my concern with policy, practice and personal behaviour change in the NHS.

Key aspects of neoliberalism and their impact on the NHS

The changes of the 1980s reframed inclusion and participation as artefacts of the market. There was an increasing sense of society as being predicated on "us and them" rather than "we". This increases inequality and leaves the vulnerable (and the unproductive) marginalised. The changes of the Thatcher government were designed to revitalise British capitalism by privileging finance via,

> the adoption of the free-market nostrums of the newly assertive free-market economists. A free-market culture then manifests a persistent individualism which goads us into believing that the only route to happiness is through consumption. Britain had to rediscover the verities of the age of Adam Smith; the state was to be rolled back; and the felicitous invisible hand of market forces was to be ungloved.
>
> (Hutton 1996: 11)[20]

The wave upon wave of attacks on the NHS that follow this sort of free-market change seek to sidestep a frontal assault on its values, including mutuality and co-operation (personified in the funded collectively and "free at the point of need" mantra). This stealth attack seeks to create a situation where, "the structures that provide health must be the closest simulacrum to the market as possible. The NHS can be reduced to a brand that houses a hyper efficient network of private sector deliverers competing for contracts" (Hutton 2019: 46). The NHS is seen by those making such attacks as an organisation that has become an inefficient monopoly of production and delivery that must be broken down by the insertion of private sector companies. The neoliberal assumptions underlying such attacks are about:

- The naturalness of the market
- The primacy of the competitive individual
- The superiority of the private over the public

Some key manifestations of these assumptions will be followed up below and how they translate to the NHS context will be considered, for example an inclination to grow by acquisition and deals, not by new investment, and a casualisation (or increasingly putting work out to tender) of the work force to enable fluctuations of the market to be more easily responded to by expansion or retrenchment; and continuing extravagant remuneration of senior managers.

Categorising neoliberalism and considering how it might impact on our actions

In this section, I will consider different ways of understandings neoliberalism and the way neoliberalism can impact on conceptualisations of the self[21] and, via these conceptualisations, the ways we interact with others.

Neoliberalism has become a go-to term on which to hang the shortcomings of social policy. As I have argued above there was much wrong before the advent of neoliberalism and some of the things that have been attributed to neoliberalism appeared to have been in place before it. Other things attributed to neoliberalism do not exhibit a convincing causal link, or they require us to identify why there is such variability in behaviours, why some things have changed, and other things have stayed the same? Further, the neoliberal project is not a monolith, and its analysts are far from agreeing on what is central to it (see Ward and England 2007). Table 2.1 summarises a range of views as to what neoliberalism is best understood as.

The more state-oriented understanding of neoliberalism, and neoliberalism as governmentality, present with different agendas over time. There are complex constructions about how they impact on the individual, on the conception of the

Table 2.1 Different understandings of neoliberalism present within the existing literature

Understandings of neoliberalism	Key aspects	What actions follow	Illustrative references
As elite power. An international class-based hegemonic project to bolster elite power	Projects a specific interpretation of the world that includes an inherent ideological justification for social and economic inequality.	Privatisation, fiscal austerity, deregulation and the hollowing out of labour rights	Hall (2011) Cahill (2015)
As replacing the state with the market. A concerted attempt to roll-back the state, often justified by the idea that opening collectively held resources to market mediation engenders greater efficiency.	Focuses on the transfer of ownership from the state or public holdings to the private sector or corporate interests. The destruction and discrediting of state services and the introduction of market mechanisms in their place.	New economic management systems, social agendas centred on urban order, privatisation, deregulation, liberalisation, depoliticisation (saying these are administrative matters, not political ones) and monetarism.	Peck and Tickell (2002), Springer (2012)
As governmentality. The push to construct and regulate social life through principles that originate in the market.	Underlines the tension between market freedom and an authoritarian state.	Authoritarianism and surveillance. A redefining of conceptions and functions of the self.	Foucault (2008), Rose (1996)

scope for autonomy and on the functioning of the self. In state-oriented understandings, we have seen 'Roll-back' neoliberalism, associated with Thatcher and
Reagan in the 1980s and exemplified by the privatisation of state assets and deregulation of the economy; and we have seen "roll-out" neoliberalism, associated
with Third-Way doctrines of the mid-to-late-1990s in the US, UK and Germany.
The roll-out manifestation involves new forms of state building, as well as the
marketisation of public services and assets (Peck and Tickell 2002).

There are other analyses of neoliberalism that identify different stages in its development; Ball uses a three phase analysis: classic small-state neoliberalism, post-
neoliberalism where the market acts as "a powerhouse of public sector reform" and
then post-austerity neoliberalism (Ball 2012: 95). This is a valuable formulation
in the context of considering the dynamic role of neoliberalism's marketisation/
privatisation of health and social care and I return to it below.

Neoliberalism as governmentality, looking to Foucault's formulation, is also a
dynamic entity, but not so much in terms of its resulting policy emphasis. Here the
dynamism is played out in the interaction between the state and the individual:

> The subject constitutes himself in an active fashion, by the practices of the
> self, these practices are not something that the individual invents himself.
> They are patterns that he finds in his culture and which are proposed, sug-
> gested and imposed on him by his culture, his society and his social group.
>
> (see Foucault, 2008: also Rose 1999: xxi–xxii)

Miller and Rose (2008) add to this analysis of the constitution of neoliberal subjects an examination of how these subjects are being produced. Regimes of power
include distinct processes of subjectivation and regulation which changes:

> relations with themselves and with others...who they thought they were,
> what they wanted to be, the language and norms according to which they
> judged themselves and were judged by others, the actions they took upon
> themselves and that others might take.
>
> (Miller and Rose 2008: 258)

Importantly, governmentality does not rely upon their being certainties and
unequivocal decisions; there is a continuous reciprocity between aggregate and
individual actions. Neoliberal ideology, as manifest in this arena of reciprocity,
privileges the individual over the social, and personal choice over collective action. This is a conceptual fit of value to those who seek to, 'pursue the marketisation of welfare for ideological purposes' (Nettleton 1997: 220). But to get people to
act in a way consistent with the hegemonic project of neoliberalism some mediat-
ing mechanisms need to be invoked. These take two main forms:

- The government of the self – via the manipulation of subjectivity.
- The invocation of risk.

Together these manipulate the ethical self, and it is this manipulation that is the conceptual bridge that links reform of health care with a change in the personal interaction of giving care, and it is this that makes space for the breakdown Francis reported in Mid-Staffordshire Hospital. I will return to this reading of neoliberalism below when I consider in more detail individual and attitudinal change (Chapter 6).

Is there a late neoliberalism?

In the aftermath of the international financial crisis of 2008 austerity impacted, and continues to impact, on the many. But, after a little inconvenience, elites quickly resumed the actions that characterised the pre-crisis years. Austerity was incorporated into neoliberalism (see Ball 2012: 95). It might have been anticipated that the crisis would highlight the chimera of market mechanisms as an adequate way to steer the economy. But neoliberalism is flexible, "austerity is…recouped and rearticulated as a means of restoring the market-state in a revised form" (McGimpsey 2017: 70). Thus the crisis does not undermine the legitimacy of the market; rather, it reconfigures the state in the context of accepting austerity as the new normal. That reconfiguration sees a shift of public services into the remit of civil society, the Big Society agenda (Sage 2012). It can be argued that at a political level the shift to civic society as the provider of public services is a device to redirect criticism for the effects of austerity from the government of the day. How far this is considered successful may depend on how far you see late neoliberalism being replaced by a popularism that re-engages with the role for the state, the economy and the relationship between them (see Greve 2021).[22]

A general election in 2019 resulted in a comfortable Conservative majority. That majority was obtained by a populist appeal to "get Brexit done", to leave the European Union. It was a position supported by a new sort of voting configuration that brought together some traditional Labour supporters, particularly in the Midlands and the North, with Tory's hostile to the EU. A new political imperative followed, to reconfigure the priorities of the government to keep this coalition intact. An early manifestation of this was the budget in 2020 which, the chancellor argued, delivered the biggest fiscal boost for nearly 30 years, public investment was going to become the highest it had been since 1955. This was something of a return to Keynesian economics. It was not enough to correct "the social carnage of the past decade", local government will miss out on this new largesse and, "The increases in current public spending will redress only about a quarter of the cumulative loss in health and education spending since 2010" (Hutton 2020. 4)), government grants to local authorities fell by 77% between 2010 and 2019. But it was a budget that marked a significant step from austerity and from the economics (and politics) of neoliberalism. (It also was a budget whose impact was subsumed in the measures announced very soon afterwards by the new Chancellor of the Exchequer Rishi Sunak to respond to the economic impact of the coronavirus epidemic.) Leading free-market think-tanks[23] who, since the Thatcher years, had backed tax-cutting, privatisation agendas and, in recent years, austerity accepted the necessity of public spending in the context of the epidemic and, in effect, heralded either the end or a pause in an era of austerity. Hutton has argued that we now see shifts in government policy catching up with what he says is a shift that has been occurring in economic theory from "the 'market is magic' doctrines that have defined the past 40 years". The policy he identifies as signalling this shift is the 2022 White Paper "*Levelling Up the United Kingdom*" (Dept of Levelling Up, Housing and Communities 2022). But he also notes that, if the analysis in the White Paper marks a shift, the White Paper's policy is still trapped in "the suffocating veto of Rishi Sunak's Treasury" (Hutton 2022). A shift in diagnosis with no change of prescription is a pyrrhic victory over the neoliberals and far from confirming the demise of their hegemony.

I will discuss the impact of the pandemic in some detail in Chapter 5 and have already previewed the case I will make that Covid-19 was a neoliberal epidemic and that the retreat of the pandemic from centre stage saw a return to neoliberal orthodoxies, albeit now infused with elements of populism.

Populism

What if neoliberalism is no longer dominant in the economy and in politics? This may not have an immediate impact on those attitudes and behaviours that shape our personal or professional contacts with others. It takes some time for system to colonise lifeworld when there is any sort of system change. But a move away from neoliberalism does impact on what changes can be introduced to address challenges to improving care. A recent reawakening of populism is perhaps the strongest candidate to replace neoliberalism.

Populism, through history, has taken different forms – it may be that this contemporary form is best seen as a mutation of neoliberalism, played out in the political domain. A hegemonic economism has remained in place or had remained in place until the impact of Coronavirus. The pandemic led to a revival of the State's role in the economy – a Conservative government found itself obliged to borrow, tax and spend, as the route to save its enterprise economy. The post-pandemic period will have to deal with the consequences of this intervention and with the potential reappraisal of the balance between the size of the state and private enterprise. Major rises in fuel prices and the impact of the war in Ukraine; rising inflation, very high levels of debt, and the risks of recession may see a more interventionist state remain longer than the ideologues of neoliberalism would want (see Garrard 2022 on the arguments for the centrality of the State). Or they may see a reassertion of a tax-cutting populism that also shifts us back to the neoliberalism whose demise was short-lived. Following the departure of Boris Johnson as Prime Minister in 2022 the Tory leadership election was fought on familiar neoliberal terrain – the management of the debt and the control of inflation on one side and the belief in the stimulus effect of tax cuts on the other (Sunak and Truss, respectively).

A short history of populism

The term dates to the nineteenth century,[24] it is defined by the Oxford English Dictionary as "a political approach that strives to appeal to ordinary people who feel that their concerns are disregarded by established elite groups". It is also a political approach that characteristically occurs at times of economic challenge, President Theodore Roosevelt, at the beginning of the twentieth century said, "Populism never prospers save where men are unprosperous". It is often a political approach that allies itself with an established "host" ideology, sometimes of the left, more frequently [in the twentieth and twenty-first centuries] with the right.[25] When political approaches become social movements they create atmospheres and spaces of resonance and they cultivate ethical dispositions (Touraine 2001). These are not always positive atmospheres and convivial spaces!

There is a long history of populism in the US. Churchwell (2018) charts this through tracing the history of key phrases that had been appropriated by Trump as candidate and then as President – "America First" and the "American Dream". The idea of returning to a golden age is a key part of this reading of populism, in the case of Trump this appears to be sometime in the early 1960s when there was an economy confident in its post-war buoyancy. It would have to be before the arrival of the Kennedy's and their Camelot culture, before the Vietnam War, political assassinations and civil rights riots.[26] The 1960s also saw George Wallace and Richard Nixon trying to turn the language of working-class majoritarianism against liberalism and later, in the 1980s, US Republicans tried to equate the will of the people with the operation of the market. This was a specific example of neoliberalism's use of populism; in reality they were trying to sell plutocracy (Churchwell 2018).

But, in the US, there are other sorts of populism:

- Sometimes it promoted democracy, for example the 1890s when it was pushing for wider democratic participation by mobilising black farmers alongside southern whites (see Goodwyn 1978).
- Sometimes it is against capitalism/big government but is also racist, for example around the First World War arguing against US involvement, denouncing oil cartels but also being openly racist.[27]
- Populism isn't always against pluralism or opposed to the democratic order. Sometimes it's of the left, labour-union populism of the 1930s, or movements seeking to widen popular alliances – Jesse Jackson in the 1980s building the "rainbow coalition" or Bernie Saunders from 2016 in his attempts to secure the Democratic nomination for the US Presidential elections. Mouffe (2018) identifies a "Left populism" – this posits a political frontier between the people and the oligarchy, it is a discursive strategy that can reanimate a moribund political culture, a productive antagonism between "us" and "them" that is central to a healthy democracy.

The rise of contemporary populism

While Roosevelt pointed to poverty as the root of populism there are other candidates.[28] Gamble argues for the importance of the poverty of the traditional political offer (in Perryman 2017). "The rights unchanging offer of 'small state, low taxes, free trade'…has become a hard one to sell after 10 years of austerity and squeezed household incomes and 30 years of rising inequality". Mark Lilla has a different candidate in mind, the liberal left, which he characterises as having targeted identity politics instead of focussing on universal programmes, or at least very wide-reaching ones. The danger in this is a separation of the alliance between the working-class and middle-class liberals (Pettersson 2017: 7) as many working-class voters felt they were left without a voice. Lilla sees this shift by the left into the politics of the particular as a feature of the hegemony of neoliberalism.[29]

But what will the final stage of neoliberalism look like? There are two general views, the first that it will go with a whimper, shifts in fiscal policy and a move to more state intervention, the second that it will go with a bang. The work of US philosopher Richard Rorty now looks prescient, although his identification of the "strongman" as coming from the left underestimated the propensity of the right to seek such a figure. In lectures delivered in 1997, he presented thoughts on the endgame. The left, hampered by a preoccupation with cultural politics rather than the politics of class would lose faith in any political alliance forged with the middle classes and would seek a populirist "strongman" who was "willing to assure them that, once he is elected, the smug bureaucrats, tricky lawyers, overpaid bond salesmen and postmodern professors will no longer be calling the shots" (Rorty 1999).

Rawnsley, says that into the rhetorical space left by the poverty of conventional politics an argument emerged that the status quo was too metropolitan; it was too managerial; more and more focus on markets left people behind; it was indulgent of the excesses of high finance and impotent to do anything about stagnant incomes for most and obscene gains for some; it was mesmerised by the power of globalisation and resistant to giving enough thought to those left behind. This set of far from consistent arguments mobilised electoral majorities across the West to argue for a "nativist authoritarian position", posing this as the debate of the age as it took on "globalist liberals" (Rawnsley 2018: 49). It was accompanied by an attack on the elevated status given to "experts", explicitly voiced in the UK by prominent politicians, "people in this country have had enough of experts" (Secretary of State for Justice Michael Gove 2016, see Deacon 2016) and by the rise to a discursive prominence of the terms "fake-news" and "post-truth".[30] A new electoral coalition was being shaped and it was accessible to the manipulation of populist politicians. It was a coalition that saw the rise of the "Trumpenproletariat" who had achieved a majority for what Hilary Clinton, during her presidential campaign, had termed "the deplorables" (Müller 2017: 20–21), a terminology that perhaps best illustrates that gap between liberal elites and the working class voter and helps explain her defeat.[31] The new populist electoral coalition might appear to constitute a different sort of politics but it has antecedents in the long history of populism and in other political formulations that better fit into the nomenclature of the far right.[32]

But populism is a volatile construct, as well as the opposition to elites and to experts there is a case made for identifying a technopopulism. Bickerton and Invernizzi Accetti (2021) identify failings in traditional party democracy eroding its legitimacy and creating a space for turning government over to "independent experts". Policy making is replaced by "problem solving" and the unity of the people is restored as those promoting divisive party politics are replaced. Their examples include the UK under New Labour and France under President Macron – times when leaders represent themselves as neither left nor right but separate from the politics of the past.

Surveillance capitalism

Bauman (1999) says that in late modernity the major tool that elites used to keep order was the scrutiny offered by the Panopticon in which the few can observe and control the many. This has been replaced by the Synopticon where the many watch the few, via social media and enhanced technological surveillance, those who transgress can be castigated by those seeking to channel what they call the voice of the (previously neglected) majority. One of paradoxes of our age is the opportunity for rapid and widespread communication via the internet and the realisation that internet discourse has become tighter, more coercive, as huge corporate interests extend control, in part via scrutinising our choices, coming up with a sense of who we are (the self as the consumer self), and seeking to perpetuate that self, "you bought that so we think you would like this".

Perhaps then Zuboff's *Surveillance Capitalism* (2019) is also a candidate to replace neoliberalism. She argues that a new mutant form of capitalism uses our own raw data to predict and manipulate human behaviour for commercial gain. This new form of surveillance, "unilaterally claims human experience as free raw material for translation into behavioural data". That data is used to predict future choices, what you will do now, soon or later, and then this is traded to produce profits. Zuboff sees this as a new stage in capitalisms long evolution: from making products, then mass production, then managerial capitalism, financial capitalism and now the trading of behavioural prediction covertly derived from the surveillance of users. In the same way that Bentham, Foucault, Bauman and others have observed the changing nature of surveillance Zuboff is now identifying how digital technology is separating the citizens in all societies into two groups, the watchers and the watched, with an asymmetry of knowledge that translates into asymmetries of power.

See Boxes 2.4 and 2.5 on the shifting populist position across the West (and elsewhere).

This rise of populist government is, in part, a response to the financial crash of 2008 and in part, it is a product of more deep-seated contradictions in neoliberalism. It is like other reactionary backlashes that follow periods of rapid social

Box 2.4 From hubris to austerity via the financial crash: the rise of populists in government in Europe and across the world from 1998 to 2019

The number of Europeans living under governments with a populist in the cabinet – 1998 – 12.5 million: 2018 170.2 million in 11 countries. In 1998, 7% of votes cast in national elections went to populist parties, by 2018 the figure was more than 1 in 4.

Situation in 1998: In the UK, Tony Blair's New Labour has a big majority, it goes on to win two more elections. Clinton was in his second term in the White House and the SPDs Gerhard Schroder was German Chancellor – he served two terms. The moderate left was in government in two-thirds of EU countries. Up to the crash of 2008 the level of hubris that believed the economy was now a self-regulating system that functioned in a domain separate from messy domestic or international politics was high; consider Prime Minister Tony Blair, in 2005, asking, why "debate globalisation? You might as well debate whether autumn should follow summer"[33] or Alan Greenspan (former chair of the US Federal Reserve saying, in 2007, that it didn't matter who was US President, "we are fortunate that, thanks to globalisation, policy decisions in the US have been largely replaced by global market forces" (see Tooze 2018).

By 2018: there was a right-wing and populist government in Poland – the Law and Justice (PiS) party (re-elected in 2020) under President Andrzej Duda, and in Hungary there was Viktor Orbán and his Fidesz party. French socialists were decimated in their election, the right-wing candidate for the Presidency, Marine Le Pen, was supported by one in three French voters (her party changed its name from the French National Front to National Rally). There were the worst results for the moderate SPD in Germany since the establishment of the Federal Republic in 1949, and a rise of right-wing parties – the national populist Alternative for Germany (AfD) party captured 94 seats in the Bundestag. The Northern League made progress in Italy, Matteo Salvini, its secretary was deputy Prime Minister from June 2018 to September 2019, the Five Star Movement, led by Beppe Grillo became the largest single party in the Italian Parliament in 2018 elections. Switzerland has a long established right wing populist movement, the Swiss People's Party, the centre-left suffered electorally in Austria, the Freedom Party, a party whose stance is more familiarly far-right as opposed to populist, is a coalition partner in the government. In the Czech Republic, populist parties won 40% of the vote in the 2017 general election. This rise of populist and parties of the right was evident even in Scandinavia, with only one Scandinavian country retaining a social democratic government. (Denmark, had a Centre-Right coalition government: Mette Frederiksen's Social Democrats are unlike previous iterations of social democracy – they are to the left on the economy but on globalisation, immigration and free movement of labour, they are closer to the right populists in other parts of Europe and closer to the more unequivocally populist Danish People's Party (DPP), Sweden has the far-right Sweden Democrats who got 17.6% of the vote in the national election. Finland has the nationalist Finns Party).

Portugal after the crash had a right-wing government who introduced austerity; in 2015 this was replaced by a socialist one, led by Antonio Costa, who eased austerity.

In Greece, ten years of austerity after the crash and bailouts from the EU were characterised by tax rises, public sector jobs and wage cuts and pension cuts. In 2015, a radical leftist government of the Syriza party, led by Alexis Tsipras, was elected. He was Prime Minister from 2015 to 2019 and subsequently leader of the opposition.

In Spain, a crisis from 2012, with some recovery from 2015 with GDP growth and employment and household incomes rising, saw a right-wing government replaced by a socialist one with plans to ease austerity. It also saw, in the success of Podermos, an example of left-wing populism.

Outside Europe: Recep Tayyip Erdogan became president of Turkey in 2014, Narendra Modi, the leader of the Hindu nationalist Bharatiya Janata Party took power in the same year. In 2017, Donald Trump became US President. In the Philippines, Rodrigo Duterte was elected in 2016. In 2019, Jair Bolsonaro became president of Brazil (see Zielonka 2018).[34]

Box 2.5 Fluctuations in the fortunes of populists

In 2020/21, in the UK and US: In the UK the Brexit movement and the various incarnations of UK independence parties, led by Nigel Farage, could claim policy success but not electoral success, their platform largely taken away by a populist shift from the Conservative Party.

In the US, the Trump administration was replaced by President Biden's Democratic Party in 2021.

By 2022, all five Nordic countries were led by centre-left governments, Portugal elected a Socialist government in 2022, Germany's Social Democrats lead a three-party left-liberal coalition, there is a progressive alliance in power in Spain; in Italy, the Democratic Party is a member of the ruling coalition although that changed in 2022 when a new right wing coalition took control. Donald Trump lost the US election in 2020 and in Brazil Bolsonaro was defeated in 2022, they were succeeded by respectively the Democrat Joe Biden and by the Worker's Party led by Luiz Inacio Lula da Silva.

change, a characteristic of modernisation. Saxer argues that in the vertigo that such change generates,

> old certainties are shaken up, traditional values transvalued. Modernisation drives the pluralisation of values, the fragmentation of society and the diversification of lifestyles. Social transformation erodes traditional communities which used to give security and a sense of purpose. Authoritarians perceive diversity and disorder as a normative threat to the integrity of the moral order which they seek to remedy by kicking out foreigners and non-conformists.
>
> (Saxer 2017: 15)

In this context, right-wing popularism wants to "restore governability (order and control) of an increasingly complex world by homogenizing society". It's an alt-right agenda which argues for an interventionist "strong" state to combat the marginalisation of the "left behind" parts of the population and, in so doing, it includes leftist narratives; the people against the establishment – opposing progressive privilege. This has left the left without a coherent message and in danger of a contagion effect as they take on the social agendas of the right, for example hostility to foreign workers. Politics becomes "grey on grey" (Habermas 2017: 27).

This contemporary manifestation of populism is played out within an extant hegemonic neoliberalism. Some key ideas clash, for example the market economy of neoliberalism wanting to maximise capitalist growth and profit and a political agenda of populism wanting to make claims for the justice of the populace benefiting from growth. This makes for an unstable juxtaposition of competing ideologies. There are examples of attempts to reconcile clashes rhetorically, typically the argument is that getting the economy right will provide funds for the NHS/welfare state. But economic growth is not followed by reductions in inequality – "healthy" neoliberal economies trickle up not trickle down! There is also a moral bankruptcy in the idea that growth is the primary goal – how about fairness (or decency) – and a clash between promoting the new, and glorifying change and a nostalgia that is a common feature of popularism. In this case, as Lilla (2016) describes, it's not a nostalgia for a common bucolic past, it's about circling the wagons to repel boarders. The potential boarders are the unproductive "others".[35]

Neoliberalism and contemporary populism come together in a shared formulation that if you are needy you are unworthy. They also come together in a belief that the default position of "big government" is that it is "designed to take something from them [those in the wagons] and give it to someone who is unworthy", this was the core of candidate and then President Trumps' attack on his predecessor's *Affordable Care Act* (Remnick 2016: 62).[36] In healthcare (see Speed and Mannion 2017), this wish to protect some and cast out others is, for example, also manifest in attacks on "health tourists", people who seek health care when visiting the UK from another country.

Conclusion

People born in 1979 when Thatcher was first made Prime Minister are now well into middle age, if you were an adult in 1979 you are now over 60, a generation has been brought up under neoliberalism. No-one under 80 can remember the experiences of the pre-NHS UK. Why should we be surprised if the post-war consensus does not survive the attack it has been under? The great success story of late twentieth-century capitalism was its ability to define itself as axiomatic (whatever state of crisis it was in) and to have that definition widely accepted. (This Emperor's new clothes are the most dazzling in history). But, as with the Emperor, dominant ideas are always challenged, power generates opposition including proposals for different ways of doing things.[37]

Notes

1 See McNeill (1997) on what is meant by "The West".
2 Often "generations" are linked with shorter historical periods but these challenge Collins argument and may be better seen as transitory phases existing as interim creations while generations shift – the post-war generation (stoical, deferential) merges into the 60s generation (creative, challenging) – both "generations" lasting about 20 years. Then, by the 1980s, we get a 40 years (and counting) neoliberal generation (individualistic, competitive).
3 Roland Barthes (1982) called this process "ex-nomination". It might, for example, indicate an assumed normative that markets are the only way to organise the economy. In the past ex-nomination processes included the development of normative assumptions that are built around sexist or racist assumptions, for example that "society" is synonymous with "men" or that "white values" are the only ones that matter.
4 Jonathan Sacks (now Lord Sacks) is a religious leader – he was Chief Rabbi of the United Hebrew Congregations of the Commonwealth between 1991 and 2013 – and, as such, may have underestimated the sincerity of those people in the 1960s and after who were seeking to explore morality outside established hierarchical structures.
5 Sacks was writing before the events that precipitated the resignation of Prime Minister Johnson in 2022 but his formulation is most apt – if we consider Johnson's lies about Downing Street parties during Covid lockdowns, and about his knowledge of the past behaviour of his Deputy Chief Whip.
6 May (2018) has identified, "The dynamics between numerated and narrated selves in what are intensified, yet abstracted forces that inform our everyday lives and sense of ourselves and of others…" as a part of the forces that have increased in prominence in our lives in recent years.
7 Obama is invoking Martin Luther King whose optimism was contemporaneous both with the peak of the "we" from the Putnam and Romney formulation and with extreme racial oppression in the US.
8 Both David Ricardo and Marx saw rent seeking as a great social evil, particularly in the example of landlords who increased their lands value just by restricting access to it rather than using it productively.
9 The figure of Gordon Gekko proclaiming "Greed is Good" in Oliver Stone's 1987 film "Wall Street" becomes a subject of perverse attraction rather than a figure whose actions provide a warning of the perils of breaking the law by insider trading. There are many historical predecessors saying either that people who get wealthy both deserve it and are socially beneficial or who say we need the poor and shouldn't seek to eradicate poverty via state (or even charitable) activity – before the industrial revolution

mercantilists and those who see "a hidden hand" steering the economy excited both enthusiastic supporters and vehement critics –*The Fable of the Bees, or Private Vices, Public Benefit* by B. Mandeville (1728) being the most famous example.

10 The Beveridge Report (Social Insurance and Allied Services 1942) was a key document in the development to the UK Welfare State see Box 2.1 on the five evils.

11 I say more about and develop the idea of "ballast" in my concluding chapter.

12 The 1960s and 70s were a time of "bastardised Keynesian corporatism" (Hutton 1996, xxix).

13 It is a trope frequently invoked across history that the cash-nexus is eroding human relationships. Gray (2008) examines how "practically all aspects of interpersonal relationships seem tainted by the scent of money" in Shakespeare's *Merchant of Venice*. While this will not be surprising given the play's subject matter he argues that a monetary mindset that was becoming increasingly embedded in Early Modern England is also a significant factor in *The Comedy of Errors, The Merry Wives of Windsor, Measure for Measure and Timon of Athens*. A key date in the reconceptualisation of money was 1971 when US President Richard Nixon suspended the gold convertibility of the dollar. "For the first time since the invention of money in the ancient world, no major currency was anchored to a metallic base. Money was openly acknowledged as a political creation" (Tooze 2018a: 34).

14 Hegel thought the end of history would arrive when humans achieved perfect self-knowledge and self-mastery, when life was rational and transparent. Marx "turned Hegel on his head" – the end of history is when there are no more masters and slaves, when all are equal. Neither endpoint resonates with the neoliberal world in the years since the 1980s.

15 My focus is on the UK, with looks to the US and Europe but both neoliberalism and the 2008 crash have profound impacts across the world, far from the economic centres that had first benefited from and then recklessly ignored the dangerous economic forces they disdained to control. After the crash the World Bank and the International Monetary Fund told developing countries to cut social, health and welfare programmes and redirect resources to debt repayment (Lasker 2016).

16 Fukuyama's end of history may not even make us happier. When all political efforts were committed to "the endless solving of technical problems, environmental concern, and the satisfaction of sophisticated consumer demands" we might feel nostalgia for the "courage, imagination and idealism" that animated the old struggles for liberalism and democracy (Fukuyama 1989: see Menand 2018: 65). Marx's end of history saw us hunting in the morning, fishing in the afternoon and discussing philosophy at night – not everyone's cup of tea either!

17 The impact of epidemics across history is examined in Snowden (2020) and in Honigsbawn (2020).

18 The other change that is likely to be lasting is a shift from cash – a change that further marginalises the "precariat" – those without secure employment and housing who find it more difficult to get bank accounts and afford smart phones and their subscription costs, the new essentials for exercising economic citizenship (see Scott 2022).

19 The cosily coherent is an enemy of the democratic. Bauman (1999: 86–87) talks about the model of the agora, not just the physical public square but the sphere of communication where traffic between the public and private can occur. It's a "territory of constant tension and tug-of-war as much as it is the site of dialogue, co-operation or compromise".

20 Adam Smith didn't just argue this – he also had a political philosophy and ethical position – argued in other books – that took a different viewpoint, for example *The Theory of Moral Sentiment* (published in 1759) (see Mannion and Small 1999).

21 I am grateful for guidance in completing this section from Dr Madeleine Power, University of York. A fuller treatment of types of neoliberalism and allied conceptualisations of the self can be found in Power 2019.

22 It does not help my piece of mind as I watch the elaborate machinations of the privileged seeking to justify their continued pre-eminence despite the global economic collapse, in the context of the failure of the left to nail them for their shortcomings, and with the Trump personified rise of populism to be reminded of Yeats' poem *The Second Coming* (W B Yeats 1919) where, "The best lack all conviction, while the worst / Are full of passionate intensity". Ezra Pound said poetry is "news that stays news".

23 These think tanks included two founded to promote free market policies in the 1970s - the Adam Smith Institute and the Centre for Policy Studies.

24 Nietzsche in 1878 said that Liberal democracy will devour itself creating conditions for authoritarian rule. Disorder and instability will sow distrust in politics itself.

> Step by step, private companies will absorb the functions of the state…Even the most tenacious remnants of the old work of governing (for example, the activity that is supposed to protect private persons from one another) will finally be taken care of by private entrepreneurs.

The distinction between public and private spheres will disappear (quoted in Ross 2019: 38).

25 Some other definitions: it's a journalistic cliché and political epithet, a catchphrase for political ills (Brubaker 2017: 357); it's a "thin-centred ideology" (Mudde 2007); a political logic (Laclau 2005); a rhetorical strategy (Canovan 1999) or a political style (Moffitt 2016).

26 In the UK a good candidate year to indicate a shift would be 1967 – the year of the decriminalisation of most male homosexual activity, the Abortion Act and the year of Sergeant Pepper and the Summer of Love. The following year was tumultuous in many countries – assassinations in the US, escalation of the Vietnam War, Soviet invasion of Czechoslovakia, student protest in France and Germany – but less fraught in the UK despite clouds on the political horizon around Northern Ireland, and UK labour relations (see Sandbrook, 2009).

27 See Wolfe (1970: 38) on Senator Tom Watson.

28 W.H. Auden in his poem *Letter to Lord Byron* is speaking about authoritarianism but it's also a prescient observation on the sorts of settings that prompt a rise of populism. His argument is that it is loss of hope, when you lose faith in choice or in thought, that leads to a call for "law and order" (Auden 1937: 55).

29 Other things he thinks neoliberalism has shaped for the left include a concern in the academy with cultural pluralism, reflexivity and ideologies of difference, he says – all embraced rather than critiqued.

30 The Oxford English Dictionary made "post-truth" its 2016 "International Word of the Year" and defined it as a term that "relates to or denotes circumstances in which objective facts are less influential in shaping public opinion than appeals to emotion and personal belief". Wells (2016) argued that post-truth is a euphemism for post-trust, you can fact check things said about the past but when people are talking of the present and the future you need to trust them. Truth is both about the objective facts about the past but is also about the promises made for the future.

31 There is a considerable literature on the success of Trump in the US and the Brexit vote in the UK which, while not assuming the context are the same, do examine both economic and cultural underpinnings of recent right-wing populism. See for example Neiwert (2017), Stocker (2017), Evans and Menon (2017). Adopting a rather different viewpoint Goodhart (2017) identifies the key faultline in Britain as being between people who are rooted in a specific place or community and people who could come from anywhere – the two groups he terms "somewheres" and "anywheres". The former is socially conservative, small town or countryside, often not university educated and pro-Brexit. The latter is socially liberal, urban, university educated and opposed to Brexit (see also Goodhart 2020 on status in the 21st century).

32 If populism is the word used to capture this shift there are also elements of a much older political formulation where a search for a solution, or response to the insecurities of rapid change, is resolved albeit temporarily by authoritarian leaders seeking to use demagogy to convince others of the benefits of listening to them. There has also been a debate about how far the Trump approach to politics, including the incitement of the invasion of the US Capitol, is best described as pre-fascist, or neo-fascist (see Snyder 2017, 2018.)

33 The broader point Tony Blair was making in this speech to the Labour Party conference in Brighton was,

> I hear people say we have to stop and debate globalisation...you might as well debate whether autumn should follow summer...The character of this changing world is indifferent to tradition. Unforgiving of frailty. No respecter of past reputations. It has no custom and practice. It is repleat with opportunities, but they go only to those swift to adapt, slow to complain, open, willing and able to change.

Jon Cruddas called this approach "brutal liberalism" (2021), I have linked it with neoliberalism and the arrogance and hubris of this sort of formulation captures something of the dynamic that fuelled populism. Many people do not relish the prospects of the future belonging to the swift to change and they see tradition as a succour and frailty as an indication of a need for care. (see Harris 2019: 35) An article by Eugene V Debs, founder of the American Railway Union and Social Democratic Party and serial candidate for the US Presidency, published in 1882, spoke of the best kind of man being the "sand man":

> When a train stalled from the steepness of the incline or the weight of the freight, railroad men poured sand on the tracks to improve the grip of the wheels....Men who have plenty of sand in their boxes never slip on the path of duty.
>
> (Lepore 2019: see also Van Sciver et al. 2019)

34 While populism is useful for capturing something shared and particular about this political turn some of its emergence might be more accurately attributed to the appeal of self-styled "strongmen" politicians – in Hungary and Turkey for example.

35 In the populist mind *borders* are those lines between countries that must be protected, *boarders* are those people who seek to gain the advantages they have not contribute to.

36 One categorisation of President Trump's position on trade is that it manifests a "naive mercantilist" position which focuses on "bilateral trade imbalances as a cause of job losses" (Wolf 2019); or, to put it more simply, "The foreigner has tricked us, or has taken advantage of our weakness".

37 Karl Polyani in *The Great Transformation*, first published in 1944, wrote, "a pure freemarket society is a utopian project, and impossible to realise because people will resist the process of being turned into commodities", a complete commodification would lead to fascism.

References

Auden, W.H. 1937. Letter to Lord Byron. In, *Collected Longer Poems* 1968. London, Faber and Faber, 55.

Baggini, J. 2008. Across the great divide. *Prospect*, Jan, 38–41.

Ball, S J. 2012. The reluctant state and the beginning of the end of state education. *Journal of Educational Administration and History*, 44, 89–103.

Barthes, R. 1982. *Camera Lucida*. London, Jonathan Cape Ltd.

Bauman, Z. 1993. *Postmodern Ethics*. Oxford, Blackwell.

Bauman, Z. 1999. *In Search of Politics*. Stanford, CA, Stanford University Press.

Berger, J. 2007. *Hold Everything Dear*. London, Verso.

The Beveridge Report. 1942. *Social Insurance and Allied Services*. Cmd 6404. London, HMSO.

Bickerton, C.J., Invernizzi Ascetti, C. 2021. *Technopopulism: The New Logic of Democratic Politics*. Oxford, Oxford University Press.

Brubaker, R. 2017. Why populism? *Theory Society*, 46, 357–385.

Cahill, D. 2015. *The End of Laissez-Faire?: On the Durability of Embedded Neoliberalism*. Cheltenham, Edward Elgar Publishing.

Canovan, M. 1999. Trust the people! Populism and the two faces of democracy. *Political Studies*, 47(1), 2–16.

Carter, Z.D. 2020. *The Price of Peace: Money, Democracy and the Life of John Maynard Keynes*. Random House.

Churchwell, S. 2018. *Behold, America*. Bloomsbury.

Collini, S. 2017. Review of "Bread for All" Chris Renwick in *Guardian Review*. 9 Sept, 8.

Collins, R. 1998. *The Sociology of Philosophies. A Global Theory of Intellectual Change*. Cambridge, MA, The Belknap Press of Harvard University Press.

Cruddas, J. 2021. *The Dignity of Labour*. Polity Press.

Deacon, M. 2016. Michael Gove's guide to Britain's greatest enemy...the experts. *The Telegraph*, 10 June.

Department of Levelling Up, Housing and Communities. 2022. *Levelling Up the United Kingdom*. CP 604, Crown Copyright.

Edgar, D. 2017. *Front Row*. BBC Radio 4 2nd Sept.

Edgerton, D. 2018. *The Rise and Fall of the British Nation: A Twentieth Century History*. Allen Lane.

Elias, N. 2000 2nd Ed. *The Civilising Process*. Wiley Blackwell (originally published in German 1939 and English 1969).

Elliott, L. Opinion. *The Guardian*. 12 Apr 2018.

Evans, M., Menon, A. 2017. *Brexit and British Politics*. Polity.

Fawcett, E. 2015. *Liberalism: The Life of an Idea*. Princeton.

Foucault, M. 2008. *The Birth of Biopolitics: Lectures at the College de France, 1978–1979*. Palgrave Macmillan.

Friedman, M. 1962. *Capitalism and Freedom*. University of Chicago Press.

Fukuyama, F. 1989. The End of History. *The National Interest*.

Fukuyama, F. 1992. *The End of History and the Last Man*. The Free Press.

Fukuyama, F. 2022. *Liberalism and Its Discontents*. Profile.

Gamble, A. 1979. The free economy and the strong state. In, Miliband, R., Saville, J. (Eds) *Socialist Register*. Merlin.

Garrard, O. 2022. *The Return of the State*. Yale.

Giddens, A. 1998. *The Third Way: The Renewal of Social Democracy*. Polity

Goodhart, D. 2017. *The Road to Somewhere: The New Tribes Shaping British Politics. Politics*. Penguin.

Goodhart, D. 2020. *Head Hand Heart: The Struggle for Dignity and Status in the 21st Century*. Allen Lane.

Goodwyn, L. 1978. *The Populist Moment: A Short History of the Agrarian Revolt in America*. Oxford University Press.

Gopnick, A. 2016. Liberal-in-chief. *The New Yorker*, 23 May, 23–24.

Gough, I. 1980. Thatcherism and the welfare state. *Marxism Today*. July, 8.

Grav, P.F. 2008. *Shakespeare and the Economic Imperative: "What's aught but as 'tis valued?"* Routledge.

Greenspan, A., Wooldridge, A. 2018. *Capitalism in America: A History*. Allen Lane.

Greve, B. (Ed) 2021. *Handbook on Austerity, Populism and the Welfare State*. Edward Elgar.

Habermas, J. 2017. For a democratic polarisation: How to pull the ground from under right –wing populism. *Social Europe Journal*, 11, 24–29.

Hall, S. 2011. The neo-liberal revolution. *Cultural Studies*, 25, 705–728.

Harris, J. 2019. Crowd control. *The Guardian Weekend*, 23 Nov, 33–35.

Harvey, D. 2005. *A Brief History of Neoliberalism*. Oxford, Oxford University Press.

Haveman, R.H. 1987. *Poverty Policy and Poverty Research: The Great Society and the Social Sciences*. Wisconsin, The University of Wisconsin Press.

Hayek, F.A. 1960. *The Constitution of Liberty*. University of Chicago Press.

Hennessy, P. 2022. *A Duty of Care: Britain Before and After Covid*. Allen Lane.

Honigsbawn, M. 2020. *The Pandemic Century: A History of Global Contagion from the Spanish Flu to Covid-19*. W.H. Allen.

Hutton, W. 1996. *The State We're In*. London, Vintage.

Hutton, W. 2019. Comment and analysis. *The Observer*. 3 Mar, 46.

Hutton, W. 2022. This may come as a surprise … *The Observer*. 20 Feb, 52.

Ishiguro, K. 2016. Remembrance of things Proust. *The Guardian Review*. 25 June, 18.

Keynes, J.M. 1936. *The General Theory of Employment, Interest and Money*. Palgrave, Macmillan.

Laclau, E. 2005. *On Populist Reason*. London, Verso.

Lasker, J.D. 2016. *Hoping to Help*. Cornell University Press.

Lepore, J. 2019. The fireman. *The New Yorker*, 18 & 25 Feb, 88–92.

Levitsky, S., Ziblatt, D. 2019. *How Democracies Die*. Penguin Books.

Lilla, M. 2018. *The Once and Future Liberal: After Identity Politics*. C. Hurst and Co Publishers.

Lilla, M. 2016. *The Shipwrecked Mind: On Political Reaction*. The New York Review of Books Inc.

Macpherson, C.B. 1962. *The Political Theory of Possessive Individualism*. Oxford, Clarendon Press.

Macpherson, C.B. 1973. Elegant tombstones: A note on Friedman's freedom. *Democratic Theory: Essays in Retrieval*. Oxford, Clarendon.

Mandeville, B. [1728] 2010. *The Fable of the Bees, or Private Vices, Public Benefit*. Kessinger Publishing.

Mannion, R., Small, N. 1999. Postmodern health economics. *Health Care Analysis*, 7, 255–272.

May, T. 2018. Thinking Sociologically in Turbulent Times. British Sociological Association News. https://www.britsoc.co.uk/about/latest-news/2018/september/thinking-sociologically-in-turbulent-times/

McGimpsey, I. 2017. Late neoliberalism: Delineating a policy regime. *Critical Social Policy*, 37(1), 64–84.

McNeill, W.H. 1997. What we mean by the West. *Orbis*, Fall, 513–524.

Menand, L. 2018. What identity demands. *The New Yorker*, 3 Sept, 61–68.

Miller, P., Rose, N. 2008. *Governing the Present: Administering Economic, Social and Personal Life*. Cambridge, Polity Press.

Moffitt, B. 2016. *The Global Rise of Populism: Performance, Political Style, and Representation*. Stanford, CA, Stanford University Press.

Mouffe, C. 2018. *For a Left Populism*. Verso.

Mudge, S.L. 2018. *Leftism Reinvented: Western Parties from Socialism to Neoliberalism*. Harvard University Press.

Mudde, C. 2007. *The Populist Radical Right*. Cambridge, Cambridge University Press.

Müller, J-W. 2017. A majority of "deplorables"? *Social Europe Journal*, 11, 14–17, 20–21.

Müller, J-W. 2017a. *What Is Populism?* Penguin.

Muniz, M. 2017. Popularism and the need for a new social contract. *Social Europe Journal*, 11, 10–13.

Neiwert, D. 2017. *Alt-America: The Rise of the Radical Right in the Age of Trump*. Verso.

Nettleton, S. 1997. Governing the risky self: How to become Healthy, Wealthy and Wise. In, Petersen, A., Bunton, R. (Eds) *Foucault, Health and Medicine* (pp. 371–398). London, Routledge.

Nietzsche, F. [1878]. 1994. *Human All Too Human*. Penguin Classics.

Nussbaum, M.C. 2001. *Upheavals of Thought: The Intelligence of Emotions*. Cambridge University Press.

Nussbaum, M.C. 2018. *The Monarchy of Fear: A Philosopher Looks at Our Political Crisis*. Oxford University Press.

Offe, C. 1984. *The Contradictions of the Welfare State*. London, Routledge.

Osborne, D., Gaebler, T. 1992. *Reinventing Government: How the Entrepreneurial Spirit is Transforming the Public Sector*. New York, Basic Books.

Peck, J., Tickell, A. 2002. Neoliberalizing space. *Antipode*, 34, 380–404.

Perryman, M. (Ed) 2017. *The Corbyn Effect*. Lawrence and Wishart.

Pettersson, K. 2017. Without social democracy, capitalism will eat itself. *Social Europe Journal*, 11, 4–9.

Piketty, T. 2014. *Capital in the Twenty-First Century*. Harvard University Press.

Piketty, T. 2020. *Capital and Ideology*. Harvard.

Polanyi, K. [1944] 2002 (2nd Ed). *The Great Transformation*. Farrar and Rinehart (Beacon Press).

Power, M. 2019. *Food Insecurity and Food Aid in "Advanced" Neoliberalism: Interrogating the Trajectory of Neoliberalism through a Study of Food Insecurity and Food Aid in Contemporary Bradford*. Doctoral Thesis, University of York.

Putnam, R., Romney Garrett, S. 2020. *The Upswing: How America Came Together a Century Ago and How We Can Do It Again*. Swift.

Rawls, J. 1971. *A Theory of Justice*. Harvard University Press.

Rawnsley, A. 2018. Populists will eventually be found out – moderates must be ready for that day. *The Observer*, 11 Mar, 49.

Rawnsley, A. 2018a. Has the west lost its appetite for democracy? *The Observer Review*, 20 May, 46–47.

Remnick, D. 2016. It happened here. *The New Yorker*, 28 Nov, 54–65.

Renwick, C. 2017. *Bread for All: The Origins of the Welfare State*. Allen Lane.

Rose, N. 1996. Governing "Advanced" Liberal Democracies. In, Barry, A., Osborne, T., Rose, N. (Eds) *Foucault and Political Reason: Liberalism, Neo-Liberalism and Rationalities of Government*. London, UCL Press.

Rose, N. 1999 2nd Ed. *Governing the Soul: The Shaping of the Private Self*. London, Free Association.

Ross, A. 2019. The eternal return. In, *The New Yorker*, 14 Oct, 34–39.

Rorty, R. 1999. *Achieving Our Country: Leftist Thought in Twentieth-century America.* Harvard University Press.

Runciman, D. 2018. *How Democracy Ends.* Profile.

Sacks, J. 2020. *Morality: Restoring the Common Good in Divided Times.* Hodder and Stoughton.

Sage, D. 2012. A challenge to liberalism? The communitarianism of the Big Society and Blue Labour. *Critical Social Policy*, 32, 365–382.

Sandbrook, D. 2009. *White Heat.* Abacus.

Sassoon, D. 2006. *The Culture of the Europeans.* Harper Press.

Saxer, M. 2017. Ten theses for the fight against right-wing populism. *Social Europe Journal*, 11, 14–17.

Scott, B. 2022. *Cloudmoney: Cash Cards, Crypto and the War for our Wallets.* Bodley Head.

Smith, A. [1759] 2010. *The Theory of Moral Sentiments.* Penguin Classics.

Snowden, F. 2020. *Epidemics and Society: From the Black Death to the Present.* Yale University Press.

Snyder, T. 2017. *On Tyranny: Twenty Lessons from the Twentieth Century.* Bodley Head.

Snyder, T. 2018. Donald Trump borrows from the old tricks of Fascism. *The Guardian.* 30 Oct.

Social Insurance and Allied Services. 1942. *The Beveridge Report.* Cmd 6404.

Stocker, P. 2017. *English Uprising: Brexit and the Main-streaming of the Far Right.* Melville House.

Speed, E., Mannion, R. 2017. The rise of post-truth populism in pluralist liberal democracies: Challenges for health policy. *Integrated Journal Health Policy Management*, 6(5), 249–251.

Springer, S. 2012. Neoliberalism as discourse: Between Foucauldian political economy and Marxian poststructuralism. *Critical Discourse Studies*, 9, 133–147.

Steger, M.B., Roy, R.K. 2010. *Neoliberalism: A Very Short Introduction.* Oxford University Press.

Tawney, R.H. [1920]. 2019. *The Acquisitive Society.* Wentworth Press.

Taylor-Gooby, P. 1981. The new right and social policy. *Critical Social Policy*, 1(1), 18–31.

de Tocqueville, A. [1835] 2002. *Democracy in America.* University of Chicago Press.

Tooze, A. 2018. *Crashed: How a Decade of Financial Crises Changed the World.* Allen Lane.

Tooze, A. 2018a. Beyond the crash. *The Observer*, 29 July, 34–35.

Touraine, A. 2001. *Beyond Neoliberalism.* Polity Press.

Toynbee, P., Walker, D. 2011. *The Verdict: Did Labour Change Britain.* Granta.

Van Sciver, N., Buhle, P., Max, S. 2019. *Eugene V Debs: A Graphic Biography.* Verso.

Vernon, J. 2007. *Hunger. A Modern History.* Cambridge, MA, Harvard University Press.

Ward, K., England, K. 2007. Introduction: Reading neoliberalism. In, England, K., Ward, K. (Eds) *Neoliberalisation: States, networks, people.* Malden, MA, Blackwell, 1–22.

Wells, S. 2016. Thought for the Day, BBC Radio 4, *Today Programme*, 17/11.

Williams, R. 1983. *Keywords.* Fontana.

Wolf, M. 2019. Saving capitalism from the rentiers. *Financial Times.* 18 Sept, 9.

Wolfe, T. 1970. *Radical Chic and Mau-Mauing the Flak Catchers.* New York, Farrar, Straus and Giroux.

Wood, J. 2019. Can you forgive her? *The New Yorker*, 2 Dec, 59–64.

Wright, P. 1985. *On Living in an Old Country.* Verso.

Yeates, W.B. 1919. The Second Coming. In, *Selected Poems*, 2000, Penguin Classics, London

Zevin, A. 2019. *Liberalism at Large: The World According to the Economist.* Verso.

Zielonka, J. 2018. *Counter-Revolution: Liberal Europe in Retreat.* Oxford University Press.

Zuboff, S. 2019. *The Age of Surveillance Capitalism: The Fight for. Future at the New Frontier of Power.* Profile Books.

Part II
The impacts of neoliberalism

3 Change in action
Neoliberalism and the economics of the NHS

Introduction

Neoliberalism is more than a political philosophy enacted through economics. If we look at neoliberalism in action, and imagine a Russian Doll, the largest doll is a particular sort of economics, marketisation sits inside it and as we continue to open the doll we reveal changes to organisations and the professions that staff them and, further still, changes in social attitudes and in individual subjectivities. Sometimes the economic, political and attitudinal components of neoliberalism work in close harmony. Sometimes one component is in the ascendancy, sometimes they seem to diverge, prompting the question "is this still neoliberalism?" The complex relationship of political and economic agendas characteristic of populism offers the prime example of this, sometimes populism manifests as a modified neoliberalism, sometimes it appears antipathetic to its tenets. But marketisation and privatisation have been neoliberalism's constant bedfellows.

The marketisation of the public sector, which initially accelerated in the Thatcherite 1980s, has not only changed the organisation of the NHS but also its ethos. A massive cultural change was brought about by a new approach to applied economics but was not just economic in its impact. It was accompanied by a systematic attack on solidarities, first on the idea of collective bargaining by NHS workers and then moving on to deconstruct professional identities that claimed a legitimacy separate to that of the market – doctors solidarities as doctors for example (I will consider doctors as managers and as workers in Chapter 4).

The ideas of common purpose and shared identity are countervailing powers to a primacy of markets. They have been attacked and undermined (see Box 3.1 for some of the ways this is manifest). This has been done in our work lives but then, as the hegemonic project of marketisation progresses, in all aspects of our lives from our patterns of consumption to our sociality (often played out in our social media.) It is not surprising if this attack changes the way we see our relationship with our fellow workers and with the welfare state and changes the relationship (and responsibility) we have with those in need.

DOI: 10.4324/9781003332404-5

Box 3.1 Wealth, morals and quickly forgetting

The moralisation of wealth – The monetarists' argument is that the pursuit and possession of wealth is moral – effort should be rewarded, there are wealth creators whose efforts trickle down into benefits for all. This is, in effect, a moralisation of privilege.

Social amnesia – the sorts of social atmosphere created in neoliberal society is one that does not look to, and does not remember, the past. So, you can do things that create great damage to others and, even if you get caught, you soon can come back and do it again! Bankers can do exploitative things, reap huge rewards, create chaos, be bailed out and then quickly return to doing it again – even after the crash of 2008 banks kept paying huge bonuses, they understood that people forget and that the crash did not disrupt the hegemonic order. They can even quickly return to pontificating about what the economy/society needs.[1] In the ten years after the 2008 financial crisis, the number of billionaires in the world almost doubled (Oxfam Report 21 Jan 2019).

Moral distance – The processes of governmentality and financialisaton (described below), plus outsourcing and privatisation, exacerbate a sense of their being deserving and undeserving people accessing welfare services. Organisations, including the NHS, are impacted by this (I will consider the ethical challenges of reconciling care and profit as motives in health care below). Two sorts of processes ensue, one an active one characterised by moral distancing (May et al 2019) and the other a less overt but far-reaching one of the erosion of social solidarity (see Lister 2003). There is a developing sense of their being "less-worthy" citizens (see Patrick 2017). These shifts are overtly played out in social security systems and most clearly exemplified in the "food bank" (Power and Small 2021), but they are also evident in the relationships between carer and patient.

An ascendancy of economics

We are going about things the wrong way if we outsource identifying what we should do to economists. They will go with what they think they can measure and will tell us these are the most important things. We are also ignoring the politics inherent in approaches to economics, dressing it up as science by using maths doesn't take the politics out (Nesvetailova and Palan 2020) (see Box 3.2).

Kay and King[2] (2020) point to a search by economists for "mathematical certainty", this was fuelled by their being captured by the appeal of probability theory as a route to tame uncertainty – they wanted to be like physicists, and they wanted to make forecasts. The rise of mathematical modelling and game theory has split economics off from its pre-mathematical past (Baert 2007). Kay and King

---

Box 3.2 Cause of the financial crash 2008

The most obvious cause is the actions of financiers themselves – especially the irrationally exuberant Anglo-Saxon sort, who claimed to have found a way to banish risk when in fact they had simply lost track of it. Central bankers and other regulators also bear blame, for it was they who tolerated this folly. The macroeconomic backdrop was important, too. The "Great Moderation" – years of low inflation and stable growth – fostered complacency and risk-taking. A "savings glut" in Asia pushed down global interest rates. Some research also implicates European banks, which borrowed greedily in American money markets before the crisis and used the funds to buy dodgy securities. All these factors came together to foster a surge of debt in what seemed to have become a less-risky world (taken from *The Economist – Schools Guide*).

Other causes – failure of the US housing market/securitisation/toxic debt/deregulation/hedge fund trading in derivatives

See: John Lanchester 2010. *Whoops*. Penguin.
Michael Lewis 2010. *The Big Short*. Allen Lane.

---

point out that this concern to predict and to do so by using maths has two faults; first, the forecasts of economists are often very bad, examples include failures to either forecast the 2008 crash or to forecast the likely rate of growth after the crash. Second, the important questions are not amenable to being quantified. Those important questions are about how to make good decisions in an uncertain world, to do this we have to make narratives (or parables) about what we want to happen or what we want to stop happening, and then use economics as a tool to do those bits it is equipped to do.[3]

Two key aspects of the economics underpinning marketisation, specifically incentives and measurement, have been identified by Skidelsky (2014) as "dangerous mechanisms at the heart of economics".

1 Incentives – monetary incentives crowd out professional pride, institutional loyalty, and public spirit. They may also create incentives that make sense when judged at the single institution level but when considered in terms of the overall picture of either an individual or, for example, a health economy they appear perverse. A payment-by-results system encourages a hospital to admit a patient rather than engage with other services to reduce the need for admission for example (Paterson 2009: 26).

2 Measurement systems shape the conduct of the organisations they seek to measure, for example if you rate hospitals on patient turnover "they will turn patients over with indecent haste". "A measure is a dangerous tool, for it tends to take the place of whatever it measures. The thing itself – talent, health – disappears behind a numerical proxy" (Skidelsky 2014).[4]

The reification of data

Public sector bureaucracies have created what Monbiot calls "quantomania", an obsession with measuring (Monbiot 2019). But we could be cleverer with the numbers we choose to use and we could also empower other groups to take control of their own data, for example giving patients data about their care in such a way that they can make informed choices (Taylor 2013).[5] We could then make decisions based on a combination of what works, as evidenced by the numbers, and what works according to the experiences of patients.

But too much reliance on the numbers carries risks, even if the numbers are better numbers! Numerical values don't generate good phenomenology – they are not good at navigating the rich texture of lived reality; the perceptions, movements, interactions and expectations of our ordinary experiences (Bakewell 2016: 325).[6] O'Neil (2017) warns that if we use numbers to build models that help us make predictions those models reflect the goals and ideology of those who create them, "Models are opinions that are embedded in Mathematics" they perpetuate and reinforce inequality – algorithms and mathematical models should be tools, not masters and yet they shape so many areas of our lives; health insurance, how societies are policed, how we respond to epidemics and many other areas. There are many examples in the Covid-19 epidemic where the mantra "we follow the science" was linked to the models of the spread of infection that were being developed. While, in many cases, these models proved accurate and useful their elevation in the discourse of the epidemic promoted the (false) idea of a monolithic, uncontested science or acted as a cloak for decisions based on an assessment of political expediency. O'Neil says we have to learn to read between the lines (of code) to unlock their hidden biases (see Box 3.3).[7,8]

Being cleverer with the numbers, then means not just producing "better" numbers but thinking about the philosophical, the existential, questions that should be raised when we approach making decisions about our lives and the lives of others based on them. If there is some concern about which numbers to use there is also a question *pace* Einstein about "whether everything that matters can be counted and whether everything that matters can be counted".

Epidemiology is a word derived from combining epi and demos (above/around/besides the people), it is the science of aggregation, the science of the many. It works best when it is in step with the science of the one – medicine for example. For example, in the coronavirus pandemic, the overall picture of virus spread in any population is important but so too is the way the virus is manifest in each individual. We have to consider the collective and the individual. "The one becomes the many. Count both; both count" (Mukherjee 2020: 22).

Episodes in the history of marketisation in the NHS

Meek (2014) makes the case that the NHS hasn't been privatised in a literal sense but it "has been commercialised and repeatedly reorganised, with competition introduced, in such a way as to create a kind of shadowing of an as-yet-unrealised

Box 3.3 Predictive models and algorithms

Algorithms are integral to how computers work – they are now being used alongside big data to generate machine learning that is used to make prediction based on observations of past behaviours. But there are intrinsic flaws in the technological "solutionism", "its judgements reflect the biases in the data-sets … which can make the technology an amplifier of inequality, racism or poverty". However, despite the flaws, algorithms that can have serious downsides for society are increasingly evident across society, tech companies seem exempt from any scrutiny regarding public harm before they roll out new algorithms. Naughton calls this "tech exceptionalism" and argues that ruling elites in liberal democracies are mesmerised by them and seem oblivious to the accumulating monopolistic power of these companies (Naughton 2020: 18).

Algorithms are procedures or sets of rules for calculating or problem solving – they were used in 2020 to attribute A-level exam grades to students who had not sat the exams because of the Covid-19 pandemic. More than one-third of results in England were downgraded from those that had been issued based on teacher assessment. Protests from pupils, parents and teachers followed and the algorithm generated results were scrapped. Other examples of where these predictive algorithms are used include finance – getting a loan; Police – allocating resources by predicting who is likely to commit crimes based on past crime figures; social work – using algorithms to predict who will need child services. All these areas are rife for the risk of perpetuating data biases and stigma.

Sometimes the numbers are just wrong – on 17 March 2020, UK Chief Scientific Advisor Sir Patrick Vallance said if we keep the number of UK Covid deaths below 20,000 that would be a good outcome. By July 2022 Covid deaths in the UK reached 200,000 (Sridhar 2022). The, in retrospect, wildly optimistic 20,000 was a manifestation of seeking to predict in what was a fast-changing and novel scenario but it was also a figure that complemented and helped create a narrative then being developed.

private health insurance system". Marketisation is implemented via an encroachment of profit into a system set up to meet basic medical needs – it changes the ethos from one that is about how to provide public provision to a concern to act on a model of market exchange. "The introduction of market forces (and cash) into public services erodes the idea that health provision is a public good that cannot be captured via the price mechanism alone" (Hutton 1996: 333).

There are two key points of change in the history of the NHS that are particularly pertinent in an argument that is seeking to explore how markets might supplant traditional collective and professional values, the NHS and Community

Care Act of 1990 and the Health and Social Care Act of 2012 (see House of Commons 1990: Department of Health and Social Care 2012) (see Box 3.4).

The 1990 Act redefined the relationship between District Health Authorities and the hospitals within the geographic area they covered. Prior to the Act, there were administrative, geographical and historical ties; after the Act, the relationship between them is defined by contracts and carries no broader obligation on either side. This was the establishment of an internal market and constituted the separation of governance and service provision. It was part of a "spread of a culture of contractualism…where the disciplines of the market tend to supplant more traditional collective and professional values" (Hughes and Dingwall 1990: 296). The assumption inherent in the 1990 Act was that these were reforms that would facilitate more efficient management. The strategy was to bring to the NHS what was taking place in education, social work and in a range of public utilities, that is, facilitating the primacy of market forces in the provision of public services.

The possibility that changing culture in one area of the NHS would impact on culture in other parts, specifically in the culture of care, is what is important for the case I am making here. A primacy of markets changes the way resources are allocated (including total amounts allocated) and priorities set. It also changes the way people talk and think and this changes how they act: "A society that talks incessantly about 'productivity' but that hardly understands, much less uses, the word 'resilience' to going to become productive and not resilient" (Meadows 2008: 174). A newspaper headline from 1990 captures a new, but now more familiar, irony, "Of course I love you – it's in the contract" (Plant 1990).

The 2012 Health and Social Care Act was a shift towards further opening an already ajar door to privatisation (see Davis and Tallis 2013). What it created was a "market-driven, 'out-for-tender' mentality where care is provided by the lowest bidder" and where market bureaucracies introduce extra cost and inefficiency" (Abdullah et al. 2015). Of 3494 contracts awarded by 182 Clinical Commissioning Groups (CCGs) in England between April 2013 and August 2014, 33% went to the private sector (http://www.bbc.co.uk/news/health-30397329 accessed 9/4/2015). In relation to social care, funding reductions for local authorities have undermined their provision, consequences include longer stays in hospital because of the difficulty of finding an appropriate place to discharge patients, and more pressure on GPs and on Accident and Emergency services because of the lack of social care places to ameliorate pressures being felt by home carers. (These are changes in the relationship between hospital and social care provision that became a key point of tension during the Covid-19 pandemic in 2020 where discharge of vulnerable older people from increasingly pressured hospitals to care homes spread the virus to that sector and many deaths resulted.)

Private firms and NHS contracts

The Health and Social Care Act wasn't the only route by which the profit motive was locked into the NHS, Foundation Trusts, private finance initiatives, and the

Box 3.4 Some key steps in the privatisation and marketisation of the NHS

1989 – introduction of the idea of organising the NHS via an "internal market" in the White Paper *Working for Patients* (Department of Health 1989: see Small 1989).

1990 – NHS and Community Care Act – purchaser/provider split (including establishing GP fundholding.) 1997 – fundholding abolished but purchaser/provider split retained.

Examples of measures strengthening the internal market between the 1990 and 2012 Acts

- Use of private providers via Diagnostic and Treatment Centres, later called Independent Treatment Centres, commissioned by the NHS.
- Private finance initiative – using private capital to build public infrastructure, with long-term repayments resulting.
- Practice based commissioning – a new form of GP fundholding in which GPs in large geographically based Primary Care Trusts (PCTs) commissioned services for their patients.
- Payment by results – introduced in 2005, payments for NHS Trust services were given based on standardised tariffs for average costs for the actual work they did (previously hospitals were given a global budget based on historical usage and expenditure). This meant that NHS PCTs could buy services from any Trust.

(see Pollock 2004: Hunter 2008)

2012 Health and Social Care Act. This changed the responsibility of the Secretary of State for Health from one where they had a duty to "secure or provide free of charge a comprehensive health service for the prevention, diagnosis and treatment of illness" into one where the duty was to "promote" rather than secure (Section 75 of the Health and Social Care Act). "Promote" allows the opportunity for private companies to take over what they consider will be profitable. Governmental responsibility was shifted to ad hoc bodies, Clinical Commissioning Groups most significantly, in a move that further opened the NHS to competitive markets in which private sector organisations were seeking market share (Department of Health and Social Care 2012.)

Details of some key innovations.

The *Private Finance Initiative* (PFI) is "a form of contracting that relieves a firm of competition" (Toynbee and Walker 2017: 103). It has been around, and present in contracting a lot of services across government, since the early 1990s. Essentially it operates by encouraging private firms to build, say, a new hospital by borrowing money on the commercial market. The

NHS Trust involved then agrees to cover the borrowing charges associated with the loan and pay for the ongoing maintenance of the building. The NHS is locked into a lengthy and expensive financial commitment (even if the private company refinances the deal at more favourable rates thus achieving a healthy profit for itself). PFI was used by Tory and Labour governments, Labour arguing that it was the only way to get the needed rapid reconstruction of the old NHS estate. It is a "Trojan horse undercutting the very principle of public provision in the common interest. Providers of private finance are not Santa Claus; they seek high returns on their investment, and minimal risk" (Hutton 1996: 333).

Foundation Trusts: these legally independent organisations are Public Benefit Corporations set up under the Health and Social Care (Community Health and Standards) Act 2003 (see Department of Health 2005). The first Foundation Trusts were announced in 2004 and by the end of 2012, there were 144 (including the Mid-Staffordshire Trust). The governing Labour Parties' intention was that these new sorts of trusts would be independent from the central direction of Whitehall and, as such, would help devolve and decentralise decision making and better tailor provision to meet local needs. In pursuit of this, the trusts could raise capital from public and private sectors and retain financial surpluses to invest in new services. Monitor was set up in 2004 to authorise, monitor and regulate Foundation Trusts. In April 2016, Monitor became part of NHS Improvement (see www.dh.gov. uk/nhsfoundationtrusts).

ability of trusts to charge for a range of services were already in place.[9] Even in wider commissioning structures, there was a considerable degree of encroachment by those concerned to pursue profits. In March 2013 the BMJ estimated that one-third of board members of CCGs had financial interests in healthcare providers. But the Act offered "unheralded opportunities for numerous for profit companies" these included Virgin Care, Serco, Care UK (in 2011, 31 out of 38 CCGs in London had contracts with private firms for intensive organisational support) (see Davis et al. 2015). In 2009–10, the Department of Health paid over £26 million to private consultancies (American firm McKinsey and Company were the biggest recipient of this money).

During 2016–17 almost 70% of the 386 clinical contracts that were put out to tender by the NHS in England were awarded to private firms. (These included the seven highest value contracts) and the total value to private firms was £3.1bn – a rise from the £2.4bn of the previous year. The total of contracts tendered by the NHS for services was £7.2bn making the private sectors share 43%. The biggest single private firm winning these tenders was Virgin Care, with Care UK in second place (see NHS Support Federation 2017).[10] The NHS Support Federation also reports a series of contract failures involving the private sector.

- Hinchingbrooke Hospital – here the private company Circle pulled out of a ten year contract to run the hospital after just two years during which they encountered both financial problems and severe criticism from the Care Quality Commission.
- Serco ended its contract to provide out-of-hours GP care in Cornwall in 2013 after some of its staff falsified data about its performance.
- Coperforma's delivery of non-urgent patient transport in southern England was much criticised by health unions and it lost the contract in 2016 (see NHS Support Federation website for regular updates on contract failures *nhs-forsale.info*)

BMJ Fact Check (https://www.bmj.com/content/367/bmj downloaded 20/11/2019) looks beyond the proportion of tenders awarded to the private sector and considers the overall proportion of the NHS budget spent on private providers. They chart an increase (under all political parties) from 2.8% in 2006–07 to 7.3% in 2018–19 (the peak was 7.7% in 2016–17). The rise followed a decision made in 2000 to expand competition in the English NHS. The Kings Fund considers the 7.3% to be an underestimate reflecting a lack of detail available to interrogate the exact makeup of local contracts (Kings Fund 2019) and the Centre for Health and the Public Interest argue that both a wider view of what expenditure to included is required (to include spending on private providers by local authorities, charities, the voluntary sector and social care) and a narrower focus as to what is considered "health" spending (they argue this should not include spending on regulatory bodies or the cost of running the Department of Health and Social Care itself). Given these caveats, they argue that the proportion of the NHS budget spent on private providers is closer to 18% (Rowland 2019).

While there may have been a tactical decision by political parties that privatising core NHS services outright would not be acceptable to the electorate there was no such embargo on subjecting these services to "market disciplines". These disciplines distort priorities, for example previously existing integrated services were broken up because the benefits of continuity and cooperation were not factored into the cost-led outsourcing scenario.[11]

In a wide-ranging speech to the Royal Society of Medicine physicist Professor Stephen Hawking included criticism of NHS privatisation. He said that the £2.9bn spent every year by hospitals in England on temporary personnel to alleviate chronic understaffing has enriched private employment firms while denying the NHS vital funding. "The huge increase in the use of private agency staff, for example, inevitably means that money is extracted from the system as profit for the agency and increases costs for the whole country". He also feared that private firms have gained such a large role in treating NHS patients they are now undermining its founding principles and opening the door to the Americanisation of care.

We must prevent the establishment of a two-tier service, with the best medicine for the wealthy and an inferior service for the rest. International comparisons indicate that the most efficient way to provide good healthcare is for services to be publicly funded and publicly run.

(reported in *The Guardian* 19 August 2017)

The sort of outsourcing of NHS care that was speeded up by the 2012 reforms has been bad for health care. A report in July 2022 shows the growth in health contracts being tendered to private companies has been associated with a drop in care quality and significantly higher rates of treatable mortality – patient deaths considered avoidable with timely, effective health care. Researchers analysed data showing how much 173 CCGs in England spent on outsourcing between 2013 and 2020, in this time it grew from 3.9% to more than 6.4%. In total, £11.5bn was handed to private companies over the period, although the amount varied considerably between CCGs. The analysis shows that an annual increase in outsource spending of 1% is associated with a rise in treatable mortality of 0.38% – or 0.29 deaths per 100,000 people – the following year. Researchers claim 557 additional deaths between 2014 and 2020 might be attributed to the rise in outsourcing. The authors speculated that the higher mortality might be due to private companies "delivering worse-quality care, resulting in more health complications and deaths", or because greater competition for contracts may result in for-profit providers prioritising shorter waiting times "at the expense of quality of care" (Goodair and Reeves 2022.)

Market discipline – how profits changes priorities

McCartney (2012) asks, "what happens when you turn patients into customers?", the answer, you get "sexed-up" medicine, clinics and waiting rooms full of the healthy wanting screening or their blood pressure/cholesterol measured, pharmaceutical companies glossing over research they don't like and pushing products that are especially profitable for them (see Goldacre 2013), charities become preoccupied with raising the profile of "their disease", thousands of companies offer services and products to the anxious well and a residue of the chronic sick and elderly are pushed out to the periphery.

Davis and Tallis (2013) add to this critique in their identification of the growth of the market and of private medicine shifting central principles of the NHS such that we can no longer assume, "vocation has to have a higher value than shareholders' profits and quality must not come second to competition".

What happens when you turn hospitals into businesses? I began my Introduction with a consideration of the Mid-Staffordshire NHS Hospital Trust, its management strove for, and became, a Foundation Trust. The market ethos they engaged with as they sought foundation status led to a lack of focus on patient care, staff cuts, falling morale, over-reliance on agency staff, secrecy. Changes in priorities are also evident in other areas:

Schools teach to the test, depriving children of a rounded and useful education. Hospitals manipulate waiting times, shuffling patients from one list to

Box 3.5 Examples of marketisation elsewhere

73% of old *state industries, transport, public utilities and social utilities* are now in private hands. The five big privatisations have been the postal service, railways, water, electricity supply, and social housing. While there has been significant privatisation, there has been an even wider impact created by a process of commercialisation rather than privatisation including in the NHS (Meek 2014).

There has been a substantial privatisation of *land*, since 1979 10% of the land area of Britain has been sold by the state to the private sector, "the biggest privatisation of all is not housing, railways, or utilities but the oldest source of oligarchic power – land" (Christophers 2018). Since the 1980s millions of *council houses* have been sold and resold with social housing now privatised.

Higher Education has been marketised/commercialised/privatised (Brown and Carasso 2013; McGettigan 2013). Monitoring and accountability imposed on Universities through a succession of research assessment exercises (RAE's and REF's), universities must "justify themselves as somehow increasing national output – a requirement that denies that intellectual life has value as an end in itself and assumes everything of importance can be measured" (Grey 2016: 6). That obsession with metrics, scores, and a dubious prestige achieved through elevation via them, is a very neoliberal conceit. In universities, these changes have been contemporaneous with exponential fee rises for students that have impacted on the social mix of the student population and with very high salaries for Vice Chancellors – replacing the collegiality of the academy with a replica of a neoliberal economy (see Mckenzie 2017). It has been argued that neoliberalism is "manifest in everything from overpayment and overbearing management initiatives at the top to underpayment and insecurity at the bottom" and "ministers' insistence on ever greater levels of accountability and promotion of competition and consumerism" (Jump 2018: 5).

Example of markets in *childcare* – Troubled Families programme (Dept of Communities and Local Government 2012) for families with multiple problems included payment by results for local authorities – the result is they focussed not on those with greatest need but on those most likely to ensure payment is triggered (Thoburn 2013). An evaluation of the work of the Troubled Families Unit by the National Institute for Economic and Social Research in 2016 found that despite £1 billion spent on the programme it had failed to have a significant impact.

Three-quarters of children's homes are privately run and around a third of children are placed with foster families using private agencies. One in five privately run homes is classified by Ofsted as "not good enough".

Private homes are more expensive – Manchester City Council, for example reports that it can pay up to £6700 per week per child for a place in a private home, compared with just under £4000 in its own homes (Sodha 2019: 52). The Competition and Markets Authority report that private equity providers are making extremely high rates of profit and carrying concerning levels of debt that risks the stability of homes for children in care. Josh MacAlister, chair of a government-backed independent review of children's social care summed up, "the market of care for children is broken. Profiteering, children being moved far from their communities and a shortage of homes that meet children's needs are all urgent problems which need fixing" (*The Observer* 26 June 2022).

another. Police forces ignore some crimes, reclassify others, and persuade suspects to admit to extra offences to improve their statistics. Universities urge their researchers to write quick and superficial papers, instead of deep monographs, to maximise their scores under the research excellence framework.

(Monbiot 2019)

How marketisation changes the way we talk and think about patients and about health care

I began this chapter by saying neoliberalism is more than just the enactment of a particular sort of economics. It is also more than just changes in how money is allocated and how organisations work. It carries with it another agenda, to change individuals. Core to achieving that is shifting responsibility for welfare from the state to individuals by a promotion of the idea of "active citizenship". The neoliberal citizen (Galvin 2002: 6) is autonomous, active, and responsible. The dependent citizen (Kisby 2010) is reliant on others, passive and not contributing to the economy. It follows from this dichotomy that the active citizen needs to be protected (or be able to protect themselves) from moral and economic contagion that might spread from the dependent (Jensen and Tyler 2015), now, "not quite" citizens.[12]

"Privatisation within the NHS has only added to the problem: now that patients are seen as consumers, the old and chronically ill have become an underclass-degenerates or unregenerates whose continued existence doesn't merit much investment". [They are] bed-blockers. But "it's not only in hospitals that old people are ignored, written off and abused" (Morrison 2006) and it's not only in recent times. Shakespeare saw, "unregarded age in corners thrown" (in *As You Like It*) and there are widespread (and continuing) attitudes that the poor are feckless and the sick irresolute or ignorant.[13]

Intellectual history, across time and place, has engaged with the extent to which beliefs (sometimes categorised as ideologies) generate and sustain an approach an individual has to the society they live within. There is an "opinion corridor" – a narrow range of views that "respectable people" hold. The views in the corridor are not constant; over time they can pass from social democracy to neoliberalism for example, but whatever they are at any moment they constrain thinking from outside the bounds of the currently acceptable.[14]

Weber's analysis of *Protestantism and the Spirit of Capitalism* (2010: 1st published 1905) examines how a belief (or ideology), like the moral value of hard work, can infuse a society via its families, educational institutions and mass media to generate and then sustain an approach a person has with the society they live in even if they are not active participants in things like wealth creation. It can attribute worth and moral standing and cast out to the economic and moral periphery any who deviate from the orthodoxy. These sorts of processes continue, and, over time, the way we talk about public provision impacts on our views about health care and about patients, a prevailing ideology shapes how we make sense of things. The language we use might appear to be descriptive (summative), but it can be formative, it can constitute experience rather than just representing it and, at the same time, it can constrain or eliminate knowledge. It has an epistemic role (Foucault 1972).

> The replacement of citizenship defined as concern with the public good by citizenship reduced to the citizen as homo oeconomicus... eliminates the very idea of a people, a demos asserting its collective political sovereignty. the way neoliberalism differs from classical economic liberalism, is that all domains are markets and we are everywhere presumed to be market actors.
>
> (Brown 2015)

As such this new citizen replaces homo politicus and, in so doing, "eliminates the open question of how to craft the self or what paths to travel in life" (Brown 2015: 41).

Notes

1 Sajid Javid was on the board of Deutsche Bank during the financial crisis – a bank that was at the heart of much of the mis-selling that collapsed the global economy. He moved on to be the UK's Chancellor of the Exchequer (and subsequently to be Secretary of State for Health and Care).

2 Mervyn King was Governor of the Bank of England.

3 It's important to choose whose narratives or parables we listen to – not all are benign. Some narratives can cause great change in economies – a catastrophe narrative can generate a catastrophe for example. Nobel laureate Robert Schiller's 2019 book on *Narrative Economics* is sub-titled "How stories go Viral and Drive Major Economic Events" (Schiller 2019).

4 Goodhart's Law – "When a measure becomes a target it ceases to be a good measure", Charles Goodhart, former Chief Economist of the Bank of England, developed his "law" in the 1980s in the context of Margaret Thatcher's targeting the money supply to control inflation. What followed was that inflation ran out of control even when the government had a tight grip on money supply.

5 Taylor was one of the founders of the Dr Foster company and it was its identification of the failings of Stafford Hospital together with the voices of patients' relatives at that hospital, including Julie Bailey who founded the campaigning group "Cure the NHS",

which eventually led to the Francis inquiry. It is worth noting that extensive efforts were taken by the West Midlands Strategic Health Authority to undermine Dr Foster's data (see Small 2023).

6 I have referred to E M Forester's thoughts on this and also Sherry Turkle's plea to "Reclaim Conversation" in my considerations of dignity and trust in Chapter 8.

7 Data isn't neutral, and big data creates a spurious legitimacy for one way of seeing the relationship between knowledge and power. There are others (see Noveck 2015, 2016: 6). The seduction of big data, or of complicated numbers, is captured in the saying that "people with a hammer see all problems as needing nails".

8 If mathematics and their models characteristically get away without the scrutiny their ubiquity ought to prompt this is even more the case with the internet. In 2001, Hubert Dreyfus discussed the Internet as the technological innovation that most clearly reveals what technology is. Its infinite connectivity promises to make the entire world storable and available but in doing so it removes privacy and depth from things. Everything, above all ourselves, becomes a resource. In being made a resource we are handed over not just to another individual like ourselves but to an impersonal "they" who we never meet and can't locate.

When Heidegger discussed technology in 1953, he was thinking about typewriters, film projectors, cars, farm machinery, he said that technology isn't just an aggregation of clever devices it says something fundamental about our existence – we have to think about it philosophically it relates to how we work, how we occupy Earth, how we are in relation to Being (see Bakewell 2016: 324). By 2022, his thoughts have become all the more urgent! Tech-evangelists, including those who saw the internet as an irresistible global force for democracy should be chastened if they consider how connectivity elides into surveillance (see Zuboff 2019) and if they consider the huge accumulation of wealth in internet/tech companies.

9 There is a much wider contribution to the NHS from private firms than I consider here. My focus is on contracts for direct care or for organisational support/consultancy. I have not looked at private sector profits from pharmaceuticals or from building projects for example. See Davis et al. (2015) on the NHS and Toynbee and Walker (2017) for the wider societal picture, including the NHS.

10 The NHS Support Federation is an independent group of researchers campaigning since 1989 for fair and universal access to health and supporting the NHS.

11 In February 2019 NHS England called for a repeal of Section 75 of Lansley's Act in a bid to promote integration in the NHS. A "best value" test, they argued, would allow commissioners to decide when to use procurement and competitive tendering replacing the requirement so to do (Iacobucci 2019).

12 There is of course evidence for a disdain of the sick in previous times:

> I think it is high time that Mr Bunbury made up his mind whether he was going to live or to die. This shilly-shallying with the question is absurd. Nor do I approve of the modern sympathy with invalids. I consider it morbid. Illness of any kind is hardly a thing to be encouraged in others. Health is the primary duty of life.

Lady Bracknell says in Oscar Wilde's *The Importance of Being Earnest*, Act 1. (1st performed in 1895).

A political controversy was prompted in April 2021 during the Covid-19 pandemic by reports that the Prime Minister had said he would be prepared to see bodies piling up in the streets rather than instigate another lock-down of the economy, the Prime Minister denied saying this. At best, this sentiment reflects a realisation of the harm, including to the wider health of the public, that lock-downs cause. At worst it is a manifestation of the prioritisation of business and the economically productive over the older and economically marginalised sections of society, the groups most likely to end up in the pile of bodies.

13 The work led by Dr Madeleine Power on food banks has identified the resilience of these attitudes – see Power 2022.
14 This was discussed in relation to Covid-19 policy by Nick Cohen in *The Observer* 24 May 2020, 48.

References

Abdullah, S. and 140 others. Letter to the Editor *The Guardian*, 7 Apr 2015.

Baert, P. 2007. Contextualising Max Weber. *International Sociology*, 22(2), 119–128.

Bakewell, S. 2016. *At the Existentialist Café*. New York, Other Press.

Brown, W. 2015. *Undoing the Demos: Neoliberalism's Stealth Revolution*. Brooklyn, NY, Zone Books.

Brown, R., Carasso, H. 2013. *Everything for Sale: The Marketisation of UK Higher Education*. Routledge.

Christophers, B. 2018. *The New Enclosure: The Appropriation of Public Land in Neoliberal Britain*. Verso.

Davis, J., Lister, J., Wrigley, D. 2015. *NHS for Sale: Myths, Lies and Deception*. Merlin.

Davis, K., Stremikis, K., Squires, D., Schoen, C. 2014. *Mirror, Mirror on the Wall, 2014 Update: How the US Health Care System Compares Internationally*. New York, Commonwealth Fund.

Davis, J., Tallis, R. 2013. *NHS SOS: How the NHS Was Betrayed – and How We Can Save It*. Oneworld.

Department of Communities and Local Government. 2012. *The Troubled Families Programme*. London, Department of Communities and Local Government.

Department of Health. 1989. *Working for Patients*. Cm 555. London, HMSO.

Department of Health. 2005. *A Short Guide to NHS Foundation Trusts*. Dept of Health Publications 271433 Gateway 5591. Crown Copyright.

Department of Health and Social Care. 2012. *The Health and Social Care Act*. London, HMSO.

Dreyfus, H.L. 2011. *On the Internet*. Routledge, New York and London.

Foucault, M. 1972. *The Archaeology of Knowledge*. New York, Vintage.

Galvin, R. 2002. Disturbing notions of chronic illness and individual responsibility: Towards a genealogy of morals. *Health: An Interdisciplinary Journal for the Social Study and Health, Illness and Medicine*, 6(2), 107–137.

Goldacre, B. 2013. *Bad Pharma: How Medicine is Broken, and How We Can Fix It*. Fourth Estate.

Goodair, B., Reeves, A. 2022. Outsourcing health-care services to the private sector and treatable mortality rates in England, 2013–2020: An observational study of NHS privatisation. *The Lancet Public Health*, July. https://doi.org/10.1016/S2468-2667(22)00133-5

Gray, J. 2016. Review of "Anti-Education: On the Future of Our Educational Institutions" *The Guardian Review*, 9 Jan, 6.

Heidegger, M. 1953. The question concerning technology. Lecture published in, *The Question Concerning Technology and Other Essays*. 1977. New York, Harper.

House of Commons. 1990. *NHS and Community Care Act*. London, HMSO.

Hughes, D., Dingwall, R. 1990. Sir Henry Maine, Joseph Stalin and the reorganisation of the National Health Service. *Journal of Social Welfare Law*, 5, 296–309.

Hunter, D. 2008. *The Health Debate*. Bristol, Policy Press.

Hutton, W. 1996. *The State We're In*. London, Vintage.

Iacobucci, G. 2019. NHS England sets out plan to revoke Lansley's competition rules. *British Medical Journal*, 2–19, 364, 1990.

Jensen, T., Tyler, I. 2015. 'Benefits broods': The cultural and political crafting of anti-welfare commonsense. *Critical Social Policy*, 35, 470–491.

Jump, P. 2018. The threat to standards. *Times Higher Education* (Leader), 12 Apr, 5.

Kay, J., King, M. 2020. *Radical Uncertainty*. The Bridge Street Press.

Kings Fund. 2019. Is the NHS being privatised? October. https://www.kingsfund.org.uk/publications/articles/big-election-questions-nhs-privatised

Kisby, B.E.N. 2010. The big society: power to the people? *The Political Quarterly*, 81, 484–491.

Lanchester, J. 2010. *Whoops*. Penguin.

Lewis, M. 2010. *The Big Short*. Allen Lane.

Lister, R. 2003. *Poverty*. Cambridge, Polity.

May, J., Williams, A., Cloke, P., Cherry, L. 2019. Welfare convergence, bureaucracy, and moral distancing at the food bank. *Antipode*. http://dx.doi.org/10.1111/anti.12531

McCartney, M. 2012. *The Patient Paradox: Why Sexed Up Medicine Is Bad for Your Health*. Pinter and Martin Ltd.

McGettigan, A. 2013. *The Great University Gamble: Money, Markets and the Future of Higher Education*. Pluto Press.

McKenzie, L. 2017. The middle-class academic elite are totally out of touch. *Times Higher Education*, 7 Sept, 38–39.

Meadows, D.H. 2008. *Thinking in Systems: A Primer*. London, Earthscan.

Meek, J. 2014. *Private Island: Why Britain Now Belongs to Someone Else*. London. Verso.

Monbiot, G. 2019. Neoliberalism promised freedom – instead it delivers stifling control. *The Guardian*, Opinion, 10 Apr.

Morrison, B. 2006. "I said to the nurse, please feed her" http.www.theguardian.com/society/2006/jan/07/health.familyandrelationships (accessed 1/7/2015).

Mukherjee, S. 2020. How does the Coronavirus behave inside a patient? *The New Yorker*, 26 Mar.

Naughton, J. 2020. From viral conspiracies to exam fiascos, algorithms come with serious side effects. *The New Review: The Observer*, 6 Sept, 16–18.

Nesvetailova, A., Palan, R. 2020. *Sabotage: The Business of Finance*. Allen Lane.

NHS Support Federation. 2017. https:www.nhscampaign.org

Noveck, B.S. 2015. *Smart Citizens, Smarter State: The Technologies of Expertise and the Future of Governing*. Harvard University Press.

Noveck, B.S. 2016. Enough of experts: Data, democracy and the future of expertise. Annual Sage Publishing Lecture for the Campaign for Social Science, London 22 Nov. Published in *Academy of Social Sciences Professional Briefing*, Dec 2016, Issue 10.

O'Neil, C. 2017. *Weapons of Math Destruction: How Big Data Increases Inequality and Threatens Democracy*. Penguin.

Paterson, L. 2009. Darzi's reforms and the recession. *Health Matters*, 77, 25–26.

Patrick, R. 2017. Wither social citizenship? *Social Policy and Society*, 16(2), 293–304.

Plant, R. 1990. Of course I love you – it's in the contract. *The Times*, 29 Jan, 12.

Pollock, A.M. 2004. *NHS plc: The Privatisation of our Health Care*. London, Verso.

Power, M. 2022. *Hunger, Whiteness and Religion in Neoliberal Britain*. Policy Press.

Power, M., Small, N. 2021. Disciplinary and pastoral power, food and poverty in late-modernity. *Critical Social Policy*. https://doi.org/10.1177/0261018321999799

Rowland, D. 2019. Flawed data? Why NHS spending on the independent sector may actually be more than 7%. London School of Economics and Political Science. October. https://blogs.lse.ac.uk/politicsandpolicy/nhs-spending-on-the-independent-sector.

Schiller, R. 2019. *Narrative Economics*. Princeton University Press.

Skidelsky, E. Review of Philip Roscoe "I Spend, Therefore I am: The True Cost of Viking Economics. Review in *Guardian Review*, 25 Jan 2014.

Small, N. 1989. *Politics and Planning in the National Health Service*. Buckingham, Open University Press.

Small, N. 2023. *Failures in health and social care: Governance and Culture Change*. London, Routledge.

Sodha, S. 2019. How did children's homes become centres of profit-making and abuse? *The Observer*, 29 Dec 2019. 52.

Sridar, D. 2022. As Covid deaths in the UK surpass the grim milestone of 200,000 what have we learned? *Guardian Opinion*, 13 July.

Taylor, R. 2013. *God Bless the NHS. The Truth Behind the Current Crisis*. London, Faber and Guardian Books.

Thoburn, J. 2013. "Troubled families", "troublesome families" and the trouble with Payment by Results. *Families, Relationships and Societies*, 2, 471–475.

Toynbee, P., Walker, D. 2017. *Dismembered: How the Attack on the State Harms Us All*. London, Faber & Faber.

Weber, M. (2010: first published 1905) *The Protestant Ethic and the Spirit of Capitalism*. Oxford, Oxford University Press.

Wilde, O. (1895) 2007. *The Importance of Being Earnest* London, Penguin Classics.

Zuboff, S. 2019. *The Age of Surveillance Capitalism: The Fight for. Future at the New Frontier of Power*. London, Profile Books.

4 Changing organisations and the impact of neoliberalism on health professions

Introduction

The introduction and expansion of the market in health care, with its associated assumptions and practices derived from the business world, can be at odds with an established bureaucratic paradigm. Further, business and market disciplines change the professions that contribute to the NHS. Both in organisational practice and in professional identities hybrids emerge and it is these hybrids that will be examined in this chapter. Specifically, I will consider how, and if, NHS organisations can combine a public service and market-oriented approach and how the professions of management and of nursing and medicine are manifest under neoliberalism, including a consideration of when clinicians become managers. My argument will be that organisational changes and changes in the professions reflect the hegemonic position of neoliberalism that has shaped our perceptions of the possible and the desirable. The generational impact of neoliberalism is important as there is a cumulative effect created by its many changes and an ongoing and self-perpetuating reframing of the discursive world to privilege its assumptions.

Neoliberalism's impact on the NHS has both structure and practice components and, as such, connects with Habermas's system and lifeworld distinction (explored in detail in Chapter 6) which examines how the external world colonises the internal. But it also resonates with Parson's systems theory, albeit with a slightly different focus. Parsons discusses instrumental and consummatory (symbolic) functions as routes to how both culture and personal behaviours/choices are changed by externally decided adaptation and goal attainment (see Parsons 1951). Habermas and Parson's categories are summarised in Box 4.1.[1] What Habermas and Parsons both do is recognise that the process of change in organisations is about the context within which the organisation exists, the dynamics of the organisational form itself and the individual values that are made manifest and changed within the organisation. In the Parsonian system adapting to market changes and to the goals these set shapes organisational cultures and individual behaviours so that they are aligned with market ideals. Habermas, in a similar way, sees the lifeworld, including an individual's values, colonised by an economic and political system such as neoliberalism (Table 4.1).

DOI: 10.4324/9781003332404-6

Table 4.1 Habermas and Parsons

	Instrumental functions	*Consummatory functions*
External problems	Adaptation	Goal attainment
Internal problems	Latency/Pattern maintenance	Integration
System world (material production)	A Economy/money	G Political system/political power
Lifeworld (symbolic reproduction)	L Fiduciary System/value commitments	I Society/communities/influence

Neoliberalism, bureaucracy and markets

There is a well-established literature that argues bureaucracies develop an interest in self-perpetuation alongside an interest in carrying out the task they were established to fulfil (Weber 2013 [1st published 1922]). This is a process that offers a justification for those who believe it is always possible to cut spending without damaging the principal services offered because the bureaucratic elements of these services will have expanded to serve their own interests (Niskanen 2007).[2] I will discuss funding levels and the impact of austerity on health care in Chapter 5 but here note that those seeking to pursue market approaches conjure up this so-called "waste" and link it with an appeal to improve efficiency, understood as getting the same (or more) output with less input. The drive to privatise and marketise public services is justified by its proponents as promoting efficiency, but they also argue that it enhances freedom. These are claims that the neoliberals believe they can make because they transpose what they think happens in the private sector into the public and assume this transposition to be an axiomatic good. But this is an argument that is flawed in its foundation assumptions. Markets do not promote freedom – they promote freedom for some, freedom for finance capital but not for workers, for example collective bargaining and other forms of worker agency or routes to worker protection are dismissed as an infringement on the freedom of the market. The second flawed assumption is that the private sector is a shining beacon of efficiency. Even a recent history that captures booms and busts, excess profiteering and company collapse, inflation and recession undermine this assumption. Some private firms do well, the private sector as a category is much more compromised in both its efficiency and social utility. It is an irony that the virtues of the private sector are habitually extolled even when the economy had been plunged into crisis by the speculators in the banks.

Compare this social damage with the NHS which, despite all its difficulties, still comes high in league tables of performance and cost efficiency across developed countries. We need to proselytize the merits of the public sector to the failing private sector (Davis et al. 2014).

Organizational structure needs to reflect the tasks to be performed and the environment operated in. Simply transposing an approach from one setting to another does not work. Some approaches are inherently unsuitable for some settings, for example you cannot measure intellectual work by mechanical devices – it tells

Table 4.2 Systems of management

Mechanical	Organic
Decisions made in a tightly controlled normative framework. Employees functions are well defined. Control, authority and communication are hierarchical. Interaction is vertical (between subordinate and superior)	There is continual adjustment and redefinition of tasks through interaction with others. Communication is characteristically lateral, involves people of different rank and is based on consultation rather than command

you nothing about being a doctor to measure how long he or she takes to examine a particular person. Burns and Stalker (1961) for example identified mechanical and organic systems of management. Mechanical systems, they argued, were only suitable for stable market and technological conditions. If things were changing and there arose unforeseen circumstances, tasks cannot be adequately described functionally, or distributed automatically through a clearly demarcated structure. In such settings, an organic system was required (Table 4.2).

Perhaps within large organisations, it is possible to identify areas where organic systems are required but there is some normative framework shaping other areas of practice. In such situations appropriate mechanisms for communicating and resolving conflicts between different parts of the organisation are essential (Lawrence and Lorsch 1967). Management needs to be contingently matched to organisational context and tasks (and not the other way around). It is a mistake to think that introducing a business paradigm for example will ipso facto improve any organisation, and it will damage it if the organisational task becomes distorted to meet a management need, for example if running at a surplus becomes more important that guaranteeing optimum care.

Bureaucratisation and commodification

In the NHS, we can see a conflict between the wish to improve accountability and quality via the hierarchical mechanisms of clinical governance, NICE guidelines, clinical audit, National Service Frameworks, performance management, gold standards, targets and protocols (Harrison and Ahmad 2000) and the care imperative of tailoring service to individual circumstance and preference. Equating "best practice" simply with sticking to the protocol reduces the salience of care. Downie (2012) has argued that these sorts of encroachments on individual professional judgement constitute a shrinking of the profession, and a reordering of the sorts of knowledge that shape its practice from an emphasis on judgement to one on adherence to a particular type of evidence.

Guidelines, pathways and protocols do more than their ostensible purpose. They are seen as capturing something that is real – they produce the experience they initially were seen as just describing, a person's experience is fitted into the structures they "ought" to be conforming to. Cussins (1998) called the way images and records appear to create and control both medical practice and the patient's medical experience "ontological choreography".

If the bureaucracy of top down instruction and the choreography of protocols impinge on health work so does commodification. Commodification can be pursued via command and control principles or it can be pursued via neoliberal self-governance. The latter may not be seen by professionals as a threat to autonomy if they have incorporated ideas that the right thing to do is in harmony with the changes proposed (this would be an example of Foucault's governmentality in action) (see Moffatt et al. 2014 and a fuller exposition in Chapter 6).

Ritzer (1996 and 2008) has used the example of fast food outlets as a mechanism to view a broader social change, something he terms the "McDonaldisation of Society". McDonalds' aims for a uniform service wherever they are based, the most efficient processes for each stage of acquiring, preparing, selling and clearing up food and a speedy throughput of customers. Many people value the speed and the familiarity of McDonalds, they may welcome similar characteristics in other areas, some of the appeal of day surgery for example may be because it replicates a construct of speed equating to desirable, it also disrupts the normal as little as possible, you can be back in your home that evening (see Rhodes et al. 2006). But a uniform approach geared to efficient "throughput" doesn't fit everywhere, including where the intention is care not cure.

Organisational ethics

As well as priorities and principles changing there are other key changes to consider when private and third-sector organisations deliver NHS and social care services. One area is how to accommodate the shift in organisational ethics that occurs. Organisational ethics are, "a process or strategy for adjudicating different stakeholder views in an organisation" (Spencer et al. 2000). When some stakeholders are health professionals, some are patients, and some are shareholders and directors of commercial companies there is a potential for conflicts of interests and a need for clarity about how these conflicts are reconciled.

There is a long history of considerations of the role of money in healthcare encounters. In the US in the late 1980s and the 1990s a shift to "Managed Care" made overt a dual responsibility in these organisations to provide health care and to run as a business. There were concerns about reconciling healthcare ethics and business ethics in a way that safeguarded the integrity of each (Pearson et al. 2003) and, it was decided, the route to achieve this reconciliation was via the development of standards by a Joint Commission on Accreditation of Healthcare Organisations (Schyve 1996).

In the UK, the Health Act of 2009 required all bodies providing NHS services, including third-sector and private providers, to "have regard" to the 2009 NHS Constitution (Department of Health 2009), including acting fairly and effectively. Frith (2013) argues that adherence to the NHS Constitution does not resolve all the issues that private sector involvement in the NHS creates, for example private sector providers may have a different relationship with the staff they employ. She argues that existing clinical ethics committees could be augmented with specialists in administration and business and then extend their remit to encompass organizational ethics. An example of this sort of approach is in the "IntegratedEthics" programme of the Veterans Health Administration in the US. This programme embraces three levels of ethics: decisions and actions (broadly clinical ethics as currently perceived); systems and processes (considering those aspects of systems and processes that create ethical issues); and, environment and culture (this includes how leadership can promote an ethically aware organisation – for example performance targets could include ethical dimensions and aspects of culture could include fostering ethical behaviour and priorities as much as organisational efficiency) (Frith 2013: 21: see also Fox et al. 2010.)

Impact on healthcare professionals

New work practices

Consider the most successful of the new breed of capitalists, companies like Apple have introduced very close monitoring and control of their workers, other companies were set up with a labour force who were classified as being independent contractors, Uber for example. This sort of arrangement includes zero-hour contracts that epitomise the "gig economy".

Philosopher Byung-Chul Han (2017) considers that neoliberal work practices such as these internalise exploitation, "Everyone is a self-exploiting worker in their own enterprise". This is an argument that links with Foucault's presentation of the emergence of homo oeconomicus (introduced above and considered in more detail in Chapter 6), and with ideas of self-regulation and introjected surveillance, a "panoptical regime of monitoring and assessment" (Monbiot 2019: 4). Monbiot calls this sort of regulation and surveillance "neoliberal theology" and it impacts on both the structure of the public sector, including the NHS, and on the available scope for professional practice. These technologies of power distort priority setting, they engender stress in the workforce and destroy staff morale as staff realise they are not able to exercise the professional autonomy (constrained by the new bureaucracy and finance-driven imperatives) or the compassion they previously saw as core to their professional identity. (It's difficult to express compassion in truncated, bureaucratised, encounters with patients.)

McKinley and Arches (1985) believe that the logic of the market and commercialisation leads to the proletarianization of doctors. There are two interrelated aspects of proletarianization; the first is to do with the context in which care is provided, specifically the way the delivery of care is shaped by bureaucracy. The second is to do with the process of care, McKinlay and Arches sum this up as: "… the process by which an occupational category is divested of control over certain prerogatives relating to the location, content and essentiality of its task activities and is thereby subordinated to the broader requirements of production under advanced capitalism" (1985: 161).

They argue that there is a (possibly) irreconcilable difference between professional and bureaucratic authority. Some of the complaint's physicians make about the advance of bureaucracy into their professional domain include; the dangers of lay evaluation in domains that involve complex professional judgements, the imposition of managerial imperatives, government intrusion, inappropriate criteria for organisational decision making, the erosion of autonomy (McKinley and Arches 1985: 182).

Proletarianization is an idea originating in Marx and Engels' considerations of factory workers in nineteenth-century Europe, but the process is not restricted to such settings. Neither are the psychological processes that accompany such a shift, for example false consciousness. "Many physicians simply cannot see that what they are involved in is not independent of capitalist initiatives". Their perceptions are masked by "both their false consciousness concerning the nature and significance of their own everyday activities and also by their elitist conception of their role" (McKinlay and Arches 1985: 190).

As well as changing the priorities the NHS sets, the logic of the market and commercialisation also produces an ennui in staff, a feature of constant changes in work, disturbance of social relationships and everlasting uncertainty. In such a situation "venerable ideas and opinions, are swept away". One consequence of this is that people feel an alienation that is characteristic of those who are forced to describe their activities in misleading terms – cuts described as efficiency savings or even as "quality improvement programmes" for example (see Collini 2012).[3] This alienation is further exacerbated by a sense that the organisation is constantly undergoing reorganisation, is preoccupied by one crisis after another and, despite repeated initiatives, does not seem to make headway on resilient problems, waiting lists for surgery and waiting times in casualty for example.

Nursing also experiences the sorts of role changes and role confusions that can produce ennui and alienation, not least through living with the contrast between what nurses say they do and what they actually do. What nursing says it does, or at least what underpins its contemporary ethos, is to offer a holistic model of care, informed by bio-psycho-social scholarship, that places therapeutic relationships at the heart of practice (Allen 2015). But what they do when those practices are scrutinised rather than just questioned is, in many cases, different. For example, a study in 2012 found that District Nurses claim to spend much of their time talking to patients about their wishes for end-of-life care, but the observed reality was quite different and they were seen to focus mainly on practical nursing tasks (Walshe et al. 2012). Middleton-Green (2017), in a study on care of older people in hospital, described competing ideologies, one was of care and the other was shaped by adherence to organisational regulatory processes. Furaker (2009) identified an activity generically called "organising work" that accounted for more than 70% of the work that nurses do.

Allen (2015) has argued that there is a need to better understand these different aspects of the nurses' role, what they do at work, and why this work is seen as necessary. She suggests a paradox and a competing paradigm. The paradox is that

> for the last forty years, nursing's claim to professional expertise has been expressed in terms of its care-giving function. Informed by a distinctive

'holistic' approach, models of nursing identify therapeutic relationships as the cornerstone of practice. While 'knowing the patient' has been central to clinicians' occupational identity, research reveals that nurses not only experience significant material constraints in realising these ideals, but their contribution to healthcare also extends far beyond direct work with patients.

(Allen 2014: 131)

That contribution, Allen argues, is one centred on organisational rather than therapeutic relationships, nurses 'holistically' mobilise and sustain the networks through which care is organised.

Rolfe has analysed shifts in nursing towards a graduate-only profession suggests a concern with research and evidence-based practice detracts from the performance of what he calls, "basic nursing tasks" (Rolfe 2015: 141). He presents an argument for a shift to a human sciences paradigm in which the evidence that informs practice derives largely from practice itself. Nursing and nursing education should, "focus on the endeavour to understand and relate to individual persons rather than to make broad prescriptions for practice based on statistical and other generalizations" (Rolfe 2015: 141). This is an approach he locates in Gadamer's "hermeneutic conversation", a route to coming to an understanding via dialogue (Gadamer 1960: 388).

But pursuing Gadamer's hermeneutic conversation sits at odds with an increasingly task-focussed academy. A shift to funding by student's fees rather than government funding increases instrumentality and consumerism in the academy. Students are reconfigured as customers, and customers who feel they should say what they want, and how they want it delivered. These changes impact on academic roles, foster a preoccupation with student satisfaction, a short-termism – initial job destination as a marker of course success, an expedient curriculum and a wariness about academic rigour.[4] These are all manifestations of a market-led shift in the academy, as is a sense of vulnerability in academics often employed on short-term contracts, an increasing workload and a dislocation between what they think they should do and what they actually do that is an experience shared with doctors and nurses.

A sense of insecurity that accompanies the new work practices means that the worker doesn't complain or demand because they feel vulnerable if they do.

Box 4.1 Becoming a doctor (Becker et al. 1961.)

This looks at socialization in medical schools, how new students become doctors and the role of student culture in that process. There is a latent culture that students bring with them, but also a process of slow assimilation of medical values through peer pressure and example. It is the shaping of attitudes as expressions of the student's collective situation, rather than their individual values and immediate feelings, that are important in shaping the sort of doctors they will become.

The sustained attack on trade unionism that has been a feature of neoliberal-ism exacerbates this vulnerability. Collective bargaining and support for work-ers in voicing concerns about their work reduces, with adverse consequences for safety. Despite rhetorical encouragement of whistle-blowers those who do speak out about damaging workplaces face hostility and discrimination (see Small 2023).

What we expect our doctors and nurses (and our academics) to do has changed, as has what they think they are doing. These changes are a consequence of broader macro social and structural changes, but they are passed on in the micro-relations they have with each other, with those people who train them and with their patients. Like all of us, doctors' and nurses' attitudes are shaped by prevail-ing paradigms and the care they offer is provided within the organisational and economic context extant at any one time. This has always been the case (see Box 4.1 summarising Becker and colleagues' picture from the end of the 1950s of how the collective prevails over the latent views of the individual). Growing up in neoliberalism shapes latent views, when these interact with an increasingly marketised health care, we may see a different sort of doctor and a different sort of nurse practicing a different sort of medicine.

I will conclude this section with two examples, one from 1992 and one from 2020. They illustrate the sorts of changes I have been discussing.

> When a candidate at interview is asked why she [sic] chose nursing, the correct answer is no longer 'I want to help people'. If that is what she feels it would be more prudent to talk about social obligations, nursing being a profession which involved relating to others, career mobility, academic and emotional gratification. The value on care remains high, but care is no longer 'tender' and 'loving', it is a specifiable commodity … A nurse no longer has a vocation; she has a profession. She is no longer dedicated; she is professional. She is no longer moral; she is accountable! [One of the differences between accountable and moral is that the former is satisfied if you tick the boxes – if you do the necessary (you don't have to do the unspecified, the unspecific – things that are integral to the art of care)].
>
> (Inglesby 1992: 54 quoted in Fox 1995: 112)

Around 28 years later: An example discussed in my University Faculty of Health Studies, although not related to a former student from that faculty, is of a qualified healthcare worker who went to the home of a vulnerable elderly patient to take care of a medical need. The worker became aware that there was no food in the house and no way of getting any that day (the neighbour who did the shopping was temporarily away). The worker left after doing the clinical procedure – it was not their job to shop – they didn't inform the safeguarding team of the persons' situation. Why didn't they go to the shops?

- System concerns – so busy that they would not have been able to see the remainder of their caseload that day. This is in effect a reasoned utilitarian position (and a compassionate one within that worldview). This may be best seen as a resource issue (although they could still have alerted the safeguarding team).

- They saw their task as a clinical one and not as a more generic one to respond to any needs. This reflects a narrow construct of the professional task.
- Their concern was to meet the criteria and targets set by their employer – these were the most pressing concerns – a prioritisation of responsibility to employer and not patient. This is the sort of explanation that might be characterised as a culture issue.
- They may have had no money – or have been embarrassed about asking the patient for money: they may have thought it was the persons' fault for not planning and that they were not responsible for that. These seem to be selection, training and supervision issues.

While issues of empathy and anxiety impact on working practices so do the more prosaic, specifically the considerable demands made on healthcare worker's time by other activities. One way of emphasising flexibility and compassion might be to ingrain that in the curriculum and the everyday practice of their university experience so when they encounter this sort of situation they can have the sorts of dialogue Gadamer was talking about with those involved as parties to the decision the worker had to make, and to its consequences. But Universities are under financial pressures that have stripped out support staff in favour of the increasingly ubiquitous computer algorithms and they have academic staff with higher workloads. Despite best efforts, these circumstances mean that the idea of close pastoral or even tutorial support that would have given a student a grounding in the sorts of decision making that the circumstances of his home visit required are far from the everyday experience of all but a few of our university students.[5] (See Table 4.3 for other ways of thinking about education.)

A priority of improving quality and ensuring safety is one of two prevalent tropes about the contemporary hospital – the other is a competing one which depicts hospitals as on the "verge of chaos and collapse". One feature of recent years has been a proliferation of books narrating lives of healthcare professionals. They are frequently moving, sometimes funny and always treading the divisions between the task and the context in which it has to be delivered. They also remind us that we are talking about settings where the most challenging of life's vicissitudes are encountered (see Table 4.4).

The proletarianization of doctors and the changes in nursing roles impact on their relationships with other healthcare personnel, including managers, and it impacts on relations with patients and with the public.[6] In the rest of this chapter, I will consider new managerialism, itself an artefact of neoliberalism, and the relationship between managers and clinicians - particularly the idea of hybrid managers

Table 4.3 What is education for?

The vocation of education. It is "to inculcate serious and unrelenting critical habits and opinions". Other agendas have arisen that get in the way of this – a "ubiquitous encouragement of everyone's so-called individual personality" and a surrender of any claim to autonomy as education submits to the imperatives of the state. In talking about education Nietzsche (2015 [1872]) uses the German word *Bildung* which means "the formation of culture and individual character".	*Education as "revolutionary futurity".* Education can be a hopeful practice of liberation. That it is usually not is largely down to what Friere (1968) describes as the "banking" model of education – students are taught to master knowledge and skills "deposited" by authoritative teachers and then "withdraw" them to bankroll their smooth integration into the existing social system. The alternative is a dialogical education of critical consciousness that enables people to formulate questions about the system, understand the nature of power in society and produce knowledge that is challenging to this power. For Friere the vocation of human beings is to act on the world such that they open new horizons of untested feasibility, this is the route to becoming progressively more human.

Table 4.4 On being a professional in health services

On the strains of working in the contemporary NHS: describing an inner city A&E waiting area Watson (2018) says, "The poverty is palpable. There are drunk mothers and skeletal fathers. The room smells of body odour and of the metal of old blood".

What it means to be a nurse and what it means to care: nursing isn't really about chemistry, biology, anatomy and so on its much more about philosophy, psychology, art, ethics and politics. Examples of care – a 9-year-old girl who died in a house fire – the nurses wash her hair so she doesn't smell so acutely of the smoke which took her life – it's the sort of action that will shape the memory the family will have of saying goodbye to the girl.

She also talks of the care her own father had from his nurse when he was receiving palliative care at the end of his life – the nurse became his closest confidant, his friend – something thousands of nurses do every day.

Books on being a *junior doctor*, some are structured around amusing anecdotes but characteristically also include a sense of unacceptable workloads, lack of resources and of the challenge of reconciling your limited knowledge with the profound needs you encounter – Kay (2017), Pemberton (2008), Clarke (2017).

Managers

There has been a rise in the centrality of managers and management thinking in health care since the 1980s. In a DHSS consultation document in 1979, it appeared self-evident then that the role of management was to support doctors, dentists, nurses and other health professionals to provide the care, cure and promotion of health that the NHS was engaged with (DHSS 1979). But by the time of the NHS reforms of the late 1980s and early 1990s a major shift had occurred, a new sort of manager was in the ascendancy, one who was leading reform and rather than supporting health professionals was furthering an agenda for change that required overriding the views of those same professionals. The rationale for these changes, and the role of managers in championing them, has been summarised by Ham:

> (the) new breed of general managers started the process of making services more patient centred. The system under which doctors who shouted loudest got the biggest share of resources was turned upside down, and the NHS was transformed from a professionally dominated bureaucracy to a social business … Not only this, but managers were also the shock troops who had a key role in implementing the NHS reforms of 1991.[7] In face of concerted opposition from doctors, nurses and other staff, the reforms could not have been introduced so quickly [without them].
>
> (Ham 1995: 15)

New public management (NPM)

New Public Management promotes competition in public services and introduces private-sector management techniques in the name of increasing efficiency and reducing costs (Osborne and Gaebler 1992). An accompanying "important conceptual shift involved regarding the users of public services as customers, rather than citizens" (Schrecker and Bambra 2015: 103). Neoliberalism's cocktail of monetarism, supply-side economics and public choice theories (de Vries 2010: 2) needed intermediate mechanisms to transfer economic theory into practice change. NPM was one such mechanism.

NPM emerged at the same time as neoliberalism. Its predecessor, perhaps we could call it "old public management", was conceptualised using public administration theories. But there was also PPA [Progressive Public Administration][8], a style of "providing all public services through 'semi-anonymized' organizations within a single aggregated unit, with detailed service-wide rules, common service provision in key areas of operation, detailed central control of pay bargaining and staffing levels" (Hood 1995: 95–97).

In contrast to both old public management and PPA, NPM emphasised an entrepreneurial approach in which public organisations were equated with private organisations. Somewhat perversely the argument was that old public management had argued for the separate analysis of public organisations (as distinct from organisations in general) because it was necessary to consider their political context. NPM argued that you should take the politics out. The perverse aspect of this is to suggest that seeing public organisations like private ones is taking the politics out!

Dunleavy (2005) identified three important characteristics of NPM – disaggregation, competition and incentivisation – and each of these separately, and especially together, will have a considerable impact on the practice of the public sector. Take disaggregation as an example, this sees public organisations becoming,

> separately managed "corporatized" units for each public sector "product" (each identified as a separate cost centre, with its own organisational identity in fact if not in law, and greater delegation of resource decisions in a movement towards "one-line" budgets, mission statements, business plans and managerial autonomy).

In health, this sort of disaggregation makes care planning that includes a number of different service providers more difficult. Dunleavy's two other features of NPM add further degrees of difficulty. Competition and incentivisation encourage a stress on parsimony, finding less costly ways to do things, and a stress on having an interventionist management style to ensure that this sort of finance-led ethos is achieved. The incentivisation is characteristically around cost containment, not clinical or care-based outcomes. In making public services more like private sector businesses therefore some elements are weakened – specifically, common service provision, settled staffing levels and a clear focus on patient outcomes.

I'm aware of the Pollyannaish danger of suggesting all was well before NPM.[9] In the early years of state-organised public services Beatrice Webb conjured up the template for public-sector managers, they were to be a "Jesuitical corps" of ascetic zealots (Hood 1995: 94). These did not materialise, but like the Sir Humphrey character of "Yes Minister" defending entrenched interests and batting away the challenges of the new,[10] or like budget-maximising bureaucrats or the gung-ho businessmen and women of the NPM years, each of these tropes captured elements of the truth and each left residues for their successors – they constitute the accumulating sedimentary layers of public sector management history.[11]

Like its predecessors NPM will be superseded by a new management approach. Dunleavy argues that we need to see the form of public management in the context of both "the level of autonomous citizen competence and the level of institutional and policy complexity" (see de Vries 2010: 3). If NPM is not solving the problems of delivering public services, and if this is accompanied by a mistrust of both bureaucracies and traditional representative democracy, there is a tendency for the rise of popularist parties, critical of experts and without clear programmes, to offer "simple" solutions via disjointed, episodic reform programmes. This constitutes, continuing to use NPM terminology, a disaggregation of governance as well as of management.[12]

Hybrid management

New managerialism, business style management approaches in health, while initially pursued in the face of protests from the health professions, now involves many of those same professionals via clinical manager positions (see Harrison and Ahmad 2000). The new public management approach has been enacted by a management cadre many of whom are also (or have recently been) clinicians. Hybrid managers who combine managerial responsibilities with clinical or medical duties outnumber full-time managers by four to one in the contemporary NHS (although there are relatively few clinicians in senior posts such as Chief Executives of hospital trusts). In a typology developed by McGivern et al. (2015) some of these are identified as willing hybrid managers, they have engaged positively and proactively with management. Others may be involved in management because they think it's their turn or they want to protect their colleagues from encroaching managerialism – they are incidental hybrids exercising a "passive obligation" to fulfil a management role. What has not happened, even with hybrid managers, is a simple elision between managers and clinicians.

The shift of clinicians into management roles for the incidental hybrids does not mean that they lose a primary identification as clinicians, nor do they see service improvement, change management or risk in the same way as do the full-time "professional" managers or their "willing hybrid" counterparts (McGivern et al. 2015). McGivern et al. (2015) argue that hybrid attitudes towards both managerialism and professionalism are mediated via what they call "identity work", that is the way organisational demands and public service, both when they are in accord and when they are not, are enacted in practice. This will be influenced by how far one is an incidental or a willing hybrid, that is how far one will follow organisational demands even when they may conflict with professional ethics. The incidentals continue to represent and protect traditional institutionalised professionalism while the willings seek to develop an identity that incorporates professionalism and managerialism, although there appears an assumption that the latter will take precedence.

This hybrid system is likely to experience conflict (or stasis) when an organisation is seeking to pursue competing priorities or when priorities are not clear. For example, the Mid-Staffordshire Trust was pursuing competing objectives. Ensuring the highest standard of care for patients and seeking organisational recognition as a Foundation Trust were not complementary objectives. They may be complementary objectives in other organisations where the pursuit of the latter maximises efforts to enhance the former. Crucial in Mid-Staffordshire was the practice of cutting back on staff in the interests of propping up the finance of the trust and hence improving its potential to achieve Foundation Trust status (see Chapter 1 and Small 2023).

The attitude one takes to hybridity and to the challenges of resolving its contradictions (for those who are not ensconced in either camp) are shaped by your attitude to each of the parts, management and professional, and by your thoughts about how each might best benefit, or defend, the patient.[13] It could be argued that today it is axiomatic that everyone wants better management. A language of management infuses all debates within health, so that; "Management seems natural, necessary and self-evident for health services" (Learmonth and Harding 2004: viii). But managerialism is "a particular way of looking at the world which stresses, first that the world is manageable and second that the world should be

Table 4.5 The physician is involved but not in charge

In health care increased complexity and a proliferation of specialists means old models of professionalism geared to the autonomy of individual doctors doesn't work – they have to collaborate. But this can be subverted by a pretence of collaboration. Kaiser Permanente –is now organised in unit-based teams in which the physician is a member but is not in charge. There is a "collaboratively defined 'value compass' (which) helps connect the organisational purpose with the day-to-day work of all members of staff". Adler (2019) is optimistic about the results, "Tapping into employees and supplier's creativity and knowledge necessitated a shift towards more socialist structures, making organisations more collaborative and their decision making more democratic" (Adler 2015 see also 2015a).

---

managed" (Grey 1996: 601). It also propagates the idea that managing is a neutral concept, we rarely interrogate it as a social construction, and we rarely scrutinise who the managers are. It is also axiomatic that professionalism is a good thing and that the professions are admirable, at least in relation to the profession of medicine. Master discourses are very powerful. Management is neither just technical nor neutral (Table 4.5).

Conclusion

Both managerialism and professionalization are social constructs, and as vectors to promote the public good they become problematic if the construct of the public good changes. They also may be examples of an incommensurability between paradigms (see Burrell and Morgan 1979), a scenario in which people "talk past each other" (Fischer and Ferlie 2013: 46). Manager and clinician can be placed side-by-side without being truly connected, a state of parataxis of the professions. Both managerialism and professionalization are supported, underpinned, by micro-processes that fill the space between understanding and action. While management may focus on changing these micro-processes via imposing routines and scripts that suffuse everyday practice with disciplinary power via small-scale accumulation and incremental imposition of power-knowledge, they are also processes that allow subversion, resistance, "doing things as we have always done them, not as we are now told to do them". Foucault, in his lectures at the *College de France* (2008, 2010, 2011), explored morally charged refusal and courageous resistance to normative codes, and argued that this constituted social practice through which "the courage of truth" is manifest. But these sorts of resistances can also be undertaken to underpin professional privilege and practice inertia.

The domains that might have provided some protection against the damaging impact of neoliberalism have been incorporated or compromised during the years of its ascendancy. Management has changed, the impact of New Public Managerialism, the commodification of the means of production and distribution of health care, and a more general erosion of trust across many sectors are examples here. The independence of the professions has been undermined by changes in the permitted scope of their autonomy and by a promotion of more instrumental thinking both in their training and in the monitoring of their subsequent practice.

The ascent of economics and the ontological choreography of language that is a feature of neoliberalism contrasts with an older ethos that many assume is integral to the NHS. The same sort of change in other parts of the public sector, housing, welfare, social care is competing with a more diffuse ethos. All together the sorts of changes occurring are examples of the Habermasian construct of the system world eroding communicative action (the ability to engage in public discourse) and the values of the life world. We don't know how to talk about what we think is going wrong or how to put it right (see Murray 2015). In the next chapter, I examine in more detail exactly what the consequences of the neoliberal ascendancy are for our health.

Notes

1 There are other models that one can use to look at factors that shape organisational practice, for example a socio-ecological model is envisaged with concentric circles of influence (viz Bronfenbrenner 1999) with, say, an intervention at the centre then, surrounding it an implementation plan, then the role of practitioners/ of managers/ leaders. Further out from the centre might be organisational context and that is surrounded by the policy dimension. The whole socio-ecological system exists within a chronosphere, this reminds us that systems exist, and change, across time.

2 There were earlier critiques of bureaucracy that resonate with the position of the neoliberals. In his book "Bureaucracy" published in 1944 Ludwig von Mises argued that unless it was curtailed to just the most essential of areas (defence, security and taxation) state involvement would produce bureaucracy which would inexorably expand into a bureaucratic totalitarianism. There could be no third way between capitalism and socialism, if the latter got a toe-hold- say via some state provided health care – then the flood gates would open and "free men" would be subjugated. Von Mises also offered the rather less apocalyptic position that no reforms can transform a public office into a sort of private enterprise, the value of public administration cannot be expressed in terms of money, government efficiency and industrial efficiency are entirely different things.

3 The noxious terminology of "customers" or the anodyne/mealy mouthed description of "users" are now characteristic of public services. Language used is another indication of the intrusions of the system world into the lifeworld. It is important to scrutinise the words we use. Do we see people differently if we call them client or service user rather than a patient? There are different meanings for the word patient – if we use it as an adjective, we think about someone quietly waiting, accepting, forbearing, long-suffering; as a noun it identifies a person receiving medical treatment. Service user is associated with a more active engagement with health services, it emerged from consumerist and democratic traditions and was used in social work and mental health services before becoming more widespread (see McLaughlin 2009). As I have been exploring throughout, we now use "culture" to talk about regimes of care – in the past we might have talked about the philosophy of nursing for example as opposed to a new "culture of nursing". Philosophies change but they may be more firmly embedded in a history of usage than the shifting sands of culture.

4 One example that illustrates all these changes is the escalation in the percentage of students getting first class degrees, even as academic input is being cut.

5 What education is for is a hugely contested area. Table 4.3 presents two influential, but very different, approaches that seem far away from the contemporary academy but very

pertinent to the sorts of challenges and the potential agendas contemporary health care students encounter.

6 Kaiser Permanente, the largest integrated healthcare deliverer in the US, presents an interesting example, see Table 4.5 that suggests a more optimistic reading of the potentialities of different ways of working.

7 Considered in Chapter 3.

8 Progressive here means a style of public administration that emerged in the "progressive era" of the late nineteenth and early twentieth century. It was linked to a belief that one had to keep politicians, with the inherent venality that attached to their genus, out of public services because they would seek to exploit it for their own or their friends financial gain and, further, in so doing they would inevitably produce high-cost, low-quality products (Hood 1995: 93). It's a description of the relationship between politicians, profit and health provision that might occur now – the allocation of contracts in response to the Covid-19 pandemic and the links between contract success and political connections was a widely debated topic in 2020/21 (see Chapter 5).

9 Pollyanna, in the children's book by Eleanor Porter (1913), has a very optimistic outlook, a bias towards the positive. Dixon-Woods (2019) seems to see Pollyanna's in the NHS, she notes an optimism bias in relation to Quality Improvement Initiatives, the enthusiasm for these "is particularly affected by the 'lovely baby' syndrome" – whoever's baby you meet for the first time you describe as "lovely" even if in reality the main feeling they generate in you is not quite that – just having a quality improvement initiative isn't the same as improving quality!

10 The TV series about the hapless government Minister and his scheming Permanent Secretary can also be followed in a book by Jonathan Lynn and Antony Jay (1990).

11 One example of the resilience of our metaphors is the continued centrality of the term "Trust", now a designation of an organisational form ubiquitous in the NHS but with a historical legacy traceable at least to John Locke who used the metaphor of trustee and beneficiary to capture his idea of the "Extent and End of Civil Government" (Locke 1689).

12 Within a few months in 2016 Brexit in the UK and the election of Donald Trump in the US provide examples.

13 There are alternate views and different points of focus – for example Fitzgerald (2016) has argued that hybrid clinical managers are crucial to NHS improvement.

References

Adler, P. 2019. *The 99 percent economy: How democratic socialism can overcome the crisis in capitalism*. New York. Oxford University Press.

Adler, P. 2015a. Taking the high road: How 'high-performance socialism' can work for large organisations. The Clarendon Lecture, University of Oxford. http://www.sbs.ox.ac.uk/school/news/taking-high-road-how-high-performance-socialism-can-work-for-large-organisations (accessed 30/8/2016).

Allen, D.A. 2015. 'Organizing Work': Nursing's Black Hole. Paper presented at *"Practices, Identities and Bodies at Work: A Critical Exploration of Contemporary Health Care"*. Cardiff University, 19 May.

Becker, H.S., Geer, B., Hughes, E.C., Strauss, A.L. 1961. *Boys in White: Student Culture in Medical School*. Chicago, IL, University of Chicago Press.

Bronfenbrenner, U. 1999. Environments in developmental perspective: Theoretical and operational models. In Friedman, S.L., Wachs, T.D. (Eds) *Measuring Environments Across the Lifespan: Emerging Methods and Concepts* (pp. 3–28). Washington, DC, American Psychological Association.

Burns, T., Stalker, G.M. 1961. *The Management of Innovation*. Oxford, Oxford University Press.

Burrell, G., Morgan, G. 1979. *Sociological Paradigms and Organisational Analysis.* London, Heinemann.

Clarke, R. 2017. *Your Life in My Hands. A Junior Doctors Story.* Metro Publishing.

Collini, S. 2012. *What are Universities For?* London, Penguin.

Cussins, C. 1998. Grooming, gossip and the evolution of language. *Journal of the History of the Behavioural Sciences,* 34(4), 398–399.

Davis, K., Stremikis, K., Squires, D., Schoen, C. 2014. *Mirror, Mirror on the Wall, 2014 Update: How the US Health Care System Compares Internationally.* New York, Commonwealth Fund.

Department of Health. 2009. NHS Constitution. London, DH.

Department of Health and Social Care. 2012. *Health and Social Care Act.*

Department of Health and Social Security (DHSS). 1979. *Patients First: Consultative Document on the Structure and Management of the NHS in England and Wales.* London, HMSO.

de Vries, J. 2010. Is new public management really dead? *OECD Journal on Budgeting,* 10(1), 1–5.

Dixon-Woods, M. 2019. How to improve healthcare improvement – an essay. *British Medical Journal,* 366, l5514. http://dx.doi.org/10.1136/bmj.l5514.

Downie, R. 2012. 'Honey, I shrunk the health professions'. How 'gold standards', 'assessment tools', and 'patient choice' have undermined professional judgement, and why you should care. Public Lecture, University of Bradford and Royal Institute of Philosophy, 28 Mar. http://www.brad.ac.uk/acad/ihs/seminar/royal_institute/INDEX.PHP

Dunleavy, P. et al. 2005. New public management is dead – long live digital-era governance. *Journal of Public Administration Research and Theory.* Sept.

Fischer, M.D., Ferlie, E. 2013. Resisting hybridisation between modes of clinical risk management: Contradiction, contest, and the production of intractable conflict. *Accounting, Organizations and Society,* 38, 30–49.

Fitzgerald, L. 2016. "Hybrid" clinician-managers are crucial to NHS improvement. http://www.sbs.ox.ac.uk/school/news/hybrid-clinician-managers-crucial-nhs-louise-fitzgerald (accessed 30/8/2016).

Foucault, M. 2008. *The Birth of Biopolitics: Lectures at the College de France, 1978–1979.* Palgrave Macmillan.

Foucault, M. 2010. *The Government of Self and Others: Lectures at the College de France 1983–1984.* London, Palgrave Macmillan.

Foucault, M. 2011. *The Courage of Truth (the Government of Self and Others II): Lectures at the College de France 1983–1984.* London, Palgrave Macmillan.

Fox, E., Bottrell, M., Berkowitz, K. et al. 2010. Integrated Ethics: An Innovative Program to Improve Ethics Quality in Healthcare. *Innovation Journal,* 15, 1–36.

Fox, N. 1995. Postmodern perspectives on care: The vigil and the gift. *Critical Social Policy,* 44/45, Autumn, 107–125.

Friere, P. 1968. *Pedagogy of the Oppressed.* Penguin.

Frith, L. 2013. The NHS and market forces in healthcare: The need for organisational ethics. *Journal Medical Ethics,* 39, 17–21.

Furaker, C. 2009. Nurses' everyday activities in hospital care. *Journal Nursing Management,* 17(3), 269–277.

Gadamer, H-G. 1960 (reprint 2013). *Truth and Method.* Bloomsbury Academic.

Grey, C. 1996. Towards a critique of managerialism: The contribution of Simone Weil. *Journal of Management Studies,* 33, 5, 591–611.

Ham, C. 1995. The grey suits deserve better treatment. *The Independent,* 10 June, 15.

Han, B-C. 2017. *Psychopolitics: Neoliberalism and the New Technologies of Power.* Verso Futures.

Harrison, S., Ahmad, W.I.U. 2000. Medical Autonomy and the UK State 1975 to 2025. *Sociology*, 34(1), 129–146.

Hood, C. 1995. The "New Public Management" in the 1980s: Variations on a theme. *Accounting, Organizations and Society*, 20(2/3), 93–109.

Inglesby, E. 1992. Values and philosophy of nursing: The dynamics of change. In, Jolley, M., Brykczynska, G. (Eds) *Nursing Care: The Challenge to Change.* London, Edward Arnold.

Kay, A. 2017. *This is Going to Hurt. Secret Diaries of a Junior Doctor.* Picador.

Lawrence, P.R., Lorsch, J.W. 1967. *Organization and Environment.* Cambridge, MA, Harvard Graduate School of Business Administration.

Learmonth, M., Harding, N. 2004. *Unmasking Health Management: A Critical Text.* New York, Nova Science Publications.

Locke, J. (1689 – this edition 1966). *The Second Treatise of Government.* Oxford, Basil Blackwell.

Lynn, J., Jay, A. 1989. *The Complete Yes Minister.* London, QPD Paperback.

McGivern, G., Currie, G., Ferlie, E., Fitzgerald, L., Waring, J. 2015. Hybrid manager-professionals' identity work: The maintenance and hybridisation of medical professionalism in managerial contexts. *Public Administration*, 93(2), 412–432.

McKinley, J.B., Arches, J. 1985. Towards the proletarianisation of physicians. *International Journal of Health Services*, 15(2), 161–195.

McLaughlin, H. 2009. What's in a name: "client", "patient", "customer", "consumers". "experts by experience", "service user" – what's next? *The British Journal of Social Work*, 39(6), 1101–1117.

Middleton-Green, L. 2017. *"Here There Is Nobody." An Ethnography of Older People's End-of-Life-Care in Hospital.* Doctoral Thesis, University of Bradford.

Moffatt, F., Martin, P., Timmons, S. 2014. Constructing notions of healthcare productivity: The call for a new professionalism? *Sociology of Health and Illness*, 36, 686–702.

Monbiot, G. 2019. Neoliberalism promised freedom – instead it delivers stifling control. *The Guardian*, Opinion, 10 Apr.

Murray, D. 2015. Is the West's loss of faith terminal? *Standpoint*, May.

Nietzsche, F. [1872] 2015. *Anti-Education: On the Future of Our Educational Institutions.* New York Review Books.

Niskanen, W.A. 2007. *Bureaucracy and Representative Government.* Aldine Transaction.

Osborne, D., Gaebler, T. 1992. *Reinventing Government: How the Entrepreneurial Spirit Is Transforming the Public Sector.* New York, Basic Books.

Parsons, T. 1951. *The Social System.* London, Routledge and Kegan Paul.

Pearson, S., Sabin, J., Emanuel, E. 2003. *No Margin, No Mission: Health Organizations and the Quest for Ethical Excellence.* Oxford, Oxford University Press.

Pemberton, M. 2008. *Trust Me I'm a (Junior) Doctor.* Hoddor Paperbacks.

Porter, E.H. [1913] 2012. *Polyanna.* Wordsworth Editions.

Rhodes, L., Miles, G., Pearson, A. 2006. Patient subjective experience and satisfaction during the peri-operative period in day surgery: A systematic review. *International Journal of Nursing Practice*, 12, 178–192.

Ritzer, G. 1996. *The McDonaldization of Society.* Thousand Oaks, CA, Pine Forge Press.

Ritzer, G. 2008. *The McDonaldization of Society 5.* Thousand Oaks, CA, Pine Forge Press.

Rolfe, G. 2015. Foundations for a human science of nursing: Gadamer, Laing, and the hermeneutics of caring. *Nursing Philosophy*, 16, 141–152.

Schrecker, T., Bambra, C. 2015. *How Politics Makes Us Sick. Neoliberal Epidemics.* Palgrave Macmillan, Basingstoke.

Schyve, P. 1996. Patient rights and organisational ethics: The joint commission perspective. *Bioethics Forum*, 12, 13–20.

Spencer, E., Mills, A., Rorty, M. et al. 2000. *Organizational Ethics in Healthcare.* Oxford, Oxford University Press.

Von Mises, L. 1944. *Bureaucracy.* Yale University Press.

Walshe, C., Ewing, G., Griffiths, J. 2012. Using observation as a data collection method to help understand patient and professional roles and actions in palliative care settings. *Palliative Medicine*, 26, 1048–1054.

Watson, C. 2018. *The Language of Kindness: A Nurse's Story.* Chatto and Windus.

Weber, M. 2013 (first published 1922) *Economy and Society.* University of California Press.

5 Consequences
How neoliberalism makes us sick

Introduction

I have considered what neoliberalism is and have looked at economics and organisational change in some detail. In subsequent chapters, I will consider neoliberalism's impact on the sorts of relationships we have with the more vulnerable
sections of society. In this chapter, I will look at the argument that neoliberalism,
and the economics and politics that accompany it, come with another sequela –
an adverse impact on our physical and mental health.[1]

Considering the impact of economic policy on health also encourages us to engage with how external events and contexts get inside the body (sometimes inside
the cell) and lead to the sorts of changes that can make us sick and shorten our
lives. There are distal – "situated away from the centre" (of the body) factors and
proximal factors, those "situated towards the centre" (of the body). Specifically, I
will consider the distal factors of inequality and austerity and the more proximal
impacts of stress. I will also consider epidemics, neoliberalism and populist politics by looking at the arrival of Covid-19.

Inequality and austerity

Inequality is not new, Scheidel (2017) points out that the proportion of wealth
held by the top 1% in the US has only just reached what it was in 1929 (and the
relationship between richest and average citizen is not dissimilar to what it was in
Rome in 400AD.) Piketty (2014) showed that the return on capital is greater than
growth, over time, which means that capital and inequality inevitably increase.
There are ways governments can intervene to address increasing concentrations
of wealth. But there are points in history where politics and capital accumulation
go hand in hand and we have a politics of divergence, the rich getting richer and
the gap to the poor grows. In the years between 1945 and 1973, general living
standards increased and there was some convergence between the rewards accru-
ing to labour and capital growth. But since, and increasing since the 1980s, any
growth in the income of the economy has gone to very few people.

Like Piketty, Nobel Prize-winning economist Joseph Stiglitz identifies the 1980s
as a key time point, specifically the election of Ronald Reagan as US President in

1981. Reagan's policies of deregulation of the financial system and a reduction in the "progressivity" of the tax system, were key events that precipitated a rise in inequality. Deregulation led to "the excessive financialization of the economy – to the point that before the 2008 crisis 40% of all corporate profits went to the financial sector". Cuts to high earners tax (Reagan cut the top rate of tax from 70% to 28%) heightened income inequality. Chief Executive Officer (CEO) pay now is 200 times greater than the pay of a typical worker. In the UK in 2016 CEOs of the top 100 FTSE companies, on average, had been paid more between the 1st and 5 of January than the average worker is paid in a year.[2] "On average, countries with less progressive taxation have more inequality … societies with more economic inequality tend to have more political inequality". "Financialization" enhances job insecurity because finance chases short-term gain rather than investing in long-term projects that might generate job and income security. Shifting from progressive taxation reduces the income available to invest in public services. Job insecurity reduces the ability of people to accumulate resources for any health need, reduction in public services takes away a health safety net (or at the very least leaves major holes in it) (Stiglitz 2013: xxxi–xxxiii).

Austerity is bad for the poor and good for the rich. In the UK, the rich doubled their wealth in the years between 2008 and 2015 (Marmot 2015: see Reid-Henry 2016 on how the tyranny of an economic model preoccupied with growth is bad for us). Between 1980 and 2016 the poorest 50% of humanity captured 12% of global income growth, the top 1% captured 27% (World Inequality Report 2018). The richest 85 people in the world own more wealth than the roughly 3.5 billion who make up the poorest half of the world's population (Cassidy 2014).

In the US, 95% of income growth in the economy between 2010 and 2012 went to 1% of the population. In the UK, a report from The Equality Trust (2019) identified a "story of Ferraris and food banks". Six billionaires at the top of the UK "wealth league" had a combined fortune of £39.4 billion which was roughly equal to the assets of the poorest 13.2 million. Philip Alston, UN rapporteur on extreme poverty and human rights (Alston 2018, see also Alston 2019 – his final report) identified 14 million people in the UK (a fifth of the population) living in poverty: 1.5 million were destitute (meaning they did not have the money for essentials): there was a predicted increase of 7% in child poverty in the years up to 2022, with up to 40% of children likely to be affected. Alston was particularly critical of the disproportionate effect austerity had on women, the disabled and families with disabled members. Nearly half of those in poverty, 6.9 million, were from families with a disabled person. Disabled people were more likely to be in poverty, and were more likely to be unemployed, in insecure employment or to be economically inactive. They had also been some of the hardest hit by austerity measures. Financial support introduced in the 1990s to cover the extra costs of care and mobility needs had been replaced by a much harsher benefits regime including the bedroom tax, universal credit and "fit for work" tests. The latter led to cuts in benefits, they were based on criteria that are far from being fit for purpose, in 2018 70% of disabled people judged "fit for work" overturned this decision on

appeal (Ryan 2019). Alston was also critical of limits on benefit payments that pe-
nalised people who had three or more children, he also saw cuts of 50% to council
budgets as something that was slashing at Britain's "culture of local concern" and
was "damaging the fabric of society".[3]

The austerity that followed the 2008 crash impacted on the populations' health
in ways that Marmot and colleagues in University College London's' Institute
of Health Equity have explored. They published a review in 2010, *Fair Society
Healthier Lives* (Marmot 2010), and then revisited the same terrain in 2020 in
Health Equity in England: The Marmot Review 10 Years On (Institute of Health
Equity 2020). The picture they present is clear, public expenditure on policies
through the life course could act on the social determinates of health to reduce
health inequalities. But, under the banner of austerity, public expenditure was
cut from 42% of national income in 2009–10 to 35% in 2018–19. Further, if you
measure health by looking at life expectancy, not a bad measure, there has been
a dramatic slowdown from 2011, indeed life expectancy has fallen in some parts
of England, specifically amongst women in deprived communities in the north.[4]

Marmot, in many publications (see, e.g. Marmot 2004, Marmot et al. 2008,
Marmot 2015 and also Commission on Social Determinates of Health 2008), has
explored how social standing directly effects your health. Money is important
(especially if you don't have much) but so is relative inequality, where you stand
in comparison to others. Also important is the autonomy you have – lack of
autonomy produces stress, as does the extent of social integration in the society
in which you live (see Mullainathan and Shafir 2014). Inequality is bad for our
health. Further, while it is particularly bad for the health of the most vulnerable,
no one gets away without paying some of the cost, it is bad for us all – both as individuals and collectively in terms of the overall health of a population (Wilkinson
and Pickett 2009). It is also bad for our community life, for trust and for a willingness to help others (Wilkinson and Pickett 2018). "In the worlds more equal
countries, more infants survive, and people are generally healthier and happier.
Equality pays dividends at every stage of human life, from babyhood to old age"
(Dorling 2012: 13).

Two studies published in 2021 provide further evidence of the impact of austerity following the 2008 crash and the Conservative and Coalition government's austerity policy choices. Funding available for health and social care in
the NHS and in local government reduced in real terms, as well as direct service
provision, prevention initiatives and a range of local government services that
impact on public health. Martin et al. (2021) report that an extra 57550 people
than would have been expected died in the five years from 2010 to 2015 (Alexiou
et al. 2021).

Disability Free Life Expectancy (DFLE) – measures both quantity and quality
of life, asking are extra years of life healthy or unhealthy ones? While life expectancy had been going up DFLE (the years before we live with a disability) had also
been increasing, but more slowly. DFLE also shows marked differences by social
group, it varies between affluent and more deprived areas, varies by gender and

varies by ethnicity. Amongst the White British population, there is a distinct gender difference in DFLE – men's is 61.7 years, that is 2.4 years less than women. DFLE in Pakistani women is 55.1 years, in contrast to white British women (64.1 years). Chinese men and women in Britain enjoy the longest disability-free period with a DFLE of 64.7 for men and 67 for women (see Wohland et al. 2015).

Many older people live with long-term chronic health conditions such as cardiovascular disease, diabetes and coronary heart disease (Jagger 2015: 3). But the poor, and particularly poor people from ethnic minority groups, may experience more complex co-morbidities earlier in their life. The impacts this has on them, and those around them, will differ – a Pakistani women developing disabilities at 55 may still have children at home and she may also be caring for her parents.

The austerity that was a particular response to the financial crisis of 2008 included policy choices to adopt public sector cuts as a priority and, in so doing, this exacerbated economic, geographic, social and health inequalities. The hollowing out of public services is accompanied by a neoliberal mantra that there are those who benefit from economic "opportunities" and there are those on benefits and the latter are a drag on the market economy.[5] (For a different perspective on austerity see Box 5.1.)

Between 2010 and 2014, constraints on public expenditure on health care and on social care have been associated with higher than expected numbers of deaths compared with pre-2010 trends. Most of this excess was in people aged over 60 and this could be linked most closely to cuts in social care spending and with changes in nurse numbers. From 2001 to 2010 nurse numbers rose by an average of 1.61% every year, from 2010 to 2014 they rose by 0.07% – 23 times lower than in the previous decade. Watkins et al. (2017) estimate that austerity can be linked to 120,000 extra deaths since 2010 and projecting these trends into the future to 100 extra deaths every day in the coming years. Between 2010

Box 5.1 Tony Judt on austerity (Judt 2010)

In the UK in the years after the Second World War (the years when the NHS was established) austerity was not just an economic condition but also something that "aspired to a public ethic". During a period of austerity under Prime Minister Atlee, we saw the greatest age of reform in modern British history. "The opposite of austerity is not prosperity but luxe et volupté" (luxury and voluptuousness). "We have substituted endless commerce for public purpose" … in the war Churchill offers "blood, toil, tears and sweat", but President Bush in the wake of the September 11, 2001, attacks on the US asked the American people to "continue shopping". "This impoverished view of community, the togetherness of consumption, is all we deserve from those who now govern us. If we want better rulers, we must learn to ask more from them and less for ourselves. A little austerity might be in order" (Judt 2010: 30–32).[6]

Box 5.2 The impact of austerity on disabled people

The Centre for Welfare Reform calculated, in 2013, that disabled people have experienced nine times the average burden of austerity cuts (the figure rises to 19 times for the most disabled.) There are 14 million disabled people in Britain and, in 2018, 4 million lived "below the breadline". There are three ways that this burden has been exacerbated:

1 Changes to benefits that have removed funding for the extra costs of care and mobility needs.
2 Increasing use of sanctions – for example cutting benefits if someone is declared "fit for work". (In 2018–70% of people judged fit for work successfully overturned this on appeal.)
3 Rhetorical positions that argue that many disabled people are not really disabled

Underpinning all three, Ryan argues, is a wish on the governments' part to reduce the welfare bill which they characterise as "bloated" and to do this by demonising the disabled.
(Ryan 2019).

---

and 2014, the NHS in England had a real terms annual increase in government funding of 1.3% despite rising demand and increasing healthcare costs. Real terms spending on social care fell by 1.19% every year during the same period despite increases in the number of over 85s in the population – the groups most likely to need social care.

Neoliberal epidemics

In *How Politics Makes Us Sick* Schrecker and Bambra (2015) consider "neoliberal epidemics" – epidemics that are associated with, or exacerbated by, neoliberalism. Here I will consider just one of the examples they offer, stress. I will then look at populism and medical emergencies before combining these two to look at how far Covid-19 is a neoliberal epidemic.

Stress

How can neoliberalism increase stress, how can it make us more anxious and why can we characterise it as a neoliberal epidemic? We have seen how neoliberalism and austerity disproportionately affect poorer people including how income inequality increases and how poorer people are disproportionately impacted by reductions in public provision. Further, factors that are damaging to health not only cluster, but they accumulate over time (Graham 2009: 14: see also Bell et al.

2012) and both neoliberalism and austerity have been around long enough to create this cluster/accumulation effect.

Stress is greater in "lower level" jobs, it is disproportionately a condition experienced by the poor and powerless[7] (Ferrie et al. 1998; see The Whitehall Study 1 and 2 – Marmot et al. 1991). There is a long-established literature that shows jobs with high psychological demands coupled with low levels of control were associated with increased exposure to stress and ill health (Karasek and Theorell 1990). Psychological pressures are linked with time pressure, a high pace of work, high workload, conflicting demands, lack of variety, a challenge in terms of utilising or developing the skills you have and low levels of control. These "high stress" jobs are called "demand-control" jobs by Karasek and Theorell and they are contrasted with "active work", jobs with high demands but also with high control. Here the worker can manage his or her workload and has a high degree of choice and autonomy over how the work is undertaken. They are also able to learn new skills, and this helps mitigate the stress of high demands. It is also possible to mitigate the ill-health effects of work via the presence of social support from co-workers and supervisors (Johnson and Hall 1988), but this social support has been the target of attacks under neoliberalism through their undermining organised labour and their encouragement of outsourcing and short term/zero-hour contracts. There is clear evidence of the increase in stress under neoliberalism. A US study found rates of stress increased by 18% for women and 24% for men between 1983 and 2009 (Cohen and Janicki-Deverts 2012). Case and Deaton (2020), with a focus on the US, have identified a rise in premature deaths amongst working-class white US citizens without at least four years' university education. They link these deaths to a weakening position of labour, a growing power of corporations and a healthcare sector that redistributes working-class wages to the wealthy. Other, more general, factors include globalisation and automation. They argue that capitalism has lifted countless people out of poverty but it is now destroying blue-collar America. That destruction, the deaths by despair, are evidenced by alcohol and drug abuse and by rates of suicide.

Nursing and care work could fit into Karasek and Theorell's demand control category or it could fit their active work category. Staff cuts, increasing demands on staff, casualisation and privatisation increase demand control activity (and erode the mitigating effects of social support) as do changes in ethos (or perhaps culture) within the workplace, or more broadly in society. Thus, we can see that stress relates to the nature of work and the power structures of the workplace, things that predate neoliberalism, but that neoliberalism fosters a shift of work into more stressful types, including in nursing and care work.[8]

Neoliberalism, populism and Covid-19

Covid-19

The way Covid-19 was made manifest in society and the nature of the responses to it indicate that it is a neoliberal epidemic, with some manifestations of medical populism. I have already considered some of the features of the epidemic that support this assertion and I will return to a consideration of Covid-19 at many points in what follows, including arguments that it is the prevailing culture in a country that shapes the responses to the epidemic and the extent of its spread. Here I will first summarise the case that it is possible to cast this as a neoliberal epidemic and then I will look at populism and responses to Covid-19.

At the outset of this look at Covid-19 a cautionary note is needed. The full picture of the epidemic's impact and of the effectiveness of responses to it is not yet available. This is still a pandemic in progress. It is not my intention to do more than consider how, in its initial expression, it manifested neoliberal and populist characteristics. My focus will be largely on year one of the pandemic (see Table 5.1).

It is clear that there is wide variation in terms of the impact of the pandemic across countries and considerable variation within countries. When the UK recorded its 100,000th death New Zealand had 25, Taiwan 7, Australia 909, Finland 655, and Norway 550. Near the top of population size-adjusted figures on death rates, with the UK, are the US and Brazil –together these three are flag bearers of neoliberalism and, if not flag bearers, examples of populism. By 2021 (and bearing in mind differences in how figures are recorded, and the validity of some infection and mortality figures) it looked as if the UK (and England in particular) had the world's highest death rates, Belgium was another contender. The Office

Table 5.1 During the first year of the pandemic

Free and global markets and a worldwide pandemic.

Government seemed to not be able to reconcile the danger of deaths from Covid and potential damage caused by shutting down the economy, including limiting movement across borders. This vacillating position appeared to result from a need to reconcile libertarian conservative politicians and those whose priority was the furtherance of free-market enterprise regardless, pitting the present and long-term vigour of the economy against the immediate needs of public health, and the picture and policy recommendations emerging from science and clinical practice. The consequence was that the UK was:

- slow to lock down internally; and,
- border policy was less strict than that of many other countries – people were initially admitted with no-checks and no quarantine (more successful countries closed borders), subsequently a "travel corridors" policy in the summer and slow closure of borders in early 2021 meant that many people still entered the country.

Privatisation, outsourcing and a resulting lack of coordination. Some consequences:
- March 2020 – community testing was stopped; this was resumed later but instead of local public health it was passed to the private sector.
- No effective test/trace/isolate policy.
- Lack of appropriate personal protective equipment (PPE) 883 health and social care workers had died from Covid by the end of 2020. There was a notable lack of PPE in care homes and early discharge of people from hospital without testing into care homes.

for National Statistics reports excess deaths – death rates compared with those of previous years – and using this widely accepted measure that considers age profiles of populations – reported that between the end of February and middle of June 2020 England had 7.5% excess deaths, Scotland had 5.1%, the UK overall had 6.9% and Spain, for example, had 6.7%.

Within the UK, the impact of the pandemic in terms of severe illness and death has been disproportionately felt by older people and by people with disabilities. Further factors impacting the likelihood of severe illness and death are the existence of co-morbidities, being a member of a black or ethnic minority community and being in an economically disadvantaged social class. Many of these factors cluster – more ethnic minorities in economically disadvantaged social classes for example, and more have co-morbidities like diabetes and obesity (see Table 5.2). In this way Covid replicates and exacerbates long-term social divisions. This was vividly illuminated in a report by the NHS Race and Health Observatory which looked at the way the Covid-19 pandemic exacerbated long-established health inequalities, associated with ethnicity, inequalities that existed before Covid at every stage through the life course from birth to death (Kapadia et al. 2022). Other examples of Covid-19 exacerbating inequalities have been assembled by a group, *Covid-19 Bereaved Families for Justice*, who have identified many examples of people with learning disabilities being passed over for potentially life-saving treatment (covidfamiliesforjustice.org). One of these people was Susan Sullivan who was not admitted to intensive care and died in her bed in a general ward, she was 56 and had Down's syndrome. A doctor had written in her treatment plan that she might benefit from a higher level of care but that was not made available to her (see *The Observer* 10 July 2022, 19).

The Covid-19 serious illness and death figures replicate the picture of damage done by the promotion, over 40 years, of neoliberal policies that have been to the detriment of groups marginal to the market economy ethos it promotes. The way Covid-19 manifests in the body places older people at enhanced risk, but the extent of the resulting serious illness and death can be linked to government policies, over the long term, which have shaped the prevention and care environment and political decisions in the short term about balancing risk to the economy and risk of the spread of infection (see Box 5.3). Both these are policy areas that are shaped by neoliberalism. For example, by early January 2021, 26,000 people had died in care homes, a quarter of all UK deaths (this was eight times the rate of death in German care homes).

One aspect of the rhetorical position adopted with the pandemic was to discuss it as an unprecedented occurrence, something that could not have been foreseen. But there were precedents, most recently the H1N1 pandemic of 2009 and 2010. Former US President Obama has considered the how lessons from that pandemic did not translate into infrastructures or procedures that could have been quickly drawn on in the Covid-19 pandemic   for example not much research had been done on vaccine development or delivery systems. Vaccine development was not seen as a money maker and hence was not a priority for drug companies. There had

Table 5.2 Within the UK, there are differences according to age, disability social class and ethnicity

Age	Disability
Impact of Covid-19 by age – increasing age is the single biggest predictor of severe illness and death. In the first six months of 2020 more than 93,000 care home residents died – 45.9% more deaths than in the previous year.	Sixty per cent of deaths from Covid-19 between January and November 2020 were of people with a disability, this group makes up 17% of the population (Office for National Statistics Feb 2021). The risk to disabled women was 3.5 times that of non-disabled women.
Ethnicity April 2020 Intensive Care National Audit Research Centre (ICNARC): 35% of critically ill covid-19 patients are from black or minority ethnic backgrounds. Asian 13.6% of critically ill (7.5% of population): Black 13.6%. (3.3%): Other 6.6. (1%) Death rates – Black men were four times more likely than white men to die if they caught covid: Pakistani and Bangladeshi men three times.	*Social Class* Of the 20283 Covid-19 deaths in England and Wales to 17 April 2020 people in the poorest areas died at twice the rate of those in the more affluent ones. There were 55.1 deaths per 100,000 population in the 10% most deprived places compared with 25.3 in the 10% least deprived (figures from Office for National Statistics, May 2020)
Increase in exposure to risk links to occupation and housing type Ethnic minorities – more crowded homes – 2% of White British households are overcrowded, one-third of Bangladesh households are overcrowded. One in five of the NHS workforce is from an ethnic minority (14% of England and Wales population). NHS workers were disproportionately exposed to the virus.	*By Income* Poorer people – more likely to have jobs that can't be done from home, more use public transport, more use extended families for child-care, less early retirement, more pensioners need to work, more overcrowded homes. Less keen to take a test if it means a positive result will mean having time off work (and less/no income). Countries like Finland and Norway provided respectively, 100% or 80% existing income to people self-isolating. In the UK statutory sick pay of £95.85 was provided and a discretionary self-isolating payment that most people did not get – so many people who tested positive still went to work.

not been much attention given to the value of pre-positioning medical supplies, protective or respiratory equipment for example and, although much was known about the wider medical and social impact of pandemics – long-term morbidity and collateral economic damage most notably – this did not raise the need to plan high enough on the policy agenda (Obama 2020). (See Table 5.3 re UK experiences of not learning from previous experiences or preparedness studies.)

Table 5.3 Before the pandemic

Impact of inequality and austerity

- Unhealthy UK population – slowing and, in some groups, reversing previously increasing life expectancy: major health inequalities, high levels of obesity and diabetes – particularly marked in some communities (Marmot 2020a, see Marmot et al. 2020).
- Shortage of nurses and doctors – unfilled vacancies – 100,000 vacancies for core NHS staff when the epidemic began including more than 10,000 doctors and 40,000 nurses. The equivalent of 1348 fewer fully qualified full-time GPs were working in the NHS in March 2020 compared to numbers in place in 2015.
- Very full hospitals – near capacity most of the year and even more so each winter (without Covid admissions).
- In 2019, the UK was spending around 10.2% of its GDP on health care compared with 11.7% in Germany and 11.1% in France.
- Hospital waiting lists were of 4.43 million in February 2020.
- Average number of beds per 1000 people in the OECD EU nations was 4.6, in the UK, it was 2.4.
- Under-resourced public health services and hostility to local government where public health had been located. Market-led services – fractured and short-term focussed: privatisation of NHS supply chains.

(Figures from the British Medical Association June 2022)

Market concerns lead to a short-term policy focus/preoccupation with Brexit planning
- Ignoring lessons from preparedness studies – Operation Winter Willow in 2007 involved 5000 doctors, nurses, police officers, soldiers and civil servants rehearsing plans to respond to a pandemic, Operation Cygnus in 2016 modelled a pandemic and made recommendations in relation to four key learning outcomes and 22 detailed lessons. It stated that "the UKs preparedness and responses in terms of its plans, policies and capabilities is currently not sufficient to cope with the extreme demands of a severe pandemic" (Public Health England 2016).
- In the summer of 2019, the Cabinet Committee named the "Threats, Hazards, Resilience and Contingency Committee" (THRCC) was scrapped on the advice of the Cabinet Secretary so civil servants and ministers could focus on Brexit (a Home Office Report in July 2018 had said THRCC was at the heart of protecting the country from a pandemic).[9]

Sridhar (2021) argued that it isn't difficult to know what to do with a new virus, the complexity is in the logistics, messaging and leadership to do something about it. She thought that Britain throughout (the first year) has been "over reliant on modelling, cynical fatalism and complicated solutions". There was also an absence of learning from the experience of other countries. These are observations that move us from a consideration of the impact of neoliberalism to consider populism and Covid-19 (see Table 5.4). The "unprecedent" event tropes that accompanied the arrival of Covid-19 are best understood then as distraction devices for political and industrial elites, part of the populist performance of the pandemic that I will come to in my next section. But the "unprecedented event"

Box 5.3 Trade-offs in the Covid-19 pandemic

At the core of much of the debate about responses to the Covid-19 pandemic in the UK, but also widely across the world, is a discussion about the priority to give to saving lives balanced against the cost to society when we seek to reduce covid deaths by lockdowns in the economy and in education. Economists use two measures, QALYs – one year of full health – and Value of Prevented Fatality (VPF) – how much would you be prepared to pay to reduce the risk of preventable deaths. Of course, the problem in looking to such measures in a pandemic is not knowing what would happen if you did nothing to mitigate the epidemic, and not knowing what groups of people would make up most of the deaths were this route to be taken. Additionally, the impact of lock-down to reduce Covid deaths may result in recession, and recession is accompanied by major health sequalae. What these will be are difficult to specify. A post-pandemic recession is likely to be different to the impacts linked to previous recessions because sectors of the economy that are most affected may differ (Spinney 2021).

But there is another approach, ditch all this talk about trade-offs and about best measures – they are not suitable for a health emergency, it is not conscionable to argue that we could do nothing.

---

narrative is also used for another purpose – in June 2022 then Secretary of State for Health Sajid Javid said, in Parliament, that the pressures on the NHS were created by the Covid pandemic. However, issues around funding, bed-capacity, staffing and recruitment predated Covid. One reason the UK was ill-prepared for the pandemic was what the British Medical Association (June 2022) has said was "historical underfunding and under-resourcing in the decade preceding the virus". Indeed, the pandemic has underlined the problems of the NHS not created them.

The "unprecedented event" and the attribution of present-day problems to the relatively short period since the pandemic began are examples of the coming together of neoliberalism and populist performance. Specifically, the use of short-term amnesia and long-term nostalgia. Neoliberalism is concerned with the present, populism with an imagined past invoked in the interests of the powerful. I will explore this next.

Medical populism

Lasco and Curato define medical populism as, "a political style that constructs antagonistic relations between 'the people' whose lives have been put at risk" and "the establishment". They argue that a proliferation of media and a preoccupation with highlighting "breaking news" and a populism that builds support by questioning the status of experts and the veracity of their definitions of truth results in, "politicising, simplifying and spectacularising complex public health issues" (Lasco and Curato 2019: 1). Health crises become the "canvas for populist performance". That performance takes two forms according to Lasco and Curato, a vertical dimension where the people are held in opposition to an untrustworthy medical establishment, and a horizontal dimension where medical populists claim to speak for the virtuous people against the dangerous "others". This is a critique that draws on the literature on moral panics (see Mannion and Small, 2019). Some moral panics foster medical populism but all medical populism includes elements of moral panic.

The traction that this sort of populism gets depends on broader conditions, and the response to some issues shifts. It is by no means certain that populist leaders will use populist responses to all crises, and some non-populist leaders may evoke populist performance around some issues. Sometimes a little populism can help reveal shortcomings in established procedures and sometimes experts can reassert the centrality of their definition and their preferred response to a health emergency.

Populists are "for the people" and against the establishment, seeking to speak over the heads of that establishment and in so doing dismissing the status of experts and the veracity of their views. I have described above the way, on both sides of the Atlantic, expert voices were dismissed – President Trump in the US and by the proponents of Brexit in England being prime examples. These are manifestations of Lasco and Curato's vertical populism. It sits uncomfortably with a mantra of "we are following the science" that characterised the rhetorical position of the government for much of the first year of the pandemic. I have commented above on the lack of clear leadership in both speed of action and clarity of messaging that has characterised the response to the pandemic in England, debate about if face coverings matter/ debate how serious Covid-19 was – was it just like "bad flu", shifting messages about "stay at home" and then "eat out to help out", the Prime Minister's advisor Dominic Cummins breaking lockdown travel rules and then not apologising and so on.[10] These, I have said, reflect the twin drivers of seeking to reduce infection, demands on the NHS and deaths on one side and the wish to sustain the economy, including trade, on the other. The populist route out of such a dichotomy is a clear manifestation of Lasco and Curato's (2019) populist performance.

That performance included daily press conferences from Downing Street in which a politician, frequently the Prime Minister or the Secretary of State for Health, were flanked by experts from "science" and medicine. They used graphs and also answered press questions (and questions from members of the public). This was, at the same time, being led by science and co-opting science in "performing" government. Co-opting here meant occluding "science" and policy so that the latter was cloaked in the assumed veracity of the former while the opportunity of science opposing the political was subdued. Outside the theatre of the press briefing the performance was more clearly populist.[11] Two examples

Table 5.4 Populist performance

"The best place to be".
Jeremy Hunt (former Secretary of State for Health and subsequently Chair of
Parliament's Health Select Committee) early in the epidemic said, "if I had to be in any
country during an epidemic, it would be the UK" (citing its centralised NHS). By June
2020 excess deaths per 100,000 of the population in the UK were 97[12] – the highest level
in the G7 – Germany's figure was 9, I don't know if Mr Hunt has changed his mind (if
Germany isn't to his liking, he might consider life in New Zealand!) There is a danger
in idealising the NHS. While one may adhere to its founding principles and appreciate
the shortcomings of many alternate ways to deliver health care a realistic perception of
its present state must consider how it had been degraded and fractured by policy choices
across its lifespan – the rhetorical valorisation of the NHS has gone on alongside neglect
of its infrastructure and its staffing.[13]

A year later….
"Clap for Carers"
Dr Rachael Clarke, a Palliative Care doctor also working in hospital intensive care
settings, said about the weekly "Clap for Carers" – in the first wave it felt like they were
"eruptions of spontaneous gratitude and appreciation". By the third wave, "I really,
strongly did not want applause because I felt that lovely community spirit was to some
extent co-opted and exploited by the government and by Boris Johnson who stood
on the steps of No 10 and applauded us knowing that he and his colleagues had voted
against a pay raise for nurses two years previously. Their rhetoric around NHS heroes
has worn thin". *The Observer* 24/01/21.

---

illustrate, the first from very early in the pandemic and the second from almost
one year later (see Table 5.4). Both examples show a co-opting of public sentiment in the interests of the government. They also show how an image of the
NHS is conjured and exploited. The examples then are illustrative a new sort of
populism, one that combines Lasco and Curato's vertical variety – allying the
government with a perceived popular sentiment, in this case for the NHS, with
a horizontal populism in which the government is cast as one more player in the
alliance against the outside threat, in this case from the virus. This new sort of
populism carries dangers, any wider break-down in trust in political leadership
and a perceived split between government and popular sentiment could be met
on the former's part by a shift to a vertical populism that then promotes a search
for "others" to blame.

The capacities of government and the symbolism of the NHS

Both Lewis (2021) and Micklethwaite and Woldridge (2020) see shortcomings in
responses to Covid-19 as illustrative of a degeneration in state machines. Lewis
focuses on a lack of centralised decision making in the US and an excessive
caution in public health agencies, most notably the Centers for Disease Control.
Micklethwaite and Woldridge link this "degeneration" to "populist contagion"
in the UK (and elsewhere in the West)[14] and contrast this with countries such
as South Korea, Taiwan and Singapore who exhibit aggressive modernisation,

including widespread engagement with technology and a simplification of bureaucracy – less rather than weaker regulation.

There is another explanation that fits the populist paradigm for the policy choices made in the UK, and in England in particular. This explanation examines the way the NHS was seized on as a nationalist icon[15] via the invocation of a national story of collective identity and sacrifice. Davies sees Boris Johnson elevating the defence of the NHS above a defence of the public. Keeping our NHS safe, stopping it being overwhelmed, created the sort of public mood in which the rising death rates could be diverted into a "spontaneous solidarity" with NHS workers (clap for carers was one example). "Having the worst death toll in Europe clearly counts for less in the eyes of the public than the rallying around our resolutely *National* Health Service" (Davies 2020: 8). The NHS described in this process is a simulacrum, an image or representation of something conjured to serve the government.

One of the consequences of this approach was the decision in March 2020 to reduce pressure on the NHS by discharging 15,000 patients out of hospital into the community, in many cases into the care homes that soon became the epicentre of Covid deaths. The dismissal of the vulnerable in favour of the needs of the organisation is reminiscent of the discussion above about Stafford and other care settings where failures were reported (see Introduction). A populist jingoism here adds to a neoliberal elevation of organisational need in a way that suggests history repeating itself.

Short term amnesia and long term nostalgia

Neoliberalism dispenses with memory; it privileges the short term. In contrast, populism invokes an imagined history and seeks to exploit a nostalgic past. The very short-term focus is evidenced in government rhetoric by the selection of Covid-19 "success" stories and ignoring uncomfortable facts – claiming the fastest booster campaign in Europe for example and not considering the damage done by delaying the date of lockdown in March 2020. Iceland, Denmark and Israel had delivered more boosters when the UK Prime Minister made his claim about British exceptionalism. Up to 20000 people could have died because of the delay in lockdown according to Professor Neil Ferguson of Imperial College London (*The Observer* 30 Jan 2022).

Conclusion

The ascent of economics and neoliberalism's ontological choreography of language[16] is marked in the NHS because it contrasts with a more established ethos that many assume is inseparable from the institution itself. The same sort of change in other parts of the public sector, housing, welfare, social care is competing with a more diffuse ethos. The sorts of changes occurring are examples of the Habermasian construct of the system world eroding communicative action (the ability to engage in public discourse) and the values of the life world (Murray 2015).

Hayek (1960) was clear that building a market society involved breaking with some of the traditions and practices of the past. His acolytes (including Margaret Thatcher) did not always take on the implications of the economic changes they promoted. The politician-marketers dreamed of retaining (and subsequently of retrieving) a set of beliefs and practices they identified with an idealised past – family, patriotism, public service. But these are also impacted by market changes. Re-engineering public institutions on market lines helps some people get rich but it makes many people more insecure, and it impacts on their perception as to the priorities of their job via reframing the sense of self they have as public servants.

Toynbee and Walker (2017) say that the continuing attack on the state, now a 40-year phenomenon, means it has been "Dismembered". The attack has not only reshaped the way services are delivered but has also eroded a sense of social solidarity that had underpinned the growth of the Welfare State after 1945. With that it has also eroded a sense of a shared moral imperative captured in the idea that we have some responsibility for the disadvantaged. Infusing the NHS (the clearest manifestation of this shared moral solidarity) with profit seekers does more than distort resource allocations, it prises apart an idea of social spending as a social good and promotes the idea that profit for some is good and that the feckless and unfortunate are "dragging us down". It also prioritises the short term, undermining one of the rationales Keynes presented as justifying the legitimacy of state activity; the state, he said, was alone in a position to take the long view.

I have looked at what neoliberalism is, at how it impacts on the economics of health care, and how it changes the organisation and the professions of the NHS. In this chapter, I have looked at how neoliberalism makes us sick and at Covid-19 as a neoliberal epidemic, but one in which populism also shapes responses. In the next chapter, I will shift focus to look at the impact of neoliberalism on attitudes, both collectively and in individuals, and at how these attitudes shape behaviour.

Notes

1 In the *Shorter Oxford English Dictionary* sequela has two meanings, first "a consequence" and second as "a morbid affection occurring as a result of a previous disease" that latter definition seems particularly apt for the case I will make.

2 The standard measure of inequality is called the Gini coefficient – if income is shared in proportion to the population, the bottom 10% getting about 10% of the income and so on, then the Gini coefficient is zero, there would be no inequality. But if all income went to one person there would be "perfect" inequality and a Gini coefficient of (1) The US Gini coefficient is 0.48, indicating much greater inequality that any EU country (Eurostat 2012). The Gini coefficient does not properly measure the incomes of the very rich, their capacity to "hide" wealth offshore obscures the true extent of wealth inequality.

3 The prevailing definition of what constitutes poverty changes over time – sometimes because a particular definition suits a political position, sometimes because more meaningful definitions emerge from critiques of the nature and lived experience of poverty – a definition of the poverty line as being living at, or below, 60% of median UK income has been challenged by a new measure from the Social Metrics Commission which defines the poverty line not just in relation to median income but also to the resources a family has available to engage adequately in a life regarded as the

norm in society. This wider measure should remove the anomaly in relying on median income that during the 2008 financial crash as overall incomes fell it appeared that family poverty also fell.

4 2018 Office for National Statistics Report (Institute of Health Equity 2020) report a dramatic drop in previously observed increases in life expectancy – since 2011 the rate of improvement had gone down by about three-quarters for men and by 91% for women – a faster decline than other leading industrial countries except "free-market" US.

5 Tempany (2016) has vividly highlighted the disdain authorities had for the working class. British football was characterised as "a slum sport played in slum stadiums and increasingly watched by slum people who deter ordinary folk from turning up". In 1989, 96 (later 97) supporters of Liverpool football club died in a crush in a badly designed, maintained and policed stadium, Hillsborough in Sheffield, the dead and injured were demonised by sections of the press (Beckett 2016).

6 A little austerity might help support an ecological appeal to reduce consumption – perhaps it is materialism rather than neoliberalism, or even capitalism, that constitutes our greatest risk in society. There is a literature that argues that the health benefits of austerity need to be acknowledged – the impact of reduced transport use on air quality and accidents, the reduction in those health harms resulting directly from some forms of work, a change of consumption patterns and so on, this literature is summarised, and contested, in Uphoff et al. 2018.

7 This does not dispel a prevalent conceit of the rich and powerful that they deserve the great financial rewards they get because of how stressful it is being a captain of industry or a high-flying entrepreneur.

8 I have discussed the allied shifts to McDonaldisation and proletarianization of work in Chapter 4.

9 The UK was far from alone in lack of preparedness – Lewis (2021) describes the USA's Centers for Disease Control and Prevention as trapped by an institutional surfeit of caution that he says amounted to a sort of recklessness. More generally he describes the way the pandemic revealed a whole governmental structure in the US mired in a malaise that meant it was not clear who should instigate action, "There's no one driving the bus", he says.

10 My focus on the first year of the pandemic excludes the Downing Street parties during Covid lockdowns that would have provided a further, and striking, example.

11 The work by Debord in describing a *Society of the Spectacle* is relevant here and is examined in more detail in my Conclusion. Distracting dazzle depletes everyday life and instils passivity and isolation (Debord 1995: see also Reynolds 2022).

12 Excess deaths compare deaths with those recorded in previous years. In 2020, there were 697000 deaths in the UK; this is nearly 9,100 more than the average for the previous five years (population growth and age structures are considered). At 1.5% this was the largest rise in excess deaths for over 75 years.

13 It is a commonly used rhetorical trope to invoke a grand narrative to deflect from a focus on contemporary shortcomings. I will return to this at various points but here note Davies (2020: 7) discussing government responses to the Covid-19 pandemic – elevating talk about keeping our NHS safe "was an ingenious piece of political rhetoric, side-lining the methodological and morbid question of body counts, and replacing it with a national story of collective identity and sacrifice".

14 Given the differences in Covid figures in Western countries, it should also be noted that the patterns of state response varied; again early in the epidemic, the UK was liberal – up to the individual to make the right choices – whereas France reverted to a more statist approach where people were told what to do, filling in a form before you left your house even for short trips for example.

15 The idea of Britain (or England) as a single imagined community is not new – it is a recurring feature of our history (or histories) – from Henry V's appeals to the troops before Agincourt to Churchill's Second World War speeches. Edgerton (2018) makes a

case that the welfare state, from its inception, has been incorporated into this project. (I have discussed the choices and compromises made when the welfare state was established and the way they have resonated through its history in Chapter 2 and have looked at the use of "clap for carers" (Table 5.4) to invoke imagined communities – even when this did reveal a real felt bond between the public and health workers).

16 Brown (2015) argues that neoliberalism isn't just bringing economics into a more prominent role in public policy, it is destroying the very institutions of democracy and changing the way we talk about politics.

References

Alexiou, A., Fahy, K., Mason, K., Bennett, D., Brow, H., Bambra, C., Taylor-Robinson, D., Barr, B. 2021. Local government funding and life expectancy in England: A longitudinal ecological study. *Lancet Public Health*, 6(9), Sept, e641–e647.

Alston, P. 2018. *Statement on Visit to the United Kingdom by Professor Philip Alston, United Nations Special Rapporteur on Extreme Poverty and Human Rights*. United Nations General Assembly.

Alston, P. 2019. *Report of the Special Rapporteur on Extreme Poverty and Human Rights*. United Nations General Assembly.

Beckett, A. 2016. From 'slum sport' to domineering cultural force. *The Guardian*, 4 June, 7.

Bell, R., Aitsi-Selmi, A., Marmot, M. 2012. Subordination, stress and obesity. In, Offer, A., Pechey, R., Ulijaszek, S. (Eds) *Insecurity, Inequality and Obesity in Affluent Societies*. Oxford, Oxford University Press for the British Academy.

Brown, W. 2015. *Undoing the Demos: Neoliberalism's Stealth Revolution*. MIT Press.

Case, A., Deaton, A. 2020. *Deaths of Despair and the Future of Capitalism*. Princeton University Press.

Cassidy, J. 2014. Forces of divergence. *The New Yorker*, Mar, 69–73.

Cohen, S., Janicki-Deverts, D. 2012. Who's stressed? Distributions of psychological stress in the United States in probability samples from 1983, 2006 and 2009. *Journal of Applied Social Psychology*, 42, 1320–1334.

Commission on Social Determinates of Health. 2008. *Closing the Gap in a Generation: Health Equity through Action on the Social Determinates of Health (Final Report)*. Geneva, World Health Organisation.

Davies, W. 2020. Flags, face masks and flypasts. *The Guardian Review*, 16 May, 6–9.

Debord, D. 1995. *The Society of the Spectacle*. New York, Zone Books.

Dorling, D. 2012. *The No-Nonsense Guide to Equality*. Oxford, New Internationalist Publications.

Edgerton, D. 2018. *The Rise and Fall of the British Nation: A Twentieth Century History*. Allen Lane.

Eurostat. 2012. http://appsso.eurostat.ec.europa.eu/nui/show.do?dataset=ilc_di12&lang=en (accessed 5/03/2012).

Ferrie, J.E., Shipley, M.J., Marmot, M.G., et al. 1998. An uncertain future: The health effects of threats to employment security in white-collar men and women. *American Journal of Public Health*, 88, 1030–1036.

Graham, H. 2009. *Understanding Health Inequalities*. Maidenhead, Open University Press.

Hayek, F.A. 1960. *The Constitution of Liberty*. University of Chicago Press.

Institute of Health Equity, 2020. Health equity in England: The Marmot review 10 years on. London. http://www.instituteofhealthequity.org/the-marmot-review-10-years-on (accessed 24/02/2020). (Authors: M. Marmot, J. Allen, T. Boyce, P. Goldblatt, J. Morrison).

Jagger, C. 2015. News. *Society Now*. ESRC, Autumn 3.

Johnson, J.V., Hall, E.M. 1988. Job strain, workplace support and cardiovascular disease: A cross-sectional study of a random sample of the Swedish working population. *American Journal of Public Health*, 78, 1336–1342.

Judt, T. 2010. *The Memory Chalet*. London, William Heinemann.

Kapadia, D., Zhang, J., Salway, S., Nazroo, J., Booth, A., Villarroel-Williams, N., Bécares, L., Esmail, A. 2022. *Ethnic Inequalities in Health. A Rapid Evidence Review*. NHS Race and Health Observatory.

Karasek, R.A., Theorell, T. 1990. *Healthy Work Stress: Productivity and the Reconstruction of Working Lives*. New York, Basic Books.

Lasco, G., Curato, N. 2019. Medical populism. *Social Science and Medicine*, 221, 1–8. https://doi.org/10.1016/j.socscimed.2018.12.006

Lewis, M. 2021. *The Premonition: A Pandemic Story*. Allen Lane.

Marmot, M. 2004. *Status Syndrome*. London, Bloomsbury.

Marmot, M. 2010. *Fair Society, Healthy Lives: The Marmot Review; Strategic Review of Health Inequalities in England Post-2010*. The Marmot Review.

Marmot, M. 2015. *The Health Gap*. Bloomsbury.

Marmot, M., Friel, S., Bell, R. et al. 2008. Closing the gap in a generation: Health equity through action on the social determinates of health. *The Lancet*, 350, 235–240.

Marmot, M., Stansfield, S., Patel, C., Head, J., White, I., Brunner, E., Feeney, A., Davey-Smith, G. 1991. Health Inequalities among British civil servants: The Whitehall II study. *The Lancet*, 337(8754), 1387–1393.

Mannion, R., Small, N. 2019. On folk devils, moral panics and new wave public health. *International Journal of Health Policy and Management*, 8(12), 678–683.

Martin, S., Longo, F., Lomas, J., Claxton, K. 2021. Causal impact of social care, public health and healthcare expenditure on mortality in England: Cross sectional evidence for 2013–14. *BMJ Open*, 11, e046417. http://dx.doi.org/10.1136/bmjopen-2020-046417.

Micklethwait, J., Wooldridge, A. 2020. *The Wake Up Call: Why the Pandemic has Exposed the Weakness of the West – and How to Fix It*. Short Books.

Mullainathan, S., Shafir, E. 2014. *Scarcity: The True Cost of Not Having Enough*. Penguin.

Murray, D. 2015. Is the West's loss of faith terminal? *Standpoint* (May).

Obama, B. 2020. *The Health of a Nation*. New Yorker, 2 Nov, 24–39.

Piketty, T. 2014. *Capital in the Twenty-First Century*. Harvard University Press.

Reid-Henry, S. 2016. *The Political Origins of Inequality: Why a More Equal World Is Better for Us All*. University of Chicago Press.

Reynold, S. 2022. Serious Mayhem. *London Review of Books*, 10 Mar, 19–24.

Ryan, F. 2019. *Crippled: Austerity and the Demonisation of Disabled People*. Verso.

Scheidel, W. 2017. *The Great Leveller: Violence and the History of Inequality from the Stone Age to the Twenty-First Century*. Princeton University Press.

Schrecker, T., Bambra, C. 2015. *How Politics Makes Us Sick. Neoliberal Epidemics*. Basingstoke, Palgrave Macmillan.

Spinney, L. 2021. Has Covid changed the price of a life? *The Observer: The New Review*, 16(2), 22–23.

Sridhar, D. 2021. Here are five ways the government could have avoided 100,000 Covid deaths. *Guardian Opinion*, 27 Jan.

Stiglitz, J.E. 2013 (2nd Ed). *The Price of Inequality*. London, Penguin.

Tempany, A. 2016. *And the Sun Shines Now: How Hillsborough and the Premier League Changed Britain*. Faber.

Toynbee, P., Walker, D. 2017. *Dismembered: How the Attack on the State Harms Us All.* London, Faber & Faber.

Uphoff, E., Small, N., Pickett, K. 2018. Using birth cohort data to assess the impact of the UK 2008–2010 economic recession on smoking during pregnancy. *Nicotine & Tobacco Research.* http://dx.doi.org/10.1093/ntr/nty083

Watkins, J., Wulaningsih, W., Da Zhou, C., Marshall, D.C., Sylianteng, G.D.C., Dela Rosa, P.G., Miguel, V.A., Raine, R., King, L.P., Maruthappu, M. 2017. Effects of health and social care spending constraints on mortality in England: A time trend analysis. *BMJ Open.* http://dx.doi.org/10.1136/bmjopen-2017-017722

Wilkinson, R., Pickett, K. 2010. *The Spirit Level: Why Equality Is Better for Everyone.* London, Penguin.

Wilkinson, R., Pickett, K. 2018. *The Inner Level: How More Equal Societies Reduce Stress, Restore Sanity and Improve Everyone's Well-Being.* London, Penguin.

Wohland, P., Rees, P., Nazroo, J., Jagger, C. 2015. Inequalities in health life expectancy between ethnic groups in England and Wales in 2001. *Ethnicity and Health*, 20(4), 341–353.

World Inequality Report 2018 (Coordinated by Alvaredo, F. et al.) World Inequality Lab.

6 How ideological shifts are manifest in society

In collective social attitudes and in individuals

Public man and private subjectivities

In this section, I will consider approaches to understanding the relationships between the economy and society and individuals' public positions and private subjectivities. This returns us to the lifeworld/system world interaction described by Habermas and addresses the central question about how a change in the economy and society might impact individual understandings and behaviour.

The individual level

Writing in the early days of neoliberalism, and before its impact was likely to have become entrenched in the lives of individuals, Ignatieff is concerned with the more underlying manifestations of modernity. He asks: "What is modernity doing to our identities? Are we becoming more selfish, less capable of political commitment, readier to pull up the drawbridge on our neighbours?" (Ignatieff 1986: 20). He cites the philosopher Castoriadis who points out that,

> Development or changes in society are ipso facto changes in the structure of individuals, the way they act, the way they behave. After all, everything's social. But society as such has no address. I mean you can't meet it. It's in you and me, in the language, in the books and so on.
>
> (Castoriadis, quoted in Ignatieff 1986: 21: see also Castoriadis 1986)

Even further back, Foucault (1972) approaches the same phenomenon, although here attributed to the market: nothing is fixed – just mediated by the market where the discourses of the market, "systematically form the objects of which they speak" (Foucault 1972: 49).

Norbert Elias in *The Civilising Process* (revised edition 2000: originally published in English 1969), argued that civilisation is a process whereby external restraints on behaviour are replaced by internal moral regulation – there is a civilising process rather than civilisation because there is always a constant and endless processual flux in all social relationships.[1] If internal moral regulation is eroded and external restraints on behaviour are shifting from a regulatory or

DOI: 10.4324/9781003332404-8

legalistic paradigm to an economic "imperative" then we might argue that the processual flux is, at present, an anti-civilisation one (and that that flux is evidenced by attitudes to the sick and vulnerable).

Hookway (2012) doesn't talk about civilisation but, in a closely related way, is concerned with moral decline in the West. He personifies routes to this moral decline by identifying "cultural pessimists" and "communitarians" (see Table 6.1).[2] Cultural pessimists see a preoccupation with the self played out across what becomes a "therapeutic" culture. Communitarians see moral decline as residing in our being cut off from shared narratives, from our past, our community, our traditions and our social bonds. One of his cultural pessimists is Lasch, who I will consider below, and one of his communitarians is MacIntyre who I discuss in more detail in subsequent chapters. Here, after a brief look at MacIntyre, I will, instead, focus on another commentator on "public man", Sennett.

In the late 1970s and 1980s, just before and then in the early days of this neoliberal turn, two writers identified changes that are revealing here, one was concerned

Table 6.1 Routes to moral decline

Cultural pessimists	*Communitarians*
There is a moral impoverishment of modern culture, a weakening of cultural authorities and a rise of "psychological man". That psychological man has a preoccupation with their own internal life and with the pursuit of hedonism. Lasch calls this a "culture of narcissism", a culture that is amoral and uncaring (Lasch 1979).	Widespread individualism and a decline of community are eroding shared moral life and shared values. MacIntyre sees this as revealing a loss of access to a common moral vocabulary (MacIntyre 1981). Identity, social relations and a sense of direction for moral life are lost and with them the mutual obligations and duties embedded in role structures that, "constitute the given of my life, my moral starting point" (MacIntyre 1981: 220).
Why has this happened?	*Why has this happened?*
There has been a rise of a therapeutic ethos of self-fulfilment – a product of a 1960s liberationist culture.	The rise of, "neo-capitalism, hyper-consumption and a free-wheeling market that accompanied fears of atomised self-interest and materialistic acquisitiveness" (Hookway 2012: 842).
What can we do about it?	*What can we do about it?*
Not much! Hookway is succinct in his summing up the consequence of this position; "morality has little hope in a culture in which the individual is allowed to create their 'own set of rules', where 'no' has disappeared from our moral vocabulary, and where foundational moral laws enforced by religious tradition and higher moral authorities have disappeared" (Hookway 2012: 845).	Restore communities, neighbourhoods, civic connectedness and a sense of social responsibility.

with our public selves and a retreat from the social, the other with our inner self, which he described as increasingly "minimal".

In an examination of social change and personality undertaken by Lasch in two books published in 1979 and 1985, he looked at what he identified as *"The Culture of Narcissism"* and the emergence of *"The Minimal Self"*.

The individualism characteristic of capitalism has generated a retrenchment into a minimal self, a narcissistic self that finds the goals of life in the narrowest terms (Lasch 1985). We have seen an erosion of the idea of a public space, or a public time horizon. For Lasch, this is to do with the absence of any grand social project (from the left no idea of utopian futures: from the right no belief in indefinite progress) – we rarely encounter a project that looks further than the next budget or the next election. The forces that have shaped this shift are a breakdown of traditional working-class organisations (the trades unions, parties of the left) and an ability in capitalism to give a rising standard of living in an era of consumerism. Our private time horizon is about retirement pensions and children's education. We don't have a sense of living in a world of solid objects that will outlast ourselves (a characteristic furthered by the digital age). In part, this reflects the media defining the world of culture as a place of hallucinating images and short time frames, it's not a solid world.

Lasch was writing in the 1970s and 1980s and what has happened since, certainly in relation to communication technology, has been to further conceptualise public space as a virtual space, Facebook, Twitter, Instagram and so on (the communication of political and even public health messages on these digital platforms rather than, say, in the physical settings of our legislatures is a feature of our recent politics).[3] In relation to capitalism, being able to continue to provide a rising standard of living has not been evident in more recent years (it was only evident in the years Lasch focusses on if you consider aggregates and ignore chronic income inequalities).

Sennett, in a prescient book published in the early days of neoliberalism, 1986, and then in a subsequent works in 2006 and 2012 which looked more overtly at the culture of new capitalism (Sennett 1986, 2006), considered what he termed *"The Fall of Public Man"*, he said,

> public life has …become a matter of formal obligation. Most citizens approach their dealings with the state in a spirit of resigned acquiescence, but this public enervation is in its scope much broader than political affairs. Manners and ritual interchanges with strangers are looked on as at best formal and dry, at worst as phoney … participation in the *res publica* [bonds of association and mutual commitment that exist between people not joined by bonds of family or intimate association] today is most often a matter of going along.
>
> (Sennett 1986: 3–4)[4]

The *"Fall of Public Man"* is accompanied by "anxiety about individual feelings" (5). Sennett quotes from de Tocqueville, who is reflecting on the eighteenth-century revolutions in France and America, at the start of *The Fall of Public Man*:

> Each person, withdrawn into himself, behaves as though he were a stranger to the destiny of all others. His children and his good friends constitute for him the whole of the human species. As for his transactions with his fellow citizens, he may mix among them, but he sees them not; he touches them, but he does not feel them; he exists only in himself and for himself alone. And if on these terms there remains in his mind a sense of family, there no longer remains a sense of society.

In 2012, Sennett explored how power is detached from authority as international elites live in a global detachment from responsibilities to others.[5] In terms of capital/labour relations a new model of capitalism based on short-term contracts and constant change weakens collective bargaining for workers, pits worker in competition with worker and, in so doing, shows a contempt that engenders demoralisation. He describes how the response of the powerless is one of either "you are on your own", or "us against them", both responses, individualism or a sort of brutal solidarity that enhances anxiety, inhibits the sort of cooperation that he thinks most valuable, cooperation that begins with "dialogical thinking", listening to what people say and drawing people out in those areas they don't easily say anything about (Sennett 2012). In terms of the organisation of capitalist enterprise this model sees short terms fixes rather than long-term solutions. When it is applied to health care a "management consultant's" mentality prevails – you must do something, whatever it is – it's like ADHD, flitting from one policy to the next. The result is too many and too quick reforms, forgetting that it takes time to learn how to make things work. "Craftmanship is laid low by quick-fix fever" (Sennett 2006). Further, "It's as if health were a series of episodes rather than about a human relationship between a doctor and a patient". This sort of approach favours a particular kind of person,

> Someone who does not want long-term relationships, who is good at letting go of people, who treats life in the community in the way he treats the world of work, who see life as a set of opportunities rather than a sustained narrative.

This has been a pessimistic section, Ignatieff's question about the way social and economic change impacts individuals appears to be consistent with Elias, Lasch and Sennett who collectively identify changes that are consistent with what Ignatieff's flags as possibilities; becoming more selfish, less capable of political commitment, readier to pull up the drawbridge on our neighbours. Newspaper columnist Keenan Malik (*The Observer* 4/10/20) says we live on the surface of things, depth or meaning fade away in what he calls "Flatland".

An impoverishment of the self and a diminution of the social leaves' individuals and collectivities in a weakened position to respond to the hegemony of markets. These shifts predated neoliberalism but have been accelerated by it.

In the next section, I will consider individual and attitudinal change in more detail and then, in subsequent sections, I will return to the social.

Looking at individual and attitudinal change

The government of the self

I have introduced a reading of neoliberalism as governmentality in Chapter 2 and now return to a more detailed examination of the value of this reading in understanding individual and attitudinal change.

Personal and subjective capacities of citizens have been incorporated into the remit and ambitions of public powers. This occurs not only at the abstract level, it is also about preparing people to be amenable to the techniques of public and private sector administration and the pursuit of governmental priorities and policies. Public powers police and punish people and they encourage compliance via reward, but they also regulate the conduct of citizens by acting upon their mental capacities and propensities (Nettleton 1997). In this way, citizens of neoliberalism come to regulate themselves according to certain normativities (Rose 1999), to act in ways that ipso facto serve elite power and market mechanisms.

Rose (1992: 143–145) suggests three interlinked dimensions in which public power impacts on the personal and subjective capacities of citizens. The *political dimension* concerns the extent to which the capacities of citizens form both a target and a resource for political authorities. The *institutional dimension* relates to those sites or organisations where practices are undertaken which work upon the individuals who are associated with them. The *ethical dimension* refers to the "means by which individuals come to construe, decipher and act upon themselves in relation to the true and the false, the permitted and the forbidden, the desirable and the undesirable" (Rose 1992: 144).

The ethical self has increasingly been recalibrated according to the priorities of the economic market. Expectations of individual conduct are informed by norms and conditionality of the economy, with virtue defined by economic employment and/or austere personal financial management. We achieve the ethical self – the autonomous, competitive, free individual, fulfilled by economic activity – by the application of certain technical practices of the self. These practices see the implementation of the necessary regimes to reform or improve oneself (Nettleton 1997). The next step, looking out beyond us, is that we no longer feel a responsibility for those who do not achieve that improvement of the self.

This newly evolved individuality in late modernity and neoliberalism is largely played out within the constraints of "secondary agencies and institutions", principally the labour market and in the arena of consumption (Petersen 1997: 191). Beck argues that once the individual is "cut loose" from traditional commitments and support relationships, she must choose between a diverse array of lifestyles, subcultures, social ties and identities (Beck 1992). "Class" and the nuclear family no longer determine ideologies and identities. Central to this transformation of the self is the emerging notion of *risk*. The ascendancy of the notion of individual and controllable risk factors in contemporary forms of welfare, health and medicine (places where individuals are increasingly responsible for their own futures) contributes to the hegemony of the *active citizen*, the person who can look after themselves. In this context, the active citizen, cut off from traditional ties, floating in liquid modernity (Bauman 2000), is likely to look to the lead of a work and consumption context in which one prioritises oneself. Thus, the market gets into your head and shapes the stance you take to others, including to those you work with even when your work is caring for others.

But not everyone is changed or is changed in the same way. Individuality interacting with the conjunction of the very many aspects of the relationship between the state, the social and the subjective self allows for different people in ostensibly similar situations to behave differently, to be cruel or be kind for example. This is the area Foucault considers in elaborating what he calls the "dispositive", the various institutional, physical, administrative and knowledge structures that enhance and maintain power. The dispositive shapes the taken for granted aspects of our lives including not only what it is possible to do but also what can be imagined. Deleuze uses a different term, assemblages, to describe symbolic and material formations at all levels of scale. These assemblages are characterised by an interaction of parts, by a mobility, for example between the social, power, ethics and the self (Deleuze 1992). While dispositives and assemblages are different they both encapsulate a dynamic, a terrain characterised by the contingent, the shifting, by becomings.[6]

Talking about an era of neoliberalism does not mean that its philosophy is uncontested, Foucault argued that discourses of power carried with them oppositional movements. Ideological formulations are contested, residual beliefs and practices are maintained. Leonard Cohen put it more poetically, "There is a crack in everything, that's how the light gets in".[7]

System and lifeworld

In my introduction, I wrote of the idea that some of the ways we behave are shaped by rarely voiced but shared understandings and some are shaped by the systems we live within and between. This distinction implies that some of our morality comes from within and some from outside ourselves, from society. In this section, I will consider what this twin focus means. But, at the outset, we need to add to this bifurcation of sources of understanding and of influence a consideration of the changing relationship between society and government. Foucault described this relationship as a paradoxical one: "Society is that in the name of which government strives to limit itself, but it is also the target for permanent governmental intervention to produce, multiply and guarantee the freedoms required by economic liberalism" (Foucault 2008). Those freedoms required by economic liberalism include the creation of a new sort of "man", with a new sort of stance towards society and towards social justice and individual responsibility.

This context of the interplay between the rarely voiced and the system, infused with power and resistance, is expressed clearly in Habermas's formulation of the lifeworld and the system (Habermas 1987).[8] The balance between these is very important in the argument I am developing. Habermas's ideas are summarised in Table 6.2 and some additional readings in Box 6.1.

Table 6.2 Habermas's distinction between the lifeworld and the system. (This section draws on Frank 2014)

For Habermas the lifeworld is, "the shared common understandings, including values, that develop through face to face contacts over time in various social groups, from families to communities. The lifeworld carries all sorts of assumptions about who we are as people and what we value about ourselves: what we believe, what shocks and offends us, what we aspire to, what we desire, what we are willing to sacrifice to which ends, and so forth" (Frank). The power of lifeworld assumptions is "their 'of course' or 'taken for granted' quality. Questions about the lifeworld—why do you believe such-and-such? —can only be answered (if at all) by some version of 'because that's who I am and who we are'" (Frank). "If you press people as to why they do the things most central to their lives—enter and stay in marriages, become parents, support family and friends during crises, engage in community service, work to protect the environment, take offense at wrongs, laugh at jokes—their last, best response usually comes down to 'that's who I am/we are'" (Frank).

In contrast systems are rationalised; they emphasise efficiency, calculability, predictability, and control. The point of such rationalisation is to reduce the individuals' scope of action. Decisions are minimised and "choices" are strictly limited. Everyone involved must act as the system directs them. The rationalised systems: organisations, politics, finance, can exhibit value-commitments, but they cannot generate them. The legitimacy of the system depends on the lifeworld.

Simply looking at common terminology highlights this debate. In the lifeworld, the individual is a citizen, and the state is a place of shared identity. In the system world, the individual is a client, a user or even a customer – the state is a more or less efficient service provider.

Habermas sees the lifeworld is being eroded by the expansion of the system and particularly of its rules. For example, in health-care discussions between patients, families and professionals to reach a common understanding as to the best available course to pursue offers an example of the lifeworld. In contrast rules, protocols and targets, set at a level that is some distance from the encounter with the patient, erode the sphere of the lifeworld. Within the system decisions about what course of action to pursue are decided and imposed, "this is what is on offer". It might be that this offer is couched in terms of the evidence of efficacy, or of the optimum use of resources, but it contributes to a separation of action from values. If actions and values are not allied this fuels a legitimation crisis, and legitimacy is a prerequisite for social order.

There has been a recent history of the encroachment of the system world on the lifeworld, specifically via rationalisation and regimentation – top-down directives, protocols, performance management, the elevation of economics, the reification of effectiveness into simply a numerical (or cost) value. These sorts of system world activities, over time, define our expectations and our sense of the normal and the proper. They do not eliminate lifeworld understandings. These remain as alternative voices, even alternative narratives. For example, there has been a growth in interest in the medical humanities, contributing to and in some cases challenging the dominant explanatory models of medicine (Evans and Greaves 1999).

There is a sphere of communication which holds traffic between the life and system world (between the private and the public). Bauman borrows the Greek

---

Box 6.1: Other ways of thinking about the lifeworld

For Habermas, the lifeworld is intersubjective and culturally defined but others see the lifeworld as a phenomenological attitude, something constructed in and by consciousness. The basic act of consciousness brings together typical and enduring elements in a stream of experience and then builds up models of a shared social world (see Heller 1982 and Husserl 1970). The ethnomethodologists go a little further, for them the social world is constructed through a process of typification's which then take on an objective quality above and beyond the social groups who produce them (see Berger and Luckman 1966).

Social life and relationships are constant achievements made through the use of language – we create and recreate then continuously – we "do" things, like we "do" friendship and we do "care". Meaning comes from reference to other words and to the contexts in which they are spoken, our sense of order is created in talk. To describe a situation is at the same time to create it.

Combining lifeworld as intersubjective and cultural (Habermas) and lifeworld as constructed by our consciousness and built up into streams of experience (Heller and Berger and Luckman) allows us to consider governmentality as a mechanism that shapes consciousness and builds shared models which then has its expression in the intersubjective. Habermas and Heller would agree, Wright argues, in seeing that "rationalisation and the accompanying dislocation of traditional forms of self-understanding has been extensive, but also that this had had a major influence on the political and cultural situation in western societies" (Wright 1985: 19). This is also the place Habermas and Foucault can come together.[9]

---

term "the agora" to describe this. He sees it as a "territory of constant tension and tug-of-war as much as a site of dialogue, co-operation or compromise" (Bauman 1999: 87). This stormy agora is a place where social power and private misery interface. It's a hybrid space not a liminal one; it's embodied, quotidian, visceral. We can see the potency of this space in end-of-life care for example where the details about care of the body in hospitals, what Lawton (2000) describes as "the non-negotiable effects of the patient's bodily deterioration on their sense of self", encounters the aspirations of clinicians, organisational procedures and a construct of the "good death". One reading of Francis, Neuberger and other associated reports sees them advocating a return of the lifeworld into end-of-life care: a focus on culture including the values of NHS staff; encouraging discussion with, and scrutiny by, patients and families; developing individually tailored end-of-life care programmes; and fostering an organic learning organisation (see Small 2023).

Habermas and Foucault

Throughout this work, I have looked to Habermas and Foucault as key reference points. I am aware of the considerable amount of scholarship that has explored the differences between these two writers, sometimes that exploration seeks to argue that their insights are incompatible, sometimes that they are closer than they would appear (see Kelly 1994; Ashenden and Owen 1999, and more recently King 2009 and Mayes 2015). My approach has been to look to Habermas to explore the encroachment of the system world on the lifeworld and to build on his observation that the system world was beset by growing motivational and legitimation challenges. Foucault, on the other hand, has offered a route to understand the way power and knowledge change and in particular how governmentality, the conduct of conduct, forms the motives, desires and character of individuals through what he calls "technologies of the self". Governmentality then adds to the impacts of sovereign power – power that is manifest in coercion and repression or that is exercised via inducements. Together these regulate selves and produce what Foucault called his homo oeconomicus (see Chapter 1). It isn't just that people are constrained to act in ways that serve sovereign power it is that, through governmentality, they see only that way of behaving.

The most cited point of contention in the Foucault/Habermas debate is around what Mayes calls "normative confusions". What do these two want? Habermas clearly adheres to the critical theory approach – he considers some aspects of the social and political world to be pathological – but his remedy is essentially a moral one, he seeks the sort of society in which decisions are arrived at via the free consent of everyone arrived at after open deliberation. Foucault "uncovers some ways, not clearly apparent otherwise, in which the operation of certain social institutions on us runs counter to beliefs that many of us share about how it is valuable for us to live". He does not, however, "presume to *tell* us what valuable ways to live are" (King 2009: 308).

My approach has been to argue that Habermas's point about the colonisation of the lifeworld, by a system world (now built around neoliberal dogma), constitutes the place in which organising health via privileging market choices, coupled with austerity, makes inroads into the capacities to exercise compassionate care. Then, and in addition, we can turn to Foucault and in particular governmentality to see the mechanism whereby changes in individual behaviour come to be seen in everyday practice. Together then Habermas and Foucault offer a route to answer "why" and "how" questions related to organisational and individual behaviour evident in breakdowns in care.

There are two remaining questions, first why is there variability in staff – what makes some people more susceptible to changes and some more able to retain previous lifeworld attitudes and practices? Second, haven't there always been examples of lack of compassion in care, is the contemporary novel?

Foucault is concerned with power but also with resistance, active subjects who have different degrees of ambivalence and contingent attitudes to prevailing technologies of the self (see Lupton 1995). The impact of governmentality is not evenly spread. But there is a sense in which there is an accumulating effect. Over time governmentality tightens its grip; those who seem incapable of self-surveillance or co-surveillance are targeted for more coercive regulatory interventions; any limitations on the possibility of thinking outside of prevailing constructs become more difficult. This is control of what you do but also of the way you think, and it pushes out other ways of thinking. The atmosphere is one in which those considered dangerous are constrained by the system, where all are under surveillance and where a combination of a sense of living in a risk society and of the propagation of a particular way of thinking, of a specific perception of the possible, the acceptable, the desirable are shaped by governmentality. The grip of governmentality and the surveillance over and hostility towards those who seek to stand outside it are evident in many examples of pressure groups and whistle-blowers in the NHS and elsewhere (see Small 2023).

Shifts in collective social attitudes

Disciplinary society: the rise of tyrannese

To get compliance with either what is or with what you want to change, you: (1) get people to want what the system wants (Lyotard 1986: 62) (but that can be confusing if the system wants what are seen as conflicting things, for example compassion or efficiency; (2) you observe, "render visible, record, differentiate and compare" (Foucault 1977: 208). Then you reward compliance and punish deviation (but that risks elevating some things over others, for example it elevates tick boxes over sensitivity in the encounter with the patient because the former is easier to measure, report and compare). These routes to compliance are pursued within a broader social context in which there are norms – shared expectations of behaviour that connote what is culturally desirable and appropriate. They are attached to specific social positions and normative order is underpinned by shared value commitments, obligations of membership and sentiments of loyalty. Socially, normative order requires "normative coherence" and social harmony – normatively defined obligations must, on the whole, be accepted while collectivities must have normative sanctions in order to perform their functions and promote their legitimate interests. Professions have normalising gazes, "whose very purpose is to establish the parameters of the acceptable and so isolate the deviant for correction" (McKinlay and Starkey 1998: 5).[10]

Foucault discussed the social process whereby an action or an idea is taken as being normal and becomes taken for granted, natural in everyday life. To do this you have to create an idealised norm of conduct (which will include much detail) and then reward or punish a person for conforming or deviating from that ideal. It's a tactic that allows for maximum social control with a minimum expenditure of force, as such it is a manifestation of what Foucault calls disciplinary power (Foucault 1977).

There is a difference between a disciplined society in which individuals are obedient and conformist and a disciplinary society in which "individuals constantly escape, evade and subvert the functioning of discipline" (Miller 1987: 196). In this situation, new technologies of disciplinary power emerge. Power (2011) has argued that there is a new and pervasive micro-technology of disciplinary control that re-directs attention from ideology and values, and emphasises classifications, routines, scripts to be followed and this involves: "a shift in ontological commitment from the cognitive basis of social order to a conception of order grounded in surface habits and practical action" (Power 2011: 50). (Power's case is built around a study of accountancy but the argument is pertinent if it is transferred to care settings like hospitals.) This new form of rules-based governmentality can push aside ethics oriented social practice but it doesn't eliminate it – we can still see examples of "morally charged refusal and courageous resistance in relation to normative codes" (Fischer and Ferlie 2013: 47). This sort of refusal and resistance allows the continuation of the ethics oriented care Foucault explored in his late works (Foucault 2011). In an emotionally charged setting where there is much interpersonal engagement the conflict between rules-based and ethics-oriented approaches is likely to be "hot" (Fischer and Ferlie 2013: 47). We see a language

> almost without the power of designation, because it is used conscientiously to refer to nothing in particular. Attention rests upon percentages, categories, abstract functions…. It is not language that the user will very likely be required to stand by or to act on, for it does not define any personal ground for standing or acting. Its only practical utility is to support with "expert opinion" a vast, impersonal technological action already begun … It is a tyrannical language: tyrannese.
>
> (Berry 1983: 52)

Changing social attitudes

"British Social Attitudes" have been tracking shifts in social attitudes including attitudes to the Welfare State for more than 30 years (see Curtice and Ormston 2015). They also look at levels of trust in the general public for particular professions, including doctors, nurses and hospital managers. A report looked at shifts recorded since 2010 with the intention of considering the impact of the crash of 2008, the recession that followed it and then the period of austerity that continued up to 2014 and this report (and beyond).

There has been a long-term decline in support for welfare spending. The level of agreement with spending more on welfare benefits for the poor fell from 61% in 1989 to 27% in 2009 and 30% in 2014. Support for increasing taxes to spend more on health, education and social benefits fell from 63% in 2002 to 32% by 2010 and rose a little to 37% by 2014. The figures also show a widening gap between the attitudes of people who identify as Conservative supporters and those who identify as Labour. In 2014 17% of the former and 44% of the latter agreed that more should be spent on welfare. These long-term trends need to be considered in terms of the way attitudes are influenced by the levels of spending extant at any one time; Curtice (2010) has argued that there is a "thermostat" effect, when people think public spending is increasing, they will answer the sorts of questions put by British Social Attitudes by being more likely to say spending should go down. The reverse if also the case. The changes indicated above are, in this context, even more significant. Spending in this period was going down, reforms (cuts) to social benefits were drastic (Taylor-Gooby 2013), and yet social attitudes were shifting away from spending – the thermostat was faulty or broken.

Amongst the three health professions included in survey's questions about levels of trust the most trusted group were nurses, then doctors and, some way behind, hospital managers. In the context of the critical reports about hospital care the question asked is particularly apt, "From what you know or have heard, in general, how much do you trust [name of professional group] to put the interests of their patients above the convenience of the hospital?" Twenty-one percent of people said they "just about always" trusted nurses in 2014 compared to 30% in 2002. Having had recent contact with NHS services increased your level of trust vis a vis nurses (up to 25%) and levels of trust were also higher in older people, although they were also more likely to have had recent contact with the NHS. If you add proportions who answered, "most of the time" to those who "just about always" trusted then nurses scored over 70% (a little down from 2002), trust in doctors appeared to remain high across both time points, around 65% when "always" and "most of the time" were combined. Managers were below 30% but, at that, were a little above their 2002 figures (Appleby and Roberts 2013).

The same survey asked about trust in well-known institutions or professions, the question here varied a little but when people were asked if they "tended to trust" the proportion who answered "a great deal" was 1% for the media, 2% for government and 3% for parliament. In 2015 Ipsos MORI asked similar questions about attitudes to professions, specifically, "do you generally trust them to tell the truth", doctors were top – 89%, politicians were bottom (21%) and journalists, estate agents and business leaders were a little above politicians. Trust in the clergy is declining over time – now less trusted than "the average man or woman in the street", on a par with TV newsreaders and civil servants (Ipsos MORI 2015). (I will look at trust in more detail in Chapter 8.)

By 2022, now two years since the start of the Covid-19 pandemic, further polling by YouGov and commissioned by the Institute for Public Policy Research focussed on how robust British democracy was. Seventy-eight percent of adults said politicians did very badly or fairly badly in their understanding of the lives of voters. There is a widespread belief that the views of voters are largely unheard while "big money" interests hold most sway, 6% of voters said they thought their views are the main influence on Ministers decision making, 25% thought major doners to political parties had the most influence over policy, followed by business groups and corporations (16%). Many people were opting out of participation in party political politics. Looking across the world the report finds similar patterns (although dissatisfaction with democracy is most marked in the Anglo-Saxon democracies). In the 1990s, two-thirds of people in western Europe, North America, northeast Asia and Australasia were satisfied with democracy, by 2022 the majority in these regions were dissatisfied (Patel and Quilter-Pinner 2022.)

The social level: a risk society?

In this section, I will summarise the argument that social change and its impact on our idea of who we are is linked to risk, and I will consider how this might become manifest in health care. Risk, as a concept, helps us link transformations in the economy and social structure and changes in the enactment of the self. The argument that we live in risk society builds from an assessment that fundamental coordinates of social life are being made more transitory and uncertain. This uncertainty comes from changes in working practices and shifting patterns of family life. This then occurs in parallel with social pressure towards individualisation and with a rhetorical propensity to talk about how we live in times of great (unprecedented) change, of great crises, of impending catastrophe. The result is a life lived in a state of social unease and personal insecurity.[11]

There has been a proliferation of risk management systems, and these now provide a powerful influence and a pervasive logic for how we govern a social world we characterise as "uncertain". We think we can protect ourselves from risk by having codes and procedures and people whose responsibility it is to devise, implement and audit them. In so doing, we shift responsibility from ourselves to those we designate as risk managers, and we feel protected at least from those risks we have been able to codify. This sort of shift has been chronicled by Beck who describes the emergence of a "Risk Society" that constitutes "a systematic way of dealing with hazards and insecurities induced and introduced by modernization itself" (Beck 1992: 21). For Beck modernisation includes, "surges of technological rationalization and changes in work and organization", but beyond that includes much more: the change in societal characteristics and normal biographies, changes in lifestyle and forms of love, change in the structures of power and influence, in the forms of political repression and participation, in views of reality and in the norms of knowledge (Beck 1992: 50). Power, adopting a somewhat narrower scope, has linked a pervasive perception of risk with the growth of an audit society (Power 1997: 2004). In this analysis risk, or the invocation of risk, sets into play a whole new set of regulatory agencies and within them new professional roles to deal with anything that may be construed as a hazard, "What begins as a mere possibility of danger is converted into calculable objects of surveillance, regulation and control" (Fischer and Ferlie 2013: 30). The advent of the Coronavirus pandemic in 2020 also translates a hazard, that of contracting the virus, into calculable mechanisms of surveillance, regulation and control.

But a proliferation of rules and procedures and professions to implement them may not make us either safer or make us feel safer. We retain an anxiety that what is really a risk isn't the sort of thing we can eliminate by codifying and delegating, or that those people to whom we have entrusted the management of risk will not do it conscientiously or efficiently. While we rush around developing administrative solutions, we retain a sense of disquiet that we still face existential questions. Even more, we create new risks to worry about where once we had no concerns. Risk society is a place of paradox then, being more conscious of risk makes us more anxious about the risks we know about and fear we can't control and the risks that may be lurking beyond our having yet categorised them as risks, the known knowns and the unknown unknowns to borrow from Donald Rumsfeld.[12]

The risk of contracting the coronavirus and the risk of hospitalisation and of death resulting from Covid-19 mobilise different conceptions of risk and these are manifest in ways determined both by levels of infection in populations and by a series of demographic variables, most clearly one's age. While there has been a widespread sensation of constant risk that has impacted on our sociality and on our psyche that sensation has been manifest in withdrawal from social contacts by some people and by a minimisation of the dangers to oneself in others. While some unifying sensation of shared risk was briefly evident in the UK in the early days of the pandemic, any sense of the solidarity that can accompany shared risk reduced as a recognition that, like so many features of contemporary life, this was an epidemic whose impact was socially stratified, we were, "not in the same boat; it is the same storm, and different vessels weather it" [differently] (Perry 2020: 27).

Risk is likely to generate anxiety, "being troubled in mind about an uncertain event". This is prompted where we see that we are not in control of things that may impact on our lives. Dunant and Porter (1996) say we live in an *Age of Anxiety*[13] but other words also engage with these feelings, uncertainty for example (see Elliott and Atkinson 1998). Marris (1996) emphasises the uncertainty rather than the anxiety of the times, he argues that the nature of globalised corporate economies impacts on an individual's sense of agency. It is those with fewest social and economic resources who feel the heaviest burden around the uncertainty of their place in the labour market. That uncertainty undermines the reciprocity that is essential both to social relationships and to the ability to mobilise any collective defence to the vicissitudes of the marketplace.

Change by the regulation of risk

Thinking a little more about what risk is can help reconcile a rise in the prominence of risk talk and the resilience of a recurring propensity to do harm or allow harm to be done. Douglas (1992) has shaped the way we think about the relationship between risk and culture, a central juxtaposition for our consideration both of how the unacceptable practice in Stafford might have developed and how the insights of the Francis report might be operationalised. Risks are not necessarily ontological facts, many are social constructions and, as such, they can accumulate a meaning that is considered moral, the management of risk then becomes a form of moral government. This moral government interacts with established indigenous attitudes to risk with individuals manoeuvring between and within these different understandings, albeit within the strictures of a broader hierarchical structure. This manoeuvring might result in individuals becoming what Foucault called "docile subjects" as they internalise prevailing structures of disciplinary power and hence are subjected to technologies of power-knowledge (Foucault 1977). Or individuals might contest disciplinary power. Such people seek to determine for themselves ethical government, something arrived at through "intersubjective relations of care, along with free-spoken, practical critique". In so doing they constitute themselves as "ethical subjects" (Fischer and Ferlie 2013: 32: see Foucault 2011). Whistle-blowers and activists within pressure groups are the sorts of people who are stepping outside technologies of power-knowledge, but so too are those who engage in less demonstrably free-spoken critique, those who practice the small interactions that constitute care sensitive to the needs of the patient even when those interactions are not promoted by the risk management culture within which they work (a nurse may know that her hospital's policy is that a patient on the LCP should not be given a drink of water but will provide a drink anyway when this is requested).

These intersubjective relations of care enacted by ethical subjects might have been nurtured and sustained as part of a pre-existing indigenous system. That system might be one best described as consistent with their sense of self, with what they consider is proper – what is consistent with their way of being. But the pre-existing system might also be drawn from a professional ethic, something linked with being a doctor, a nurse or another health care professional.

A formal risk management system will claim an objectivity that is superior to pre-existing local practices for dealing with social transgressions and rule-breaking. As it is imposed it may clash with indigenous systems, such a clash might result in a hybrid system. As the two systems continue alongside each other they may prove to be complementary, or there might be a struggle that results in either the subjugation of one system or a continuing intractable conflict. In this unresolved scenario "interactions between alternative risk management systems may exert perverse and intractable effects" with the possibility of "escalating morally-charged conflict". This scenario is made more likely in clinical risk management because it encompasses two sorts of risk: what Fischer and Ferlie call first-order risks to patients and second-order reputational risk to managers and organisations. This combination of risks generates some perverse interactions (Fischer and Ferlie 2013: 31) for example when reputational risk is elevated above clinical, or when a second-order risk is reframed as a first order, for example the idea that not meeting organisational targets might put the organisation at risk of closure or might be a threat to the jobs of staff. Tensions between ways of formulating risk arise because each is appealing to a different truth regime, their proponents "talk past each other" (Fischer and Ferlie 2013: 46).

If a particular formulation of risk is propagated by the powerful in any organisation and is assigned a moral force and this formulation is met by a depleted, a cowed, alternative then we can get to the situation where staff can feel that what is important is meeting particular auditing or accountancy targets rather than exercising judgements about what is proper and desirable that come from another sort of understanding. Consider the wish to pursue business models in health care delivery as a route to both manage costs and to offer a counterbalance to professional power, specifically the power held by doctors. One result of this direction of change is a shift in risk management from an ethics-oriented clinical self-regulation to a rule-based clinical risk management system (Fischer and Ferlie

2013). That sort of system might say you can only allocate a specific length of time per patient, you can use this medication but not that, you should only provide nutrition and hydration at these times and that there are risks in so doing. In none of these specific details is it different to clinical self-regulation, one would still have to reconcile time available and demands made on that time and decide treatment based on best evidence.[14] The difference however is that much of that evidence in areas like chronic illness and end-of-life care is located in practice experience and its use is made easier by an ability to be flexible in terms of what is done and when, a flexibility inhibited by a rules-based system. A shift from being ethics inspired to being rule governed, which "micro-regulation" may prompt, may not be in the best interests of the patient, especially when clinical care relies on mobilising the sorts of care practice that is not easily codified.

Changing structures and practices because of a wish to reduce risk has the potential to demoralise and disempower professionals (Beaussier et al. 2016; O'Neill 2002 and 2002a) and if it is an approach that generates fear then this is "toxic to both safety and improvement" (National Advisory Group on the Safety of Patients in England 2013: The Berwick Report)).

Notes

1 This sort of argument requires us accepting that society is a necessary source of morality (for some the necessary source). In Chapter 8 I will discuss the different approach to ethics taken by "principlists" who see principles at the heart of moral life and "narrativists" who focus on communication. But here I am staying with a more sociological analysis about how what we hold in common may be eroded.

2 As well as reading a lot of Marx in my youth, like many others I also struggled through Oswald Spengler's *The Decline of the West* (published in 1923 – my dusty edition is from 1926.) Spengler argued that cultures have a lifespan of about 1000 years of flourishing and a thousand years of decline. The current culture, the Western, is in its wintertime, its last season. It's a useful antidote/addition to writers like Fukuyama and his end of history, not least in its more expansive time frame!

3 Some writers were attributing even more to changes in representation, Baudrillard in 1981 (published in English in 1983) described how,

> a sign could refer to the depths of meaning, that a sign could be exchanged for meaning … the whole system becomes weightless, it is no longer itself anything but a gigantic simulacrum – not unreal, but a simulacrum, that is to say never exchanged for the real, but exchanged for itself, in an uninterrupted circuit without reference or circumference.
>
> (Baudrillard, quoted in Thomas 2007 – title page)

4 Amin (2012) describes modern lives in the West as being constituted through pluralism and hybridity. There are twin effects, first a nostalgia for what is seen as an earlier time of closer personal ties and strong communities, and second anxiety over the future and a drummed-up aversion to the stranger. These strangers are not just migrants but also minorities within our midst that can include all those who do not conform or who are seen as threatening.

5 Bauman has talked of a separation of politics and power (Bauman 1999), our politicians can be "in power" but not have power. He is primarily concerned with globalisation and the power of multinational corporations but it is a point relevant to new sorts of dispersed administrative power under neoliberalism. Marx and Engels, in 1848

wrote that "The executive of the modern State is but a committee for managing the common affairs of the bourgeoisie" (in *The Communist Manifesto*, 44).

6 This is an approach characteristic of the postmodern and of poststructuralism. Postmodernism is concerned with identifying and understanding the fragility of the way we use language, including in politics. Truth is politicised and that politicisation needs to be deconstructed – what is happening, why, for the benefit of whom – the terms that we use and the standards we have are social constructions, they are dependent on contingent agreements and fragile in the face of attack. A postmodern approach is not a nihilistic or a relativist one, it is concerned with testing assertions that are made and, in so doing, defending against irrationality and exploitation, as such it is a means of defending Enlightenment values, it is not saying all truth has the same value.

7 Even in bastions of neoliberal ascendancy there are oppositional voices, most notably the mobilisations around climate change and around racism and misogyny but also in party politics; the election of Jeremy Corbyn as leader of the Labour Party in the UK and his success in mobilising enthusiastic support from both the young and from disillusioned Labour supporters, the contestation of the Democratic Party Presidential candidature by Senator Bernie Saunders in the US: in Europe, Syriza in Greece and Podermos in Spain (Knight 2016). Of course, not all oppositional forces are on the left, the UK voting to leave the European Union in June 2016 and the election of Donald Trump to the US Presidency a few months later (November) reflect oppositional movements based on mistrust of those in power and suspicion of the views of experts. The powerful and the experts who are mistrusted include the neoliberals who now populate the establishment. Similar forces appear to be at work in many parts of the world. I have considered the populist turn in politics in Chapter 2 and asked if it indicates a continuation or a shift from neoliberalism. I will also consider Holloway's depiction of the dynamic of these political twists and turns, in *Crack Capitalism* (2010) in Chapter 9.

8 There are other writers who explore similar distinctions, Bourdieu's idea of "doxa" is one (Bourdieu 1977). Doxa is that which is self-evident, it's what "goes without saying because it comes without saying". The doxa provides rules of what is and is not possible. Polyani's formulation of tacit knowledge (1966) explores similar terrain. Underlying many such concerns is Kant's distinction between a realm of objectively knowable objects of experience and an unknown realm of "things in themselves" (noumena) (Kant [1781] 2007).

9 If I have a Foucauldian reader they will know I'm playing a little fast and loose by allying Foucault with any idea of subjectivity.

10 Armstrong (1983) looked at how the subject, in his case the body, is constructed through the way it is perceived and conceptualised via "the gaze"; "A body analysed for humours contains humours; a body analysed for organs and tissues is constituted of organs and tissues; a body analysed for psychosocial functioning is a psychosocial object". My approach has been to explore if a body that is not fit for the neoliberal world, an old and sick body or a body with learning disability, is seen as a body of less worth.

11 There is a disconcerting sense of this being an a-historical position. The idea of a move from an assumed job for life security and settled nuclear family before neoliberalism is a middle-class conceit, many working-class jobs in ununionised sections of economy were vulnerable to changes in the assumed interests of the firm and even the whim of the owner. As to this being a world in crisis and a place of impending catastrophe, this ignores the very many times in the past, even in the recent past, when anxiety about crisis and catastrophe was prevalent. In the Cold War years of the 1950s and 60s school children were instructed to practice "getting under your desk for protection against a nuclear attack" for example. (I will discuss anxiety in more detail below.)

12 US Secretary of Defense Donald Rumsfeld, in a 2002 news briefing about the Iraq War, identified known knowns, known unknowns and unknown unknowns, a distinction

psychologists had used for some time via the notion of the "Johari Window" (devised by psychologists Joseph Luft and Harry Ingham in 1955). Rumsfeld and his singular formulation reappear in Chapter 9.

13 In various parts of this book, I will question the sense that current times are "special times", I am forewarned by Mann (2012) who said that we should be careful of giving the present too much of a sense of its being special when we practice, "the sociology of the last five minutes". The claims for this being an "Age of Anxiety" is one such area where we need to exercise some historical perspective – we only have to go back to W H Auden's long poem, published in 1947, to see that his "Age of Anxiety" was set in the Second World War. His protagonists include a sailor who talks about his anxiety of listening on board his ship for the noise of the submarine that might sink him and send all the crew to the bottom of the sea. Another person, Malin, is in the air force and lives with "a comprehensible comprehensive dread" that he will be shot from the skies. We might surmise that this sort of anxiety, if widespread, is more worthy of the attribute "Age of Anxiety" (Auden [1947] 1968: 272).

14 An audit or risk society may emphasise different sorts of risk than the system it replaced. But other systems, for example a clinical risk management approach, also exercised a moral order and embodied a series of power-knowledge hierarchies. For example, in this system the clinician defines the nature of risk and elevates a particular form of professional knowledge to the extent that it can ignore or over-ride patient subjectivity – telling people what is good for them or even what they feel.

References

Appleby, J., Roberts, C. 2013. How have the public's views of the NHS changed over the last 30 years? In, Park, A., Bryson, C., Clery, E., Curtice, J., Phillips, M. (Eds) *British Social Attitudes: The 30th Report*. London, NatCen Social Research, 87–144.

Amin, A. 2012. *Land of Strangers*. Polity Press.

Armstrong, D. 1983. *Political Anatomy of the Body: Medical Knowledge in Britain in the Twentieth Century*. Cambridge University Press.

Ashenden, S., Owen, D. 1999. *Foucault Contra Habermas: Recasting the Dialogue Between Geneology and Critical Theory*. London, Sage Publications.

Auden, W.H. Ed. 1947. Age of anxiety. In, *Collected Longer Poems* 1968. London, Faber & Faber.

Baudrillard, J. 1983. *Simulacrum and Simulation*. Semiotext(e) (published in French in 1981).

Bauman, Z. 1999. *In Search of Politics*. Stanford, CA, Stanford University Press.

Bauman, Z. 2000. *Liquid Modernity*. Polity.

Beaussier, A.L., Demeritt, D., Griffiths, A., Rothstein, H. 2016. Accounting for failure: Risk-based regulation and the problems of ensuring healthcare quality in the NHS. *Health Risk Society*, 18, 204–224.

Beck, U. 1992. *Risk Society: Towards a New Modernity*. London, Sage Publications.

Berger, P.L., Luckman, T. 1966. *The Social Construction of Reality*. Penguin Books.

Berry, W. 1983. *Standing by Words*. San Francisco, CA, North Point Press.

Bourdieu, P. 1977 [1972 French edition] *Outline of a Theory of Practice*. Cambridge University Press.

Castoriadis, C. 1986. *The Imaginary Institution of Society*. Blackwell.

Curtice, J. 2010. Thermostat or weathervane? Public reactions to spending and redistribution under New Labour. In, Park, A., Curtice, J., Thompson, K., Phillips, M., Clery, E., Butt, S. (Eds) *British Social Attitudes: The 26th Report*. London, Sage, 19–38.

Curtice, J., Ormston, R. (Eds) 2015. *British Social Attitudes: The 32nd Report.* London, The National Centre for Research.

Deleuze, G. 1992. What is dispositif? In, Armstrong, T.J. (Ed) *Michael Foucault: Philosopher.* Hemel Hempstead, Harvester Wheatsheaf, 159–168.

Douglas, M. 1992. *Risk and Blame: Essays in Cultural Theory.* London, Routledge.

Dunant, S., Porter, R. (Eds) 1996. *The Age of Anxiety.* London, Virago.

Elias, N. 2000 2nd Ed. *The Civilising Process.* Wiley Blackwell (originally published in German 1939 and English 1969)

Elliott, L., Atkinson, D. 1998. *The Age of Uncertainty.* Verso.

Evans, M., Greaves, D. 1999. Exploring the medical humanities. *British Medical Journal,* 319, 1216.

Fischer, M.D., Ferlie, E. 2013. Resisting hybridisation between modes of clinical risk management: Contradiction, contest, and the production of intractable conflict. *Accounting, Organizations and Society,* 38, 30–49.

Foucault, M. 1972. *The Archaeology of Knowledge.* New York, Vintage.

Foucault, M. 1977. *Discipline and Punish: The Birth of the Prison.* London, Allan Lane, Penguin Press.

Foucault, M. 2010. *The Government of Self and Others: Lectures at the College de France 1983–1984.* London, Palgrave Macmillan.

Foucault, M. 2011. *The Courage of Truth (the Government of Self and Others II): Lectures at the College de France 1983–1984.* London, Palgrave Macmillan.

Frank, A. 2014. "Notes on Habermas: Lifeworld and System". http://people.ucalgary.ca/-frank/habermas.html (accessed 12/12/2014).

Habermas, J. 1987. *The Theory of Communicative Action. (Vol 2)* Oxford, Polity Press.

Heller, A. 1982. *A Theory of History.* Routledge.

Holloway, J. 2010. *Crack Capitalism.* Pluto Press.

Hookway, N. 2012. Emotions, body and self: Critiquing moral decline sociology. *Sociology,* 47(4), 841–857.

Husserl, E. 1970. *The Crisis of the European Sciences and Transcendental Phenomenology.* Ed Biemel, W; tr, Carr, D. Evanston IL, Northwestern University Press.

Ignatieff, M. 1986. Beating the retreat into private life. *The Listener,* 27 Mar, 20–21.

Ipsos MORI 2016. Veracity Index 2015: *Trust in Professions.*

Kant, I. [1781]. 2007. *Critique of Pure Reason.* Penguin Classics.

Kelly, M. (Ed) 1994. *Critique and Power: Recasting the Foucault/Habermas Debate.* Cambridge, MA, The MIT Press.

King, M. 2009. Clarifying the Foucault-Habermas debate. *Philosophy and Social Criticism,* 35(3), 287–314.

Knight, S. 2016. Enter left. *The New Yorker,* 23 May, 28–35.

Lasch, C. 1979. *The Culture of Narcissism.* Abacus.

Lasch, C. 1985. *The Minimal Self. Psychic Survival in Troubled Times.* Picador.

Lawton, J. 2000. *The Dying Process: Patients Experience of Palliative Care.* London, Routledge.

Lupton, D. 1995. *The Imperative of Health: Public Health and the Regulated Body.* London, Sage.

Lyotard, J.F. 1986. *The Postmodern Condition.* Manchester, Manchester University Press.

MacIntyre, A. 1981. *After Virtue.* Notre Dame, University of Notre Dame Press. See also 3rd Edition 2007.

Malik, K. 2020. Welcome to Flatland, where shallow appeal ousts substance and reason. *The Observer,* 04(10), 43.

Mann, M. 2012. *The Sources of Social Power: Globalizations, 1945–2011: Volume 4.* Cambridge, Cambridge University Press.

Marris, P. 1996. *The Politics of Uncertainty: Attachment in Private and Public Life.* Routledge.

Marx, K., Engels. 1952 [1848]. *The Communist Manifesto.* Moscow, Progress Publishers.

Mayes, C.R. 2015. Revisiting Foucault's 'normative confusions': Surveying the debate since the *Collége de France* Lectures. *Philosophy Compass*, 10(12), 841–855.

McKinlay, A., Starkey, K. (Eds) 1998. *Foucault, Management and Organization Theory.* London, Sage.

Miller, P. 1987. *Domination and Power.* London, Routledge and Kegan Paul.

National Advisory Group on the Safety of Patients in England. 2013. *A Promise to Learn- a Commitment to Act: Improving the Safety of Patients in England.* London, Department of Health. (The Berwick Report).

Nettleton, S. 1997. Governing the risky self: How to become healthy, wealthy and wise. In, Petersen, A., Bunton, R. (Eds) *Foucault, Health and Medicine*, London, Routledge, 371–398.

O'Neill, O. 2002. *Autonomy and Trust in Bioethics.* Cambridge University Press.

O'Neill, O. 2002a. *A Question of Trust.* BBC Radio 4: Reith Lectures.

Patel, P., Quilter-Pinner, H. 2022. *Road to Renewal: Elections, Parties and the Case for Renewing Democracy*, IPPR. http://www.ippr.org/publications/road-to-renewal

Petersen, A. 1997. Risk, governance and the new public health. In, Petersen, A., Bunton, R. (Eds) *Foucault, Health and Medicine*, London, New York, Routledge, 340–370.

Perry, S. 2020. Risky business. *The Guardian Review*, 12 Sept, 26–29.

Polyani, M. 1966. *The Tacit Dimension.* Chicago, IL, University of Chicago Press.

Power, M. 1997. *The Audit Society: Rituals of Verification.* Oxford, Oxford University Press.

Power, M. 2004. *The Risk Management of Everything: Rethinking the Politics of Uncertainty.* London, Demos.

Power, M. 2011. Foucault and sociology. *Annual Review of Sociology*, 37, 35–66.

Rose, N. 1992. Governing the enterprising self. In, Heelas, P., Morris, P. (Eds) *The Values of the Enterprise Culture*, London, Routledge.

Rose, N. 1999 2nd Ed. *Governing the Soul: The Shaping of the Private Self.* London, Free Association.

Sennett, R. 1986. *The Fall of Public Man.* London, Faber & Faber.

Sennett, R. 2006. *The Culture of the New Capitalism.* Yale University Press. see *Times Higher Education Supplement*, 10 Feb 2006, 18–19. "Craftmanship is laid low by quick-fix fever".

Sennett, R. 2012. *Together: The Rituals, Pleasures and Politics of Cooperation.* Allen Lane.

Small, N. 2023. *Failures in health and social care. Governance and Culture Change.* London, Routledge.

Spengler, O. 1926. *The Decline of the West.* New York, Alfred Knopf.

Taylor- Gooby, P. 2013. *The Double Crisis of the Welfare State and What We Can Do About It.* Basingstoke, Palgrave.

Thomas, S. 2007. *The End of Mr Y.* Edinburgh, Canongate.

Wright, P. 1985. *On Living in An Old Country.* London, Verso.

Part III

Culture as diagnosis and as prescription

7   Culture

Introduction: "problems in culture" and "cultural change" have become ubiquitous

In recent years, discussion about change, any sort of collective change, invariably includes the word "culture". Savage points out, in relation to the NHS, that "culture has, in itself, become a cultural phenomenon" (Savage 2000: 230). When organisations get into trouble looking to something that has gone wrong in its culture is often the diagnosis and fixing the culture the prescription, it's not just in the NHS. Calls for cultural change have been made in relation to reforming banks, police departments, Downing Street[1] and many other areas of corporate and public activity. We even have the even more diffuse idea of the culture of a broad society, its "political culture", its "cultural elite" and so on.

But, in many instances, culture is conceptualised without rigour. It is used either as a taken for granted term where it is assumed we all understand what it means or as a "magic word" that explains all or can change all. It is then, characteristically, attached to another poorly conceptualised and analytically empty word or phrase (Case 1994), "a culture of openness", a culture for "quality improvement", creating "a culture of achievement", "an open culture of management", a "culture of continuous improvement", "cultural excellence" (Savage 2000: 230–232).

Sometimes synonyms are used, environment instead of culture, or an assumption that culture can be subsumed into bureaucracy. Recent examples in the US include General Motors as they responded to a major product recall crisis in 2014 with the CEO focussed on creating, "the right environment to promote accountability and head off future disasters" or the Department of Veterans Affairs seeking to respond to reports of long-waits for veterans needing critical health care by seeking change in what was identified as "a corrosive bureaucracy" (Lorsch 2016: 97–98).

Sometimes a different, but related, term is used. Perhaps what we have is an ecology of the health service. An ecology combines interdependence (e.g. through the division of labour) and cooperation and competition, in the 1930s the sociologist Robert Park called this "competitive cooperation". If the ecology is disturbed it readjusts, seeking to restore equilibrium, or set up a new equilibrium. But sometimes it can be so damaged that readjustment is not enough, more

DOI: 10.4324/9781003332404-10

drastic change is needed, the responses needed to slow or reverse climate change and habitat degradation are examples.

However ubiquitous "culture" has become, its' use is not uncontested. Critics see a focus on culture as a misreading of how change is carried out, culture change is a result of other things being done, not an intervention in itself (Anderson-Wallace and Shale 2013). A Harvard Business Review article (Lorsch 2016) reported interviews with CEOs who had led major transformations in their companies. They questioned the utility of a focus on culture – it isn't something you fix, it's what you end up with after you have put new structures and processes in place. Lorsch argues that when organisations are in crisis it's usually because the business is broken. What is needed is a new business model or a reworked strategy. A changed culture is,

> an outcome – not a cause or a fix… culture isn't a final destination. It morphs right along with the company's competitive environment and objectives. It's really more of a temporary landing place – where the organisation should be at that moment if the right management levers have been pulled.
>
> (Lorsch 2016: 98)

Another critical reading of a focus on culture is one that sees the collective subjectivity that culture assumes (shared values and beliefs), as a cloak to mask a centrist, top-down management approach. "Culture", as a site of intervention, is a soft-power device to get what management or government want. For example, Harrison and Pollitt (1994) argue that the attempts at culture change via the introduction of the Patients Charter in the NHS in 1992, in effect, strengthened management in negotiations with health professionals via undermining "the traditional claim of the professional that he or she is in touch with the patient/client and knows what they really need" (Harrison and Pollitt 1994: 11).

Using culture as both a diagnostic (it's what went wrong) and as a remedy (it is the tool to make things better) involves engaging with what Raymond Williams identified as, "one of the two or three most complicated words in the English language" (Williams 1983: 87).

Culture is layered, contested and shape-shifting. It is "inherently ambivalent… it is as much an agent of disorder as it is a tool of order" (Bauman 1999a). The complexity of culture was captured by Bauman (1999a) when he traced its modern usage to the late eighteenth century. At that point people began to see the world as a human rather than a divine creation; the way people lived was now not preordained (see Box 7.1). Culture was both now an accessible freedom and a mechanism to contain the possibility of limitless choice – culture was "self-determined determination". The tension inherent in this understanding of culture continues to inform present-day perceptions. Culture is both about "creativity" and "normative regulation". It is, "As much about inventing as it is about preserving; about discontinuity as much as about continuation; about novelty as much as about tradition, about norm-following as much as about transcendence of the norm" (Bauman 1999a: xiv).

Box 7.1 Is culture (or civilisation) a protection against "human nature"?

Are those people whose actions harmed patients in Mid-Staffordshire and elsewhere the sorts of people who need to be closely controlled? Did a breakdown in control allow their damaging behaviour to be manifest? Or are they people whose benign intentions have been distorted by the toxic context they work within?

The twin poles of the human nature argument are occupied by Thomas Hobbes, who believed that all that stood between us and violent anarchy was a strong state and firm leadership, and Jean-Jacques Rousseau who declared that man was born free and it was civilisation with its coercive powers, social classes and restrictive laws that put him in chains. Is civilisation just a veneer and below the surface, our bestial nature is waiting to break out, or are humans friendly and peaceful and civilisation with its property, war and injustice has supressed this? (Bregman 2020, see also de Waal 2006).

(Philosopher David Hume said you can't derive an "ought" from an "is", for example you can't say that humans are like this by nature therefore human society must be arranged in this way.)

Culture can be understood as concept, as structure and as praxis, and, in this third meaning, it does become a site for action – for change. But the scope for that change is determined by the society it exists within or alongside. Bauman revisits culture in the 2011 book exploring the "Liquid Modern World" (Bauman 2011). That role of culture as a homeostatic influence at the service of the status quo has now become no longer tenable in the days of liquid modernisation. Now everything solid is dissolved, "culture today consists of offers, not prohibitions: propositions not norms…it serves not so much the stratifications and divisions of society, as the turnover-oriented consumer market"… "culture is no longer about enlightenment but the seduction of its 'clients'….[it's function] is not to satisfy existing needs, but to create new ones" (Bauman 2011: 13–17).

Culture: examining this most complex of terms

In this section, I will continue to examine the complexities of approaches to culture that exist in the sociological, anthropological and management theory literature. I will look at definitions and at usage of the term. I will then look at examples of culture change in my next section.

Culture as ideational or as part of a sociocultural system

In Cultural Anthropology, amidst a plethora of definitions (Kroeber and Kluckhohn 1952, identified 164), there are two overreaching typologies that seek to capture the meaning of "culture". These typologies go back to the beginnings of anthropology as a distinct discipline. Mathew Arnold's *Culture and Anarchy* (1869) defined culture as, "the pursuit of our total perfection by means of getting to know in all the matters that most concern us the best that has been thought and said in the world". Written in part as a repost to Arnold's position, Sir Edward Burnett Tylor's *Primitive Culture* (1870 2nd Ed) had a different view. Culture was, "that complex whole which includes knowledge, beliefs, arts, morals, law, customs and any other capabilities and beliefs acquired by man as a member of society" (see Appiah 2016). This difference between culture as an ideational system and culture as a sociocultural system has continued to the present day. In the former, cultural and social realms are distinct but interrelated and culture is in the minds of culture bearers, or in the products of those minds, that is in shared meanings and symbols. (Notable proponents of this approach included Levi-Strauss and Geertz.) In the latter, if there is a sociocultural system then culture is a component of the whole, manifest as behaviour and the products of behaviour (Malinowski and Radcliffe-Brown are supporters of this position) (Keesing 1974, see also Allaire and Firsirotu 1984: 196).

In both typologies there are: (1) learned patterns of behaviour, (2) aspects of culture that act below conscious levels (like grammar and syntax in a native speaker of a language), (3) patterns of thought and perception, themselves culturally determined (Scott and Marshall 2009: 150–154). But there are differences, culture as ideational, as the best that has been thought and said, does not allow for the idea of damaged cultures, of cultures of practice that have strayed far from the heights of the possible. What happened in those problematic wards and in those damaging clinical encounters summarised in my Introduction could not be examples of a culture, we need a different term for them. But they could be "culture" if culture is sociocultural. Then knowledge, beliefs, customs and habits, and all the other components that contribute to culture, could fashion its form far from the Arnoldian ideal. For Arnold, the very title of Tylor's book *Primitive Culture* was an oxymoron, as would be the idea of a destructive or a flawed culture in need of reform (a damaged or destructive "culture" is not a culture in this definition).

Geertz, a supporter of the ideational position, was clear what culture meant to him:

> Believing, with Max Weber, that man is an animal suspended in webs of significance he himself has spun, I take culture to be those webs, and the analysis of it to be therefore not an experimental science in search of law but an interpretive one in search of a meaning. It is explication I am after, construing social expressions on their surface enigmatical.
>
> (Geertz 1973: 5)

He argues that culture and social structure are closely adjusted each to the other only in societies that have been stable over an extended period. "In most societies, where change is characteristic rather than an abnormal occurrence, we shall expect to find more or less radical discontinuities between the two…" (Geertz 1973: 144).

An example of the different consequences of adherence to ideational or sociocultural understandings of culture can be seen in an evolution of organisation and management theory from looking at managing culture and then shifting into changing culture. Managing is ideational – its outside those things that are within our purview to change but we can change what we can to accommodate it; sociocultural understandings see culture embedded in other systems and amenable to change through or with these systems.

When social structure is enacted in everyday life it is exemplified by the routines we have. The sociologist Harold Garfinkel highlighted how these routines, the "taken for granted" aspects of social reality, are skilful accomplishments. If you want to apply a rule you need to know more than just the basic rule, you need to know the context in which it is to be administered and appreciate that the context is broader and more complex than just the rule. Our behaviour enacts an interchange between rule and context. This is the interchange within which culture (as process) is enacted. If you deviate from the rules, the ordered reality of your life breaks down quickly (Morgan 1986: 131).[2] If many deviate from the rules then the ordered reality of social life breaks down quickly.

But as well as the possibilities of deviating from the rules there are times when we see a disintegration of traditional patterns of social order like common ideals, beliefs and values. In their place, there is a more fragmented and differentiated patterns of belief and practice. This creates a problem of cultural management, that is, how can society be bound together again? Emile Durkheim, and many sociologists after him, considered this question and government, religion and media have been identified as potentially having a role in doing this.

Maintaining social order or sticking to the rules may be good for "cultural management" but cultural management is not necessarily a good thing. The social order may need to change and individuals should challenge those rules they see as damaging. George Bernard Shaw said, "The reasonable man adapts himself to the world. The unreasonable one persists in trying to adapt the world to himself. Therefore, all progress depends on the unreasonable man" (Shaw [1905] 2000). If culture is best understood as ideational and if, in times of change, there is a separation between culture and social structure culture can be a protection against social and economic policies that are damaging to those things that, in the culture, are seen as taken for granted positives, caring for the vulnerable for example. If culture is part of a sociocultural system then it will change as that system changes, but it may not always change at the same speed or may not change in all groups at the same speed. A part of the vernacular when we discuss culture is to recognise the "culture wars", a mark of there being a contested culture. Culture then can be a bulwark against damaging change or it can be a harbinger of change to come, it can be a defence or a vanguard.

How the word culture is used

In all the diagnoses and prescriptions for change, we see "culture" given central billing. There is a widespread recognition that it will be difficult to change culture, a difficulty compounded by the elusive definitions of the term that I have considered above. EP Thompson described culture as a "clumpish" term. It has many meanings, and the bundle of terms identifying activities and attributes that are clumped together when "culture" is invoked are wide ranging. Three attributes of culture identified by Thompson are helpful in structuring my argument here, they are that:

- culture evolves within historically specific forms of work and social relations.
- There is an inter-generational transmission of customs that are components of culture.
- These customs, and the practices they are manifest in, can lag behind changes in work and social relations, old forms existing even when other things have changed (Thompson 1993: 13).

In a complex formulation Horlick-Jones, in considering Thompson's work on culture, said culture is "multi-layered, hysteresial, praxiological, and above all, interactional" (Horlick-Jones 2012: 1223). Multi-layered and interactional are straightforward enough, but praxiological means enacted in actions – culture is "done", its manifest in our actions, it's not something inert setting the background or context for our lives. Hysteresial captures the delay between the emergence of new work or social forms and changes in culture – the sorts of lag that can find old forms co-existing with new times.

In contrast to cultural anthropologies' typologies, Williams engages with the complexities of the word "culture" by considering the various ways it has/ is used. The early use of the word "culture" was as a noun of process i.e., tending something. Then it became a metaphor, using this tending but applying it to, for example, human minds. It developed a class meaning – to be cultivated or cultured (here culture becomes a synonym for civilised).[3] Then there was a shift to its being presented as a plural – there are different cultures, for example folk cultures, working class cultures, professional cultures and cultures of practice. With the idea of there being different cultures came claims that some cultures, by virtue of superior knowledge or refinement (either between one society and another or between different groups or practices in one society), were better than others.

Do organisations have a culture?

When we think of using culture as a diagnostic and as an instrument to effect a remedy for shortcomings in the NHS, or in other public sector bodies, there are crucial questions to consider. The first is very basic, do organisations have a culture? Allaire and Firsirotu (1984) point out that we habitually discuss organisations in anthropomorphic terms; they have "life-cycles", problematic health, have purposes and survival goals, they are strong or they are vulnerable and so on. This approach allows us to attribute to them personalities, needs and characters. In this anthropomorphic world, the "personality" of an organisation is identified as its "culture". But, with a few notable exceptions, invocations of culture are not followed by any elaboration. It is presumed that the word "culture" is a stenographic cue for "values, norms, beliefs, customs" or any other such string of convenient identifiers chosen among the vast assortment of definitions available in a random pick of terms from cultural anthropology (Allaire and Firsirotu 1984: 194).

Many management theorists see culture as a distinct entity with clearly defined attributes –variables like beliefs, stories, norms and rituals come together into a "culture". They use terms like corporate culture, dominant cultures, fragmented cultures, ostensible (visible) and hidden cultures and they posit links between leadership style and corporate culture. These are terms that prompt thoughts that, in a mechanistic/instrumental way, culture can be managed. One of the notable exceptions to mechanistic organisational theory is the way Morgan considers culture as a normative glue holding an organisation together. It suggests another set of things to focus on, "influencing the language, norms, folklore, ceremonies and other social practices that communicate the key ideologies, values and beliefs guiding action" managers "see themselves as symbolic actors whose primary function is to foster and develop desirable patterns of meaning" (Morgan 1986: 135). "The beliefs and ideas that organizations hold about who they are, what they are trying to do, and what their environment is like, have a much greater tendency to realize themselves than is usually believed" (Morgan 1986: 137).

For Morgan, culture seems more "holographic than mechanistic"[4] (1986: 139) – creating a particular ethos that pervades an organisation and that employees exude – this could be a commitment to service, innovation, or lethargy/ a sense of helplessness or futility when things are going badly. "The holographic diffusion of culture means that it pervades activity in a way that is not amenable to direct control by any single group of individuals". It's not a recipe for solving managerial problems and managers being aware of the symbolic consequences of their actions or attempting to foster shared values can only go part way.

The NHS and welfare State more generally are more than the mechanistic characteristics listed by some management theorists; Morgan's generic "ethos" seems to better capture its emotional resonance as well as its utility. The way he describes its diffusion in the staff is replicated in the attitudes of the general population, its potential and actual users, in such a way that can act as a limitation on achieving change or as a defence against groups of individuals causing it damage.

One or many culture(s)?

A second basic question is which culture are we focussing on? Is there an NHS culture, or a culture of a hospital or of a ward? Are there co-existing and perhaps competing cultures within each of these?[5] How do we locate these, structurally – an administrative culture, a medical or a nursing culture; or attitudinally – a compassionate culture or a culture of instrumentality/expediency. Is the NHS to serve goals like personal advancement via enhancing clinical skills or, alternatively via meeting targets set by ones' organisation? Or is it a place we just go to work, where we "just get through the day?" If it is either of these then we might identify an outcome-oriented, or a task-based, culture where other staff and patients can be seen as a means to an end, a vector through which organisational goals are pursued, or "objects" one carries out tasks with, or on.

One example of both different cultures within the NHS and of fluctuations in power is to consider the relationship between clinicians and managers. (I have looked at aspects of this in Chapter 4.) That relationship has seen a dominance by clinicians counteracted by a rise of managerialism within health services, pursued as an overt tactic from the 1980s to limit clinicians' power, and then the rise of hybrid managers, clinicians drawn into management positions. A majority of managers in the NHS are now clinicians. Did practice in the NHS change because of the rise of managerialism? Do clinicians who are managers act in a way that is consistent with a culture of managerialism or of their professional origins? If a new policy is introduced that originates from an assessment about desirable clinical care, like the Liverpool Care Pathway, but it then is used as a management guide is clinical judgement compromised?

Morgan uses his field of study, contemporary organisations, in ways that echo the traditions of anthropology when he talks about magical thinking and the effect of money and of statistics. These are domains that have become even more prominent, and even more accrued with magical importance, under neoliberalism and they further illuminate the different cultures, and their complex interactions, that we have to consider (Table 7.1).

The idea of there being different cultures within the same organisation is necessary if we see that much of the practice in the NHS remains effective and compassionate, while there are serious breakdowns in some places. If it is only a minority of people who are problematic, we may either have a problem with the learned patterns of behaviour of some people (level 1 in the cultural anthropology schema described in Scott and Marshall (see above (2009)) or we have a separate culture, perhaps we could call it a sub-culture, operating alongside a broader, more benign culture. Or perhaps the dominant culture has weakened and is fading away, to be replaced by the culture of self-promotion by individuals and corporate self-interest for organisations. That is, the culture of compassion is disappearing, and hospitals that prioritise corporate goals over patient care (like Mid-Staffordshire) are harbingers of a broader cultural change, already underway but not yet dominant.

More fundamentally, if we want to consider culture in a dynamic way – as something through which things can be done, are we really talking about power? There is a power dimension underlining the enactment of culture; "We all construct or enact our realities, but not necessarily under circumstances of our own choosing" (Morgan 1986: 140).

Examples of attempts at culture change in the NHS

Vincent, in considering patient safety, has elaborated the characteristics of organisational culture, arguing that this includes shared basic assumptions, group learning, teaching these assumptions to new members of the group, and identification of ways that have worked well.

Table 7.1 Accountants, statisticians and magical thinking dressed up as rationality

Morgan (1986: 131–132) has described accountants as "reality constructors" in organisations that allow money to shape its reality. "Under their influence people or organizational units, whether they be pupils in schools, patients in hospitals, or work teams in manufacturing plants, become seen as profit centres generating costs and revenues. And where financial systems become a major issue, the data generated by such systems often exert a decisive influence on the decisions that are made. Many cost-conscious, bottom line-oriented organizational cultures are actually produced through the interpretive schemes that underpin such systems of control".
In these contexts, it is the interpretive lens provided by money that is given priority in the way the organisation is to be run. – the same impact can be made if you prioritise organisational structure, rules, job descriptions, standard operating procedures, etc. These are all cultural artefacts like rules about kinship, or beliefs about magic, in tribal societies.

An essay on using statistics in public policy from 1954 by Ely Devons (republished in Devons 1961) argues that there is an "exaggerated faith" in statistics and hence "a lack of reflection and critical awareness that accompanies their use". Modern organisations are sustained by belief systems that emphasise the importance of rationality and objectivity. "Like the primitive magicians, all kinds of experts are encouraged to engage in their mysterious calculations and are allowed to preserve their credibility even when events prove them wrong. If the magician's advice proves misguided, his magic is not discredited. Failure is usually attributed to an imperfection in execution or the unanticipated intervention of some hostile force….in a similar way the technical expert is allowed to blame the model used, or the turn of events, as a means of exploring why forecasts are inaccurate. The analysis is never discredited, the appearance of rationality is preserved" (Morgan 1986: 134).

> The challenge for the system as a whole is to identify a means of ensuring a positive and common culture throughout, ensuring that the positive values and ways of doing things, prevalent in much of the NHS front-line, chases out the negative which has been found in Stafford and elsewhere.
>
> (Vincent 2010: 2710)

In this section, I will consider three examples – two from Vincent's areas of concern, safety and one arising from the impact of Coronavirus to examine how culture change has been conceptualised and operationalised. The "safety examples" show how difficult it is to eradicate errors even after a sustained focus on them. They are also examples of an approach to culture that sees it as part of a sociocultural whole, with developing a safety culture via shifts in leadership and systems change as the intervention. In the first case, developing a safety culture includes a concern with values, beliefs and norms. This example therefore includes Scott and Marshall's levels one and three – changes in patterns of behaviour and in patterns of thought and perception. The second example, handwashing, is best located in Level One. The third example is about Coronavirus. Here the understanding of culture is closer to the ideational view, it is something that is long established and sits outside, albeit alongside, political systems.

Example one: complex case: developing a safety culture

Developing a "safety culture" to minimise medical error has been a high-profile concern since an influential policy document from the US in 1999 recommended a focus on leadership and on systems change (Kohn et al. 1999). A culture of safety arises, Kohn et al. argued, from a shared set of values, beliefs and norms related to patient safety. These norms include: all staff having a constant and active awareness of the potential for things to go wrong and having both staff and the organisation able to acknowledge mistakes, learn from them and take action to put things right.

Seeking to develop a new safety culture within health systems can illustrate the complexity of the challenge and the timescale needed.

- There have been many interventions since 1999 designed to instigate or improve a safety culture in the UK (Weaver et al. 2013). But, despite this, between 2003 and 2007 1,372,062 incidents relating to actual or potential risk of harm were reported to the UK's National Patient Safety Agency (National Patient Safety Agency 2007).
- There are more than 237 million medication errors made every year in England, 2% of these could potentially result in serious harm and around 26% could cause moderate harm. These errors can be linked to 1,700 death per year and over £98 million of avoidable cost to the NHS (Elliott et al. 2019).
- In 2012–13, there were around 750 avoidable deaths in hospitals in England each month, that amounts to around 3.6% of hospital deaths.[6] Oliver commented that this is "the equivalent of a passenger plane falling out of the sky each week" (Hogan et al. 2015; Oliver 2018).
- Using preventable[7] rather than avoidable as the descriptor, a study of adult deaths in 2009 in hospitals in England identified one death in 20 has having a greater than 50% chance of having been preventable (Hogan et al. 2012).[8]

However, these deaths are categorised, and accepting the caveat that a considerable uncertainty surrounds all such figures, it is clear there is a continuing problem. It is also clear that a sustained focus on establishing a safety culture has not eliminated misjudgements and mistakes.[9]

Example two: apparently simple case: handwashing to combat infection

A shift to the omnipresence of handwashing in hospitals to combat infection appears relatively simple, helped by its intuitive link between problem and solution. Gel dispensers can be easily put in place and awareness raising (screen savers on staff computers in my local trust for example: signs above the sink in my Universities' toilets telling you to, "wet your hand, then add soap etc.") can be via simple (albeit sometimes irritating) messaging.

Although there is clear information available on optimum handwashing technique whether the sort of handwashing that follows this awareness raising is optimal is more difficult to evaluate. Is any change that is apparent in response to hand-washing guidance a new sort of conformity, I have washed my hands as "they" have told me I must, or is it a re-engaging between understanding of cause and effect and a commitment to action that reflects this understanding; "I am going to wash my hands properly because I understand the link between not washing or inadequate washing and infection?"

The extent and nature of the change can be represented in figures on hospital-acquired infection rates (not a phenomenon with a single cause but a workable proxy for the impact of improved (correct) handwashing) or it can be manifest in a sense that self-policing and peer group pressure to always do the right thing has become a new orthodoxy, a part of the "culture".

While the link between cleanliness and infection has been known for many years by 2006 articles on handwashing and hospital-acquired infection were being published and attracting attention (Pittet 2006). In 2013, Allegranzi et al. reported that compliance with recommendations about handwashing across the world was low. Where there was some evidence of substantial and sustained improvement this was only after an extensive stepwise intervention. In the UK, in 2014, NICE felt it necessary (eight years after the initial articles) to issue "quality standards on measures including hand washing, prompted by unacceptable rates of hospital-acquired infections".

About 300,000 patients develop an infection in England each year while being treated by the NHS, this approximates to 1 in 16 people treated. Risk of infection that can be linked to handwashing has been resilient to change despite the focus on it and despite the simple shifts in behaviour it requires. Changing simple procedures in meaningful ways is not simple. It takes a long time and does not work in every situation. If behaviour changes are just about following rules or guidance (level 1 change) and don't engage changes in perception as to the necessary and desirable they are less likely to be done always and done thoroughly.

In 2020 handwashing assumed a new significance as one of the most recommended behavioural responses to reduce the spread of coronavirus – we were regularly instructed about how to wash our hands and for how long (our Prime Minister suggested long enough to sing the tune "Happy Birthday to you" twice about 20 seconds, also the advice on the NHS Website).

Example three: culture and coronavirus

During the first year of the coronavirus pandemic, 2020–21, it had been clear that infection rates and death rates had varied widely between countries. Variables considered relevant to explain this included relative wealth, climate, age profiles of the population and hospital capacity. Other variables considered related to the capabilities and competencies of national governments. I have considered above the neoliberal variable – the sustained impact of neoliberalism had hollowed out state provision in key areas (public health for example), privatised and, in the process, atomised other areas (care homes), promoted short-termism linked to a preoccupation with finance capital and short term gains, and had elevated a coterie of political leaders intent on prioritising the economy and reluctant to be seen as asking too much of the populous – this is the point that neoliberalism elides into populism.[10] But just as with debate about hospital and care failures, described previously, that side-lines level of resource and policy priorities (see also Small 2023), there is also an explanation for patterns of Covid infection that shifts political and economic variables aside and offers culture as cause and culture change as a remedy.

Gelfand (2021, see also 2018) thinks the main factor underlying variation in national infection rates is cultural differences in our willingness to follow rules. Her argument is that some cultures abide by social norms quite strictly, she calls these "tight" while others live with a more relaxed attitude to breaking rules and to rule breakers, "loose" cultures in her typology. She offers the comparison between Japan (tight) and Mexico (loose) – both have similar size populations but at the point, Japan reported 5000 coronavirus deaths Mexico had 150,000. Then she offers more general comparisons between loose and tight countries – five times the number of cases and eight times the number of deaths in the former compared with the latter. Paradoxically, given these stark differences, people in loose cultures were far less afraid of catching the virus, 49% were very scared against 70% in tight. In loose cultures, fewer people exposed to a confirmed person with Covid self-isolated for two weeks and a similar smaller proportion self-isolated after developing symptoms.

Leaving aside the caveat that associations are not causations, using culture as explanation removes a route to blame and hence redress. If the government is manifesting a prevailing culture which Gelfand links to a history of previous chronic threat – countries who have faced such threats have developed stricter rules, they are tight[11] – then the delays and failures of UK Coronavirus policy are not to do with leadership, and the UK's position as having one of highest death rates in the world are not to do with the 40 years of neoliberalism or the incipient populist stance of our Prime Minister and Cabinet but are to do with our bucolic past.[12]

Just as in my hospital and care examples the "culture as cause" approach also comes with cultural change as remedy. Gelfand offers "build cultural intelligence so the threat can be outsmarted" as the prescription, and within that there are three sorts of intervention: make the threat more vivid (but do this without terrifying people); make it clear that if you shift from loose to tight its only temporary, we can all soon go back to casual rule-breaking; and, emphasise we are all in this together. The last is a difficult narrative to accept in the UK of huge differences in the impact of Covid-19 across classes and ethnicities.

Cautionary thoughts

There are many parallels between the experience of seeking to set up a culture of safety and the sorts of cultural change that have been considered in seeking to ensure compassionate care. Both include a recognition of the importance of leadership and of systems change; both want staff to be constantly aware of the possibility of things going wrong; both engage with values and beliefs; both talk about recognising mistakes and learning from them. As with handwashing, a behaviour change might help but while necessary it isn't sufficient to get the sorts of change that are needed, only a change in understanding and consequently an attitudinal change will do. Many of the indications of compassionate care will be transmitted in the tenor of the encounter between health care provider and patient, just to act as if you are sensitive doesn't mean you will be experienced as sensitive although acting sensitively may be better than being crass in the same way that washing your hands is not as good as washing your hands properly but may be better than not washing your hands at all (unless a tokenistic washing of the hands is followed by your taking risks that you wouldn't have taken!)[13]

At the very least the importance put on culture in responses to care failures, and indeed to shortcomings in a very wide area of contemporary concerns, requires us to make sure that if we invoke culture we have to follow that invocation with the recognition of the complexity of the term and the widely acknowledged difficulty of creating a culture change.

One aspect of that complexity, and something I have considered above and will return to, is the need to recognise an inherent subjectivity in the production of knowledge, and in the creation of objects/focuses for research (like culture). These objects do not exist (and certainly don't act) independently of the observer. A person's perception of a particular phenomenon will, in part, depend on their beliefs, expectations and experiences – this renders any idea of "truth" or "fact" partial (Gray 2014: see also Gray 2015).

As I keep returning to Foucault throughout this book, here it is worth noting his concern with how we categorise things, how we seek order (Foucault 1970). This order is not fixed for all time, it changes and the categories we use now are not ones that would have made sense to us in the past or that will make sense to those in the future. This is also true for what we see as constituting culture.[14] Further, what we think of as the most interesting aspects of culture may just be "surface" gloss – not the things that sustain its fundamental structures.

Culture as diagnosis of what went wrong, in the NHS for example, purports to talk about deep processes but it is not deep enough to unearth "why" change occurred, and culture as prescription is not specific enough to generate interventions. We hear so often and in so many scenarios, "the problems are so deep rooted they need cultural change" but knowing "what next" is more difficult.

Time scales for culture change

In his comic novel "*Out of Town*", J.B. Priestley's academic protagonist is concerned that the widely quoted analysis that CP Snow offered about their being two cultures (exemplified by a lack of dialogue between the scientists and literary intellectuals)[15] was inadequate:

> I must first explain how I am using the term culture. It is not something that comes and goes within a century. A culture in this sense will last several

hundred years. So – that of the Middle Ages, based on a vision of God, declined during the Fifteenth Century only to be succeeded during and after the Renaissance by another based on a vision of man, which has lasted almost until our own time. But no successor has yet emerged. We are not living with two cultures; we are only trying to live – and not happily – without one at all. This is the reason why everything seems to move so quickly.

(Priestley 1968: 280)

Art Historian William Gaunt (1949) also sees an absence of a new culture (albeit 20 years earlier than Priestley's piece). For him, the absence of a culture means an absence of there being acceptable standards. There may be much activity, even brilliance, but a new culture needs "profound affirmations" to mark its arrival.

Both Priestley and Gaunt offer a cautionary tone if we dare to think that cultures change quickly or that one can transition into another easily. Neoliberalism (or populism) might be manifestations of a period like Priestley's and Gaunt's where there is an absence of culture, or it might better indicate the febrile environment Geertz describes when we get such rapid changes in social structures that the connection with a settled culture is lost. It may be that we are seeing indicators of the arrival of a new culture, or the unresolved conflicts between cultures. Whatever is the case as we examine culture as diagnosis and prescription, it will deepen our analysis to look at things that might be seen as components of any culture, and that might be compromised in a toxic culture. I turn to such things in the next chapter.

Notes

1   The furore around Covid-19 social distancing rule-breaking in Downing Street, the "Partygate" episode, promoted calls for culture change. Elsewhere in this chapter I will consider how invoking culture allows perpetrators of wrongdoing to side-step individual responsibility and it avoids critiques of structural failings or of policy mistakes.
2   In other parts of this book the idea of the "taken for granted" is discussed as lifeworld or as doxa.
3   What or who is civilised is as contentious as the definitions of culture are complex. The quip attributed to Gandhi illustrates. He was asked what he thought of Western Civilisation and replied, "That would be nice" (see Appiah 2016 for an argument that goes further and suggests that even if we could find Western Civilisation it would not be nice to see).
4   I discuss a similar formulation – "simulacra" elsewhere.
5   There may be many types of culture within one organisation. W F Whyte (1948), in a classic study, described a sort of cultural warfare in the restaurants he studied. Differential status and working practices between kitchen staff and those working on tables (fuelled by an uncomfortable and often resented relation of dependency between groups) was at its heart. This was not an environment in which a shared culture was evident, ones' identity as a waiter was more important than ones' identity as a member of the team running the restaurant. It's a scenario that might not feel out of place in the multi-disciplinary contemporary NHS.
6   Hogan et al identify avoidable deaths by using experienced clinicians to identify those with at least a 50% probability of avoidability in the view of these trained medical

reviewers. There is some uncertainty on definitions as to what counts as an avoidable death and variation in how the details of deaths are recorded and this uncertainty is reflected in the wide range of figures – in Hogan et al (2015) the 3.6% figure when considered with a 95% confidence interval varies between 3% and 4.3%.

7 A preventable death is one caused by either failure to correctly diagnose or treat or caused by treatments that should never have been considered because of safety concerns.

8 In the USA James (2013) estimates that between 1 in 6 and 1 in 13 of all hospital deaths in the US are premature deaths (another different denominator).

9 There is another way of looking at all these figures – that the vast majority of treatment is safe. Most the figures in this section for death or serious harm are below 5%. Is this a positive story? Clearly it's not if you are in the unsafe category but also it sees that it is not seen as positive given the continuing commitment (at least rhetorically) to reduce harm. There is also a wide range of potential harms that are not featured in these figures – but that are considered throughout this book – harm in chronic illness and end-of-life care, harm in upset and distress caused and in pain endured.

10 There is a danger in idealising the past, while we may not like recent changes, we still need to critique what they replaced (see Anderson-Wallace and Shale 2013).

11 The case of New Zealand – with one of the world's lowest infection and death rates and a country with an absence of chronic threat in its history – is dealt with by describing their "cultural ambidexterity" that permits adjusting from loose to tight and back depending on circumstance.

12 Gelfand is from the US – she may not be as aware of how much the UK's national story is constructed out of fears of outside threat and of the importance of standing together and then of the country standing alone – quintessentially in the place of the Second World War in national consciousness and more recently in the strength of similar tropes evident in mobilising the movement to leave the European Union.

13 A rhetorical device designed to questions road safety assumptions saw a suggestion that the safest way to ride a motorbike was if the rider was naked. Both the rider and other road users would avoid any fantasies of invulnerability (and the risk taking that follows) from leather suits and full-face helmets. The same argument is used to criticise an assumption that wearing a helmet increases a cyclist's safety. The Covid-19 pandemic has introduced a whole new set of potential examples – mask wearing rather than social distancing is one.

14 Foucault uses the example of a "certain Chinese encyclopaedia" in a story by Jorge Luis Borges where animals are categorised in ways that seem inconceivable to ways we now order things.

15 C P Snow 1959 the Rede Lecture, University of Cambridge (see Snow 2001).

References

Allaire, Y., Firsirotu, M.E. 1984. Theories of organizational culture. *Organization Studies*, 5(3), 193–226.

Allegranzi, B., Gayet-Ageron, A., Damani, N., Bengaly, L., McLaws, M-L., Moro, M-L., Memish, Z., Urroz, O., Richet, H., Storr, J., Donaldson, L., Pittet, D. 2013. Global implementation of WHO's multimodel strategy for improvement of hand hygiene: A quasi-experimental study. *The Lancet Infectious Diseases*, 13(10), 843–851.

Anderson-Wallace, M., Shale, S. 2013. Should there be changes to NHS culture? *The Guardian*, 27 Mar.

Appiah, K.A. 2016. *Culture*. The Reith Lectures, 8 Nov, BBC Radio 4.

Arnold, M. 1869 (Reissued 2009). *Culture and Anarchy*. Oxford, Oxford University Press.

Bauman, Z. 1999a. *Culture as Praxis*. London, Sage.

Bauman, Z. 2011. *Culture in a Liquid Modern World*. Cambridge, Polity.

Bregman, R. 2020. *Humankind: A Hopeful History*. Bloomsbury.

Case, P. 1994. Tracing the organisational culture debate. *Anthropology in Action*, 1(2), 9–11.

de Swaan, A. 1990. *The Management of Normality*. London, Routledge.

Devons, E. Ed. 1961. Statistics as a basis for policy. In, *Essays in Economics*. London, Allen and Unwin, 122–137.

de Waal, F. 2006. *Our Inner Ape: The Best and Worst of Human Nature*. Granta.

Elliott, R.A., Camacho, E., Jankovic, D., Sculpher, M.J., Faria, R. 2019. Economic analysis of the prevalence and clinical and economic burden of medication error in England. *BMJ Quality and Safety*. http://dx.doi.org/10.1136/bmjqs-2019–010206

Foucault, M. 1970. *The Order of Things: An Archaeology of the Human Sciences*. New York, Pantheon.

Gaunt, W. 1949. *The March of the Moderns*. Jonathan Cape.

Geertz, C. 1973. *The Interpretation of Cultures*. New York, Basic Book.

Gelfand, M.J. 2018. *Rule Makers, Rule Breakers: How Culture Wires our Minds, Shapes our Nations, and Drives Our Differences: Tight and Loose Cultures and the Secret Signals that Direct our Lives*. Robinson.

Gelfand, M.J. 2021. Why countries with "loose" rule-breaking cultures have been hit harder by Covid. *The Guardian Opinion*, 1 Feb.

Gray, D. 2014. *Doing Research in the Real World*. London, Sage.

Gray, J. 2015. The sorcery of numbers. *The Guardian*. Essay, 14 Mar, 19–20.

Harrison, S., Pollitt, C. 1994. *Controlling Health Professionals: The Future of Work and Organisation in the NHS*. Buckingham, Open University Press.

Hogan, H., Healey, F., Neale, G., Thomson, R., Vincent, C., Black, N. 2012. Preventable death due to problems in care in English acute hospitals: A retrospective case record review study. *BMJ Quality and Safety*, 21(9), 737–745.

Hogan, H., Zipfel, R., Neuberger, J., Hutchins, A., Darzi, A., Black, N. 2015. Avoidability of hospital deaths and association with hospital-wide mortality ratios: Retrospective case record review and regression analysis. *British Medical Journal*, 351, h3239. http://dx.doi.org/10.1136/bmj.h3239 pmid:26174149

Horlick-Jones, T. 2012. Taking the bundle apart: Some reflections on the significance of Edward Thompson's work for the practice of sociology. *Sociology*, 46(6), 1223–1229.

James, J.T. 2013. A new, evidence-based estimate of patient harms associated with hospital care. *Journal of Patient Safety*, 9(3), 122–128.

Keesing, R. 1974. Theories of culture. *Annual Review of Anthropology*, 3, 73–97.

Kroeber, A.L., Kluckhohn, C. 1952. *Culture: A Critical Review of Concepts and Definitions*. Cambridge, MA, Harvard University Press.

Kohn, L., Corrigan, J., Donaldson, M. 1999. *To Err Is Human: Building a Safer Health System*. Washington, DC, National Academy Press.

Lorsch, J.W. 2016. Culture is not the culprit. *Harvard Business Review*, Apr, 96–105.

Morgan, G. 1986. *Images of Organization*. London, Sage.

National Patient Safety Agency. 2007. *NICE/NPSA Issues Its First Patient Safety Solution Guidance to Improve Medicines Reconciliation at Hospital Admission*. London.

Oliver, D. 2018. Learning from deaths in hospital. *British Medical Journal*, 361, k969.

Pittet, D. 2006. Clean hands reduce the burden of disease. *The Lancet*, 366, 185–187

Priestly, J.B. 1968. *Out of Town*. London, William Heinemann.

Savage, J. 2000. The culture of 'culture' in National Health Service policy implantation. *Nursing Inquiry*, 7, 230–238.

Scott, J., Marshall, G. 2009. *Oxford Dictionary of Sociology*. Oxford University Press.

Shaw, G.B. 2000 [1905]. *Man and Superman*. Penguin Classics.

Small, N. 2023. *Failures in health and social care. Governance and Culture change*. London, Routledge.

Snow, C.P. 2001. *The Two Cultures*. London, Cambridge University Press.

Thompson, E.P. 1993. *Customs in Common*. London, Penguin.

Tylor, E.B. 1870 (2nd Ed: reissued 2012). *Primitive Culture*. Forgotten Books.

Vincent, C. 2010. *Patient Safety* (2nd Ed). BMJ Books.

Weaver, S.J., Lubomski, L.H., Wilson, R.F., Pfoh, E.R., Martinez, K.A., Dy, S.M. 2013. Promoting a culture of safety as a patient safety strategy: A systematic review. *Annals of Internal Medicine*, 158, 369–374.

Whyte, W.F. 1948. *Human Relations in the Restaurant Industry*. New York, McGraw Hill.

Williams, R. 1983. *Keywords*. Fontana.

8 Aspects of culture that might be damaged and need repair

Introduction

I have asked "how can a particular sort of economics and politics impact on caring for the vulnerable" and I have considered if this sort of economics and politics can make us sick.

I have also considered how economic and political changes impact on personal encounters and what processes might be involved in effecting such changes. In Chapter 6, my focus was on attitudinal change and, in particular, on change in individuals. In Chapter 7, I then shifted focus and looked at culture and at culture change. This chapter examines things that might be considered aspects of culture and that might be impacted by culture change – care, empathy, compassion, suffering, dignity for example. These are all things critical to the interpersonal encounter between health and social care providers and their patients/residents. How might they have changed and how might they be changed?

The latter part of this chapter goes on to consider an aspect of culture that is also central to the social contract. Trust in those providing health care and in those deciding health policy can be impacted by events specific to health and by a more general sense of trust in society. I will examine a number of areas in which there appears to have been a breakdown in trust and I will suggest these give context to the failures in health care that are the substantive focus of this book. A concern with the state of our social contract then becomes a major focus of my conclusion. To preview where this argument is going, I will say that neoliberalism has eroded the social contract through both its structural and its interpersonal sequelae.

Foucault (1972: 49) has argued that discourses form the objects of which they speak (see Chapter 6) and neoliberalism does this both in the economy and polity that emerges from it and in individual's choices and actions. But it does not do this in a way that eliminates all counterviews. Power generates opposition – social movements for example and also residual assumptions that can counter the impact of social change in individuals. The extent to which individual agency can resist social forces is the subjects of much of our philosophy (see Table 8.1), does the means of production determine the relations of production, does existence precede essence, how far do the structures we live within, and the structure of

DOI: 10.4324/9781003332404-11

Table 8.1 Public and intangible domains.

The primacy of the public domain "There is no private life which has not been determined by a wider public life". George Eliot in *Felix Holt The Radical* (1866)	The primacy of the intangible. "…the political institutions of any nation are always menaced and are ultimately controlled by the spiritual state of that nation". James Baldwin. *The Fire Next Time*. (1963: 96.)[1]

language, determine what we can think, are there resilient levels where beliefs reside away from temporary and shifting political and economic orthodoxies, and so on? Further, are there ways people can be protected against the erosion of what they might consider the decent thing to do, to be compassionate to the vulnerable for example? What gives people the strength not to obey orders, or not to conform to norms of practice they think are at odds with their own beliefs?

Care

I have considered culture as a place things can go wrong and as a vector for change and I have emphasised how culture is a far from straightforward concept. Care is similarly conceptually complex. It can be a verb or a noun. Madeline Bunting, in her book on what care is and on the present crisis in care, identifies care as a noun, "the provision of what is necessary for the health, welfare, maintenance and protection of someone or something", and as "serious attention or consideration applied to doing something correctly or to avoid damage or risk". Care as a verb can be, to "feel concern or interest, to attach importance to something", or to "look after and provide for the needs of" (Bunting 2020: 38). In this section, I will develop ideas of what care is and of how care is done, and I will then link this with needs, wants and rights. Financialisaton, alongside austerity, generates an "economy of abandonment" (Dowling 2021). The marketisation of care impacts on what are considered legitimate needs, and neoliberalism re-examines what are seen as rights. Both needs and rights need to be recognised and defended, both are integral to what care is seen to be and what caring is done. The Care Collective (2020) argues that we should reimagine the role of care in our everyday lives, making it our organising principle and recognising it as a critique of neoliberal profit making.[2]

Caring for and caring about

Sociologists have focussed on the differences between "caring for" and "caring about" somebody (Thomas 1993) and there has been interest in understanding "caring with" (Bauman 1993: 49). They have also been concerned with the organisation of care, with care as work, with "informal care" provided by family members in the main, and with the gendered nature of care and the role of patriarchy. There are caring professions and care organisations. We call family members and peoples' friends carers when we see them doing tasks we associate with caring. One can be a carer, be cared for, or be both (sometimes at the same time). While family and friends may undertake a very large proportion of care work, they may not welcome, or even accept, being categorised as carers. A husband who is looking after his wife may find what he does is demeaned by being called "care". Bond (1991) sees care by family and friends being vulnerable to incorporation into a "care in the community" modality, invoking the risk that it will be subjected to the implementation of "expert" knowledge, specifically medical judgements as to what is "need" and what is a "successful" outcome for care. (This is another example of system world encroachment on the lifeworld.)

Care can be imposed on you, for example you can be "taken into care" if someone in authority considers you to be at risk. What you might see as intrusive and controlling might be motivated by someone wishing to care for you – many of us are likely to have had this experience. Thus, care may not be experienced as benign. The difference between control and care is, in part, a subjective one. Fox illustrates this with juxtaposing key words linked to care – how trust can become dependency for example (Fox 1995: 116). But the difference can also be one of intent, or of the assumptions one makes about what care is. Fox distinguishes between care as discipline, which he calls "the vigil of care", and care as gift. The vigil of care is about power and control, the professionalisation of care and a focus on a technology of surveillance for example. There is another care that is about love, generosity and a celebration of otherness – the "gift of care".[3]

The difficulty in giving and in receiving care is, in part, because it can feel transgressive. Twigg (2000) looked at bathing as an example of a nursing task that occurs at the intersection of day-to-day life and professional service. This intersection is even more marked when care occurs in one's own home. Bathing, dressing, eating, using the toilet, are about managing the body and are also features of the ordering of daily life. They are also signifiers of the way loss of ability changes both one's relationship with ones' body and the boundary of that body in its sociality (Twigg 2006). There is a crossing of the Rubicon when you first have to be helped in one of these activities and there is a similar transition the first time you have to help a family member, other than a child.

Care as labour

Care characteristically includes physical and emotional labour, both sorts of labour can be demanding for the person giving and the person receiving care. There is a body of research that identifies how the emotional can be displaced by the physical (or practical). James (1989) noted that in a hospice if the guiding ideology is total care, that is physical, social, spiritual and emotional then the latter two are elements of "care work" that involve domains not normally made overt in medical settings. But, while hospice staff saw emotional labour as integral to their jobs, it was this area that was lost when they were under pressure to do what were seen as required physical tasks, "'emotion' sits uneasily with workplace values of timetabling, predictability and efficiency" (James 1989: 37).

Lawton (2000) explored similar dilemmas and reminded us of the considerable demands the care of people at the end of their lives makes in terms of the physical tasks required of the carers. But also underpinning the relationship between carer and cared for were the changes arising from the non-negotiable effects of a patient's bodily deterioration on their sense of self. She questions aspects of the hospice philosophy of the good death, and of living until you die, in the context of considering both embodiment and emotion in death and dying. Pilsworth (1994) reported hospice workers often using defensive mechanisms when talking with dying patients so that they can shift the emphasis of care to symptom control and patient compliance to "make their job easier". deSwaan's (1990) study of a ward which focussed on patients with cancer reported the anxieties of staff caring for people who are dying being unacknowledged and displaced into a technical (medical) realm.

The organisation of care

Some of the challenges of negotiating physical and emotional labour are linked to the organisation of care, challenges from bureaucratisation (see McNamara et al. 1994) or from a lack of support from one's colleagues (Low and Payne 1996), or from a management that lacks skill or sensitivity or that is prioritising something other than the care they are ostensibly charged to provide. In palliative care a rise of bureaucratisation could be a manifestation of the way innovation becomes transformed over time (James and Field 1992), but it can also be created by policy choices, for example the rise of clinical auditing of services as an obligation for securing funding can change the preoccupations of an organisation, and even its care practices (Seale 1989). Bunting's thoughts on this aspect of care are stark: the "vital, unquantifiable nature of care was being squeezed to the margins", deep systemic shifts evident for three decades are seeing care degraded "in an attempt to standardise this most unpredictable of human activities". "We have distorted this vital human labour into an often grotesque box-ticking parody. At the root of our current crisis [in care] lies the historic denigration and misunderstanding of care" (Bunting 2020).

Staff are having to balance care with other demands on their time, form filling for example. The shift from a prioritising of care is an unintended consequence of a new imperative for efficiency, productivity and value for money, these are linked with having to deal with the impact of reduced resources and, together, are part of the marketisation of health. There is also a heightened concern with prioritising steps to reduce human error and reduce the possibilities of abuse being perpetrated by staff on patients. These latter concerns reflect agendas linked to the widespread condemnation of the shortcomings revealed in Mid-Staffordshire, and similar concerns elsewhere. Table 8.2 considers how the 2001 Essence of Care initiative provided care standards that included simple but useful advice and that ostensibly engaged with the patient's needs and views. But, as the group set up in response to the Mid-Staffordshire Trust's shortcomings *Cure the NHS* reported, these benchmarks did not mean shortcomings were eliminated and, further, they

Table 8.2 Benchmarking Care: The Essence of Care initiative (NHS Modernisation
          Agency. 2001)

This initiative provides guidance on standards of care which should be delivered to patients. These include communication, nutrition, privacy and dignity and record keeping. From these standards, benchmarks have been developed and detailed guidance about how to use them provided (NHS Modernisation Agency. 2010).

An example of using Essence of Care:
What needs to be done to help people who need *help to eat*?

• Have a system in place to identify who needs assistance to eat and record who gets it. If practice is not meeting the benchmark, then change practice so it does – for example put food on red trays for people requiring assistance.
• Evaluate the practice – are people being helped satisfied with the help they are getting, is there evidence that people identified as needing help are well nourished. If yes then incorporate the new practice, identify indicators and monitor if they are achieved.
• Use this evidence of achievement in reports to the regulator, to the Health Service Ombudsman, when reporting against National Service Frameworks and in reassuring Commissioners as to the quality of care.

Cure the NHS, while reporting how woefully short of achieving benchmark standards trusts like Mid Staffs were, also reports how the existence of the standards was used as a diversion: when hospitals respond to complaints about the quality of care they often use the line of saying, "issues are being addressed as part of the Essence of Care benchmarking" (curethenhs.co.uk – accessed 15/9/2017).

were used as a smokescreen to deflect criticism of continuing "woeful" standards of care.

Both the efficiency/productivity/value for money imperatives and the elevation of risk of error highlight a toxic contradiction in marketised health – efficiency, productivity and value for money cannot be meaningfully calculated without including the experience of care and to pursue efficiency at the price of damaging the care relationship is futile. Risk to the worker and risk to the institution (and only as an auxiliary concern risk to the patient) is also a toxic contradiction in the very assumptions that should underpin our Welfare State.

Autonomy and agency

There is an additional concern in care at the end of life and in care of older people. That concern is that there will be an assumption by carers that reciprocity in interactions reduces (Vernooij-Dasen et al. 2011). Frailty characteristically reduces functional performance and a person's ability to have control over their life. But it rarely eliminates their capacity for reciprocity. Recognising this helps with maintaining dignity, and quality of life. That is not to say that each patient must be a fully engaged partner in making choices about their own care. There is a danger of being tyrannical when we elevate an assumption that we should exercise autonomous agency right to the end of life into a requirement. What is wrong with just being looked after? At the end of life people may wish to feel safe and to

---

Box 8.1 Coping

Ivan Illich professed to have identified "the problems of intransitive verbs". In a paper titled "Against Coping" (published with a different title in Illich 1995), he pointed out that the term coping, as in "coping with sickness", was of recent origin. In premodern times, "Sickness, like pain, disability, tiredness and fear was suffered, born, shared, alleviated, dreaded or cured (11)". By the late 1960s to cope began to be used as an intransitive verb – a way of existence. It was used without the additional word *with*, "coping flourishes within this epistemic void (12)". "The Orphic 'know thyself' now reads 'check how your system is coping'". Illich argues that, in this context, the ego is recast as a system that can be shaped and controlled by "hazardous medicalization, socially disabling professionalism, and a debilitating ritualism". He would have health care indited, "not as a demoralizing but as a nihilist activity" (12).

While Illich's ire is directed at "coping"; he may well have also taken exception to the word culture when it is being used as an intransitive verb. If he did perhaps it would be management consultants and politicians who he would see as undertaking a hazardous manipulation, an anaesthetising ritualism.

---

be looked after, to have things done for you (perhaps to have things decided for you). (See Box 8.1 for a different and provocative perspective.)

Ignatieff, explores a scenario where a person may need help but doesn't want it, or does not know what their "real" needs are. Through reflecting, in part, on *King Lear* Ignatieff describes how Shakespeare's tragedy unfolds as Lear's needs are reframed by two of his daughters as "wants" not "needs". They then proceed to tell him what he needs and he implores them "O, reason not the need" (Act 2 Scene 4: see Small et al. 2006: 385). "There are few presumptions in human relations more dangerous than the idea that one knows what another human being needs better than they do themselves".[4] But while Lear clearly voices what he thinks are his needs at the start of the play he only discovers what he truly needs through suffering. "We learn what is enough by learning what it is like to have less than enough" (Ignatieff 1984: 11).

Needs and rights

Needs are voiced and met socially. Sometimes the reactions of others can be a manifestation of the way individually expressed needs become socially recognised rights. The vulnerable person's need for care can shape social provision to respond to it. "It is this solidarity among strangers, this transformation through the division of labour of needs into rights and rights into care that gives us whatever fragile basis we have for saying that we live in a moral community" (Ignatieff

1984: 10). The ordinary virtues are of key importance in maintaining moral order in a divided world (Ignatieff 2017).

The contextual political debate that surrounds this mediation of needs into rights is not so much to question that everyone has rights, although that is increasingly called into question by the elevation of an idea of the centrality of citizenship and the casting out of "the other" that we see in populism, but how far those rights extend. Their erosion, both in their reach across the population and in their depth, how far they extend in each person's life, is a feature of the changes of neoliberalism I have been developing and as such, offers a contributory explanation into Bunting and others' identification of "the crisis of care". One example from Bunting illustrates this point about depth and reach, she describes how home care visits are squeezed into absurdly short units of time and, even with that, resources are not sufficient to meet need and the rationing decisions that follow exclude millions of people (Bunting 2020a).

The question about "how far" rights extend is characteristically reduced to a debate about the amount of funding available to meet basic needs – food, shelter, etc. – rather than really being a discussion about how far rights extend in a philosophical or judicial sense, or about how we collectively respond to those things that are not captured through the language of rights. "There is more to respect in a person than his rights", you can respect someone's rights but demean them a person. "The strangers at my door have welfare rights, but it is another question altogether whether they have the respect and consideration of the officials who administer these rights".

> It is because fraternity, love, belonging, dignity and respect cannot be specified as rights that we ought to specify then as needs and seek, with the blunt institutional procedures at our disposal, to make their satisfaction a routine human practice.
>
> (Ignatieff 1984: 13–14)

Thus, the ability to meet the varied needs of strangers in health care settings will be influenced by both the structures of practice and the empathy of the staff.

One philosophical debate that offers the possibility of looking at structures of practice and individual actions links with a discussion of differences between Principlism and Narrative Ethics and at the skills necessary to recognise and act upon differing assumptions as to what is at the core of moral life (Table 8.3).

McCarthy goes further and asks, "Is there a communicative ethic that can unite the two?", and "What skills do we need?" to achieve this? (from McCarthy 2003: 70.) For both principlists and narrativists there are skills that might be taught, and there are many areas where skills are common to the two approaches. McCarthy argues that each approach can complement the other – both can be brought to bear on a situation if both are mediated by what he calls a "moral imagination". Thus, "a good principlist pays attention to the uniqueness of each moral situation and so has narrativist tendencies, and a good narrativist has a view to multiple stories and shared meanings and so is inclined towards principlism" (McCarthy 2003: 70).

Table 8.3 The heart of moral life

Principlists: principles are at the heart of moral life (see Beauchamp and Childress 2019)	*Narrativists: communication is at the core of moral life (see Lindeman Nelson 1997: see also MacIntyre 1981)*
To be able to step back from our intuitive response to a situation we are presented with and instead to seek to identify general norms. This needs: • Conceptual and analytic skills to identify moral issues and specify principles. • Deductive skills to apply general principles to particular cases. • Critical skills to assess and weigh principles and arguments. • Reflective skills to reason from particular experiences and cases to general rules.	To be able to step outside our received values and consider the unique stories and circumstances a situation presents us with. This needs: • Literary skills and vocabulary to understand and interpret a story. • Critical skills to fit actions within a larger frame of meaning. • Reflective skills to consider and test multiple narratives. • Communicative skills to negotiate in and between the patient and professional realm.

Comfort and consolation

The moral imagination and communicative ethic can be enacted in giving comfort and consolation. Comfort is not necessarily propositional – sometimes it can be done with a hug – but consolation needs words. Tallis (2016) (see Box 8.2) says you can't give comfort at the end of life but you can console. This is the process of giving meaning to something someone is feeling, perhaps consoling at the time of a loss, the death of a loved one, a defeat, or a sense of being overwhelmed by the world around us – in war, famine or in a pandemic we may need consoling. We may console in different ways, there are prevailing social constructs about the way consolation "should" be offered. Ignatieff (2022) talks about the consolation offered by religion, or by a sense of being helped to see the world as it – Camus saying we are consoled when we see we must cope with that. Others see a part of consoling as a diversion or distraction, taking your mind off the loss; Ignatieff cites Montaigne on consolation as a distraction and Abraham Lincoln writing to a bereaved mother that he wanted to "beguile her from grief". Ignatieff also discusses Cicely Saunders and hospice care, identifying the recognition that consolation needs time and space. The modern hospital is challenged to offer these, sometimes it does – consolation can be given and received in a few moments – but often it does not.

Empathy

Comfort and compassion rely on being made manifest and being met in the individual encounter, between nurse and patient for example. A part of that individual encounter is shaped by the mood (culture) of the collective, its expression is facilitated or curtailed by the nature of the organisation care is being delivered in and it is vulnerable to the encroachment of a changing sense of

---

Box 8.2 Comfort

Raymond Tallis (2016), talking about his 92- and 94-year-old parents, considers how he cannot give them "the comfort they had once given him, could not make them safe from what they feared most, as they had made him safe". Why can't you do for your parents what they did for you? He argues that it is because you can't give comfort against the approach of the end of life – it's existentially different to the comfort you can give to someone growing up because approaching death is irredeemable. You can't make it better (or at least you can't make its essence better).

---

who is a worthy recipient of the care that follows defining only some people as having social rights. But the individual encounter is also shaped by the capacity a person has to recognise the needs of another at a perceptual, a precognitive level of intuitive and tacit knowledge.[5] This way of knowing is often termed empathy.

For example, a nurse may recognise visual clues that a patient is suffering; grimacing, breathlessness and so on, but a response that combines the practical and the empathic allows the nurse to offer not only comfort for the symptoms but also reassurance for those aspects of suffering that are not easily categorised and responded to. The fear that these symptoms will recur, that they are harbingers of a future deterioration, that they have stripped away another bit of one's confidence to look after oneself can be as important as the physical challenge that has just been dealt with. The capacity of the nurse, or other health care professional, to respond to this wider world of suffering, these things that generate a need for reassurance and emotional warmth, will draw on things deeper than their training, they need to recognise this suffering, feel empathy for it and respond in a way that draws on their own reserves of sympathetic experience (Carnevale 2009), it requires the conscious engagement of one's intersubjectivity (Gadow 1980). Maya Angelou said, "I've learned that people will forget what you said, people will forget what you did, but people will never forget how you made them feel" Maya Angelou, (quoted in Riess 2017: 74).

Bunting (2020) identified the psychologist Edward Bradford Titchener as coining the word "empathy" in the early years of the Twentieth Century (2020: 66). It was "the power of projecting one's personality into, and so fully understanding, the object of contemplation". Empathy as a concept was used in aesthetics – knowing a work from the inside by feeling an emotional resonance with it – and, during the latter part of the Twentieth Century, shifted into being used to describe the way one can feel one's way into the experience of another person. Martin Buber described an empathic relationship as being characterised by "I and Thou" interaction, contrasted with unempathic disrespect in "I and It" interaction. The latter constitutes a situation of objectification and dehumanisation (Buber 1970). Buber's are distinctions that resonate with many contemporary accounts of breakdowns in hospital care (Small 2023).

After charting the development of the term "empathy", Bunting identified two key usages; how we can infer what another is feeling and what might move someone to help another who is suffering? "The first is about knowledge, the second is about ethical behaviour, and one cannot assume there is a link between the two – the skill of the torturer may lie precisely in their capacity for empathy" (Bunting 2020: 67).

These different aspects of empathy can also be categorised as cognitive empathy and emotional empathy and they prompt questions: can they be taught; can one sort make up for the absence of the other; how can you reconcile awareness of another's feelings when there may be several, possibly competing, feelings in various others involved in any situation?

The picture emerging from the research is complex: there are US studies on how empathy declines during medical training (Hojat et al. 2009; Nunes et al. 2011) and research that empathy can be taught to health care providers and that this can result in increased patient satisfaction, fewer medical errors and better clinical outcomes (Riess et al. 2012). Who we show empathy for varies, "Individuals tend to have the most empathy for others who look or act like them, for others who have suffered in a similar way, or for those who share a common goal" … "empathy is not always an equal opportunity benefactor " (Reiss 2017: 75 – see Kale et al. 2011). But there is also evidence that emphatic concern can be strong if one values the welfare of people even if they are dissimilar to you (Batson et al. 2007).

The dynamics of a team or an organisation (in a hospital for example) can engender conformity to prevailing norms and, in some cases, this wish to conform to the team can override intentions an individual staff member may have. Conforming to norms can be a positive force, for example the team can be a bulwark against

---

Box 8.3 Sincerity and sympathy

Can *sincerity* be considered the manifestation of an inner state reflected in a person's physical/verbal expression of it? Or can it be seen as a part of a manipulative repertoire learned as a means of succeeding, part of a politics of presentation (the "have a nice day" society). So, sincerity might be part of a social shift – towards acting a role, it's not deeply anchored and doesn't survive any strain experienced by the individual (see van Alphen et al. 2008).

Aneurin Bevan, founder of the NHS, was more concerned with outcome than process when he said, "I would rather be kept alive in the efficient if cold altruism of a large hospital than expire in a gush of warm *sympathy* in a small one" (quoted in Foot 1975: 131).

crass management or damaging policy initiatives. But conforming to norms, being loyal to your tribe, can also have a negative impact on one's relationship with "outsiders" or "strangers". Beleaguered teams in health care may see mutual support as necessary to self-preservation and, in this context, more important than responding to patient needs. (See Box 8.3 on an allied characteristic – sympathy.)

Looking to narrative ethics offers a route out of pitting "team" against "outsider".

> In ideal form, narrative ethics recognises the primacy of the patient's story but encourages multiple voices to be brought forth by all those whose lives will be involved in the resolution of a case. Patient, physician, family, health professional, friend, and social worker – for example, may all share their stories in a dialogical chorus that can offer the best chance of respecting all the persons involved in a case.
>
> (Hudson Jones 1998: 222)

I have introduced Bauman's identification of the importance of "caring with" above (Bauman 1993). He also highlights how the dignity of human life and the moral impulse to be "for the other" are denied by the morally ambivalent nature of social life. That social life under neoliberalism prizes autonomy and independence and adhering to this further divides the carer from the cared for, in this case the healthy from the sick. Brody reminds us that we have more in common than such distinctions would have us believe:

> we may fondly imagine that most people are whole and intact, unlike those who suffer from disease…Charity tends to assume that I start off whole and remain whole while I offer aid to the suffering. Empathy and testimony require a full awareness of my own vulnerability and radical incompleteness….
>
> (Brody 1987: 21–22)

Compassion

Webster's Third New International Dictionary (1986) defines compassion as; "Deep feeling for and understanding of misery or suffering and the concomitant desire to promote its alleviation; spiritual consciousness of the personal tragedy of another or others and selfless tenderness towards it". Philosophical consideration of compassion underlines the integral place of action within the concept – compassion requires one doing something, the expression of compassion creates a desire to act for others. As such compassion is an incentive to act for the alleviation of suffering either at the individual level or in pursuit of social justice (see Jones and Pattison 2016).

Like care and empathy, compassion is something you have and something you do. But how we feel compassion and how that compassion is expressed is shaped by the context we are in, including the precepts of our society. Some sorts of society are more conducive to compassion. Materialism and neoliberalism are not features of this sort of society, although living in such societies does not eliminate compassion (Thompson 2016). There is an influential case made that compassion is a collective endeavour; there have been initiatives seeking to develop and support compassionate communities and cities (see Kellehear 2013) (I return to this in Chapter 9).

Chaney (2021) persuasively argues that compassion is a recent arrival as an issue of central importance in nursing. For much of the last hundred years, "sympathy" was assumed to be the desired characteristic of the nurse's relationship with the patient. Sympathy does not carry with it the action imperative inherent in compassion – it can be "just" a virtue whereas compassion includes a task-oriented, performative dimension. Chaney has compassion emerging in the 1980s and 90s (the early neoliberal years) as the emotional aspects of care and relationships with patients were given more prominence in health care and as these became distinctly nurses work. Nurses were to do "patient-centred care" and secure their patient's satisfaction with care, a new imperative of the emerging consumer model of "businesses" and "customers". Only after an NHS Review in 2008 when compassion was explicitly introduced as an NHS value and a "Compassion Index for Nurses" was proposed (High Quality Care for All), did compassion begin to assume its ubiquity in nursing discourse.

However, "there is little in the nursing literature defining what compassion is" (Ledoux 2015: 2041).[6] It is assumed that nurses are compassionate, or that "Compassion is nursing's archetype" (Ledoux 2015: 2045: see Smith 2012 on the emotional labour of nursing). In this sense, it is a term not unlike the others I have been considering, culture, care and so on – a portmanteau concept – containing many desirable if undetermined meanings and being confined to very little that is specific (Jones and Pattison 2016). There is more on challenges – compassion deficit and compassion fatigue – and there is some literature critical of the belief that compassion is integral to health care. The argument here is that being a professional includes the capacity to be detached and disengaged, Smajdor (2013) says you don't need compassion to efficiently remove an appendix or empty a bedpan.[7] Indeed too close an engagement contributes to distress and burnout in some health professionals.[8] (I have quoted Bevan's preferences for efficiency over sympathy should he require hospital care above).[9] Smajdor's chosen examples might sound dubious for those who have had to use a bedpan – a bit of compassion with the efficiency would be very welcome to make this intrusive and embarrassing procedure more bearable!

Flores and Brown (2018) wonder if health scandals may be more common not in spite of but because of growing expectations of compassionate care. If the context to deliver compassionate care does not exist then compassion "risks becoming little more than a rhetorical and political device rather than a concept that can change or improve how services are delivered and experienced".

Compassion fatigue

This has been identified in the literature on nursing and in relation to other caring professions – sometimes it's seen as on a continuum, and just before, "burnout",

---

Box 8.4 Effects of compassion fatigue on nurses (see Ledoux 2015: 2043)

Anxiety, fear, sadness, grief, anger, rage, uncertainty, persistent feelings of vulnerability, feeling detached and emotionally withdrawn from patients.
   Physical and mental fatigue
   A questioning of the meaning and purpose of their lives, isolating themselves from others, difficulty concentrating and functioning in their role.

---

sometimes it's seen as a distinct entity. What is compassion fatigue? Two contrasting views highlight its complexity, it is, "...the final result of a progressive and cumulative process that is caused by prolonged, continuous and intense contact with patients, the use of self and exposure to stress" (Coetzee and Klopper 2010: 237). Or compassion fatigue results from feeling unable to give the care that was judged to be appropriate, including that which the individual themselves saw as appropriate. It is a form of "moral distress" (Austin 2009). "Perhaps it is not caring which creates nurse suffering but when care is obstructed", hence it "is associated more with a breakdown in the employer-employee relationship than with the nurse-patient relationship" (Ledoux 2015: 2045–2047). Experiencing compassion fatigue is not when you are required to do too much but when you feel yourself unable to do the things you wish to do. Here the link between compassion fatigue and the contemporary healthcare context becomes clearer.

   Compassion fatigue is manifest in a range of behaviours including decreased attention span, exhaustion, physical illness, apathy and anger. It appears in all sorts of settings, with all sorts of patients (see Box 8.4). Figley has argued (2002) that there is a "cost to caring" and that cost is born by the nurse, the patient and the healthcare organisation. There is a considerable literature on the ways compassion fatigue is made evident in nurses; and a more limited literature on its impact on patients (nurses making more errors, exhibiting poor judgement, being unable to maintain positive inter-professional relationships). Its impact on healthcare organisations is less widely researched although absenteeism, presentism (at work but not effectively engaging with it) and mistakes are all likely (Alkema et al. 2008).

Compassion and choice in neoliberalism

If compassion is an incentive to act for the alleviation of suffering either at the individual level or in pursuit of social justice, then political and social changes are likely to be relevant to how far compassion is evident in health care. The impact of neoliberalism on compassion includes the way its competitiveness encourages individualism, as we pursue wealth and status with this pursuit comes a sense that the better off are more virtuous, material success elides into moral worth. The elderly and the sick can slip into the unproductive, less worthy, category.[10]

Neoliberalism's impact also includes changes in the resources available to provide healthcare and the priorities that health care organisations adopt. In this section, I will look at the relationship between choice and compassion as an example of this link between context and behaviour.

Borgstrom (2015) and Borgstrom and Walter (2015) have highlighted "how discourses of choice and compassion became detached from each other in English End of Life Care policy discourse in the years after 2008" (Bergstrom and Walter 2015: 99). While choice and compassion can be linked, it is compassionate to give choice/ having choice increases the chances of compassionate care, they also exist in somewhat separate realms.

Choice was

> the dominant rhetoric in England's *End of Life Care Strategy* (Department of Health 2008) and in its public education offshoot *Dying Matters*; and "compassion" (or the lack thereof) was a dominant trope in scandals about the treatment of (primarily) frail, elderly people and in official responses to these scandals.
>
> (Borgstrom and Walter 2015: 99)

Borgstrom and Walter identify how, in practice, choice is subsumed by a more powerful imperative – to meet targets. Choice becomes a tick box exercise of recording that it was offered rather than involving a meaningful and considered balancing of a person's viable options.[11]

Compassion is, at first glance, more difficult to incorporate in the reductionist commodification characteristic of the neoliberal. But when commissioners of care devise "Compassion in Practice" guidance[12] we can see how it might be evident, even in this domain. Here compassion is one of the "6 Cs" that are sought alongside care, competence, communication, courage and commitment, all complex constructs requiring further sub-categorisations (Commissioning Board Chief Nursing Officer and DH Chief Nursing Adviser 2012). There is a Russian Doll feel to this sort of exposition – we seek to explain one complex term (compassion) with another, say courage, but we end up after several iterations with the banal (see the *Essence of Care* policy described above). Borgstrom and Walter offer a vivid example of the scope for commodification in compassion using the caring for / caring about comparison I have discussed above. They contrast "body work" and "presence", the former can be itemised and costed, so many minutes for a wash, for toileting etc., the latter – being with, expressing small kindnesses – the comfort of touch for example – cannot be costed, so the measurable pushes out the intangible.

Suffering

Paley (2013) argued that failures in care are not so much illustrative of a failure of compassion but a "failure to see suffering", compassion is only possible if suffering has been recognised. While responding to problems has included a focus on the need to improve individual virtues (via recruitment, training, in-work supervision) if the problem is not seeing suffering it may also be that institutional structures and processes, the nature of social cognition or the social psychology of the workplace, are important barriers to progress. As such this is an area that falls into the "culture" domain and within that the contemplation of the way modernity is manifest.

Cultural responses to suffering include two camps, the "face it" camp and the "fix it" camp. Some cultural traditions engage directly with living with suffering – the Book of Job in the Bible: Stoicism: African American Blues. Some cultural traditions are all for fixing things. In his novel *Scar Tissue* Michael Ignatieff (1993) considers what he terms "moral prometheanism" – a belief that a person's will can make them master of their fate. It is a belief that, as he puts it, "is hell on the weak" (66). It is also a belief that is widespread in modern medicine. A combination of justifiable optimism in the progress of medicine, of hubris and of self-regard – a belief that you can and should shape your life, right up to its end – contributes to some health care staff blaming some patients who they see as not trying hard enough.

> Sometimes it's good to struggle – to feel responsible for ones' reaction to the experience of illness – it might even improve our chances of survival. We need to feel that "we are adequate to our fate, that we have not been found wanting". But we must not think badly of person's who despair, who feel terror or horror at their own disintegration.
>
> (Ignatieff 1993: 170)

> Now that much illness has been conquered, stoic acceptance of biological fate is equated with fatalism. Suffer and be still no longer. The "last men" of modernity have junked the culture of endurance for the sake of a culture of complaint. They go into illness as rights bearers, as vigilant bundles of informed consent. The stoic tradition, on the other hand, did address itself to a question the culture of complaint cannot answer: when should I struggle and when should I give in?
>
> (Ignatieff 1993: 67–68).[13]

Suffering is not an infringement of your rights, nor is it necessarily about one's needs not being met, nor is it just another symptom to be relieved. While the medical management of problems that are associated with suffering, including pain and fatigue, may have an impact on these,[14] it doesn't necessarily relieve suffering. If we just think it's about meeting needs than the health professional may not be able to step back and consider what the patient experiences as suffering – it may be a sense of the loss of the life one was used to leading, it may be anomie, meaninglessness, or fear. Frank (2001: 358) said suffering is "a lived reality that resists articulation".

It may be that pointlessness closely links with suffering (Samuelson 2018). Pointless suffering is when there is no payoff, no reason – Sisyphus's punishment for his hubris is not that he must push the rock up the hill but that he knows his efforts will amount to nothing. The struggling nurse in the dysfunctional ward may experience this sort of suffering.

Dignity and values

Dignity is given different emphases across philosophical traditions and, not surprisingly, changes over time. In end-of-life care debates dignity is often used in the way that Schiller defined it, "tranquillity in suffering" (Schiller – see Rosen 2012; Gawande 2015). More negatively it might relate to freedom from humiliation or abasement (see Blackburn's review of Rosen 2012). It is integral to the good death debate (see Smith 2000) and is sometimes used alongside arguments about the importance of autonomy, for example the "Dignity in Dying" movement campaigns for more autonomy in how, where and when we die (dignityindying.org. uk). In this approach dignity is not just something that can be assaulted, lost or taken, it can also be claimed, asserted and regained. Protecting dignity should be a concern of the NHS.

In Classical philosophy dignity was associated with rank and hierarchy. It belongs to some people and is a characteristic to be aspired to. If you wish to have it, you should do what your superiors do. Aristotle's "great-souled man" had dignity. That sense of exclusivity, and of a hierarchy in possessing dignity, sits in opposition to a tradition, exemplified in Christianity, that makes dignity universal. If we are made in the image of God, we share the same status. The same sort of formulation as that seen in Christianity can be arrived at without God if we argue, as Kant does, that dignity exists in our common capacity for rational choice, or because we have an a priori capacity to confer value on things. The Enlightenment thinkers shared the belief in the universality of dignity, but here linked to man's capacity to exercise reason.

More recent positions, for example the 1948 United Nations *Universal Declaration of Human Rights*, see dignity as a birth right, we are born free and equal in dignity and we have rights that are essential for preserving our dignity. It is the role of the state to support these rights. As well as being a concern of international organisations and of states dignity also provides a focus for social movements – it is something that prompts action when it is seen as threatened and its restoration, or preservation, can be a sign of a movement's success.

But dignity exists alongside other formulations, autonomy, rights and respect for example. Some of these are attributes – we have rights and dignity, some are relational – we have respect paid to us or we are given respect, and we have autonomy *from* the encroachments of other people. Dignity also exists alongside two other ways of seeing, an embodied value system and an emphasis on the collective.[15] Perhaps, in this latter reading, attacking or denying someone's dignity is a necessary precursor to doing worse things to them. We strip someone of value and of dignity, and then we strip a whole category of people of value and dignity. Seeing the dying, especially the cognitively impaired dying, as not sharing our capacity for rationality risks casting them as less than fully human (as does seeing dignity as belonging to the great or the strong). This might be a necessary step towards the ascendancy of a mind-set that can perpetrate, or acquiesce in, the sorts of neglect and attacks on dignity evidenced by Francis and reported in the furore about the implementation of the LCP.

But why might we have allowed such a change to take place? MacIntyre, in his book *After Virtue* (1st published in 1981, 2007 3rd Ed) argues that we have cut ethics off from any sense that human life has a proper end or character. This has left ethics as a series of words with little definition and no context. It makes it easy to abandon what we once believed. This is the sort of context in which ordinary social practices can be "corrupted" by institutions that pursue goals external to the individual, money, power and status for example. The root of our problems, for MacIntyre, lies in the Enlightenment with what he sees as its project of making the individual the fundamental interpreter of moral questions. He offers participation in community life as the best defence against these perils of modernity. He is advancing the idea that we need a teleological view – we are people who come from somewhere and are going somewhere, and we best do this with others. (We can contrast this with individualist philosophy of the sort proposed by John Rawls (1971) who says that we should think of justice through a process of abstracting ourselves from who we are, making decisions on resource allocations for example without knowledge of how we would benefit from that decision.)

The challenge MacIntyre sets us also resonates with a related philosophical debate, one between consequentialists and deontologists, a debate I have touched on in this book's Introduction. Nagel (2021) contributes to this debate by considering how we evaluate different kinds of things – states of affairs or outcomes on the one hand and actions or policies on the other. To evaluate states of affairs we use concepts of good and bad, better or worse. To evaluate actions we use, in addition, the concepts of right and wrong. The key question then is when we are looking at right actions (or right policies in institutions) do we have to explain these instrumentally by asking, do they lead to good or bad outcomes? If we do then we term this approach consequentialism (its best-known version is utilitarianism). The opposite view is that right is independent of the good, this is the deontological position, "Deontological principles say that whether an act is morally permitted, prohibited or required often depends not on the goodness or badness of its overall consequences but of intrinsic features of the act itself" (Nagel 2021: 5). When we think about how we value others it is their state as autonomous independent beings that is central – they determine how we should treat a person rather than what we should want to happen to him or her. John Rawls also has a contribution to make here in his idea of reflective equilibrium. This is the process of putting one's moral thoughts in order by testing general principles against considered judgements about particular cases and adjusting both until they fit more or less comfortably together. I will return to these debates in my conclusion when I will refer to them in the context of considering a new ethics of care and how we protect the vulnerable from a consequentialism that might promote an economistic view of cost-benefit, for example enhancing the efficiency of the hospital in a way that damages the status of the patient as a member of a moral community, or unduly tipping the balance in the reflective equilibrium by the remorselessness of a dominant regime of truth promoting the importance of the market for all of us.

MacIntyre identified problems associated with the Enlightenment, but it's unruly children, industrialisation and capitalism, also break down certainties as to our place in the world and our relationship with those around us, the power of capitalism creates the situation where "all that is solid melts into air" (Marx and Engels 1952 [1848]). It is this sort of context in which apparent certainties can be dismissed from on high with a casual phrase, Prime Minister Margaret Thatcher's "there is no such thing as society"[16] is an often cited example (talking to *Women's Own* Magazine Oct 31st, 1987). In 2016, the editors of the Oxford Dictionary made "post-truth" its "international word of the year". Post-truth is an adjective relating to circumstances in which objective facts are less influential in shaping public opinion than emotional appeal. It is particularly associated with the stage of capitalism Zuboff (2019) called *Surveillance Capitalism* (see Chapter 2) and its huge internet/social media companies. It also links directly with trust in society, which I will consider in my next section.[17]

In "The Machine Stops", a 1909 short story by E M Forster, humans live in isolated pods and communicate through a vision-phone system – a son speaks to his mother via this but says "I see something like you … but I do not see you. I hear something like you…but I do not hear you". The simulacrum is no substitute for the real Other. Forster tells us, "The imponderable bloom, declared by discredited philosophy to be the actual essence of intercourse, was ignored by the machine".

Bringing us nearly up to date, Sherry Turkle has argued that technology creates a stumbling block to empathy, we are always distracted, always elsewhere (2017). She makes a plea that we need to reclaim conversation, in so doing giving one another our full attention (Turkle 2016.)

Both Forster's prescient story and Turkle's pointing to attention and empathy assume an extra resonance in the context of the Covid-19 epidemic as families kept in touch virtually or where experiences of care home residents communicating with their families through the closed windows of their care home became commonplace. They are also relevant when we consider the many speculations that, post-Covid, many of us will continue to work from home and communicated with colleagues on-line. We will indeed be elsewhere when we interact, and we need to be careful our Forsterian bloom does not fade away.

Trust

In this section, I will look at trust in the personal domain, in our relationships with those in authority and with the structures of civil society. I will argue that trust has been eroded in the two latter domains and I will present examples of specific areas in which this has occurred. I will also argue that loss of trust with authority and civil society also impacts on trust in the personal domain and I will describe this process as part of the colonisation of the lifeworld by the system world. These examples are thus linked to neoliberalism and populism and further link to a wider malaise, an erosion of the social contract.

Dimensions of trust

Trust has both cognitive and affective dimensions; these link in a complex interaction to ideas of competence and intentionality (see Calnan et al. 2020). We trust people who we are confident can do a good job, who we see as having the skills to deliver what they promise. But we also need to be confident about the intentions of those to whom we give our trust, are they able, and inclined, to work in our best interests with beneficence, fairness and integrity. The cognitive dimensions are therefore grounded in rational and instrumental judgements. But trust also has an affective dimension, there are people we feel are trustworthy. Sometimes this feeling is generated by the characteristics of the trustworthy person, their capacity to express empathy and to sustain affective bonds. Sometimes it is triggered by the category in which we place that person, it is not that long ago that we would have assumed that the police officer, the bank manager, the clergyman (it was a man in those days) and the doctor were intrinsically to be trusted.[18] We also assumed that the expertise of particular groups could be trusted if they had conformed to the protocols of their profession.

The priorities we give to the varied components of trust are circumstantial – as we go into hospital we might prioritise competence trust in the medical and nursing staff. But we also want the hospital to prioritise our safety as opposed to, say, seeking to save money by reducing spending on staff. We need to think they have our best interests at the heart of what they do. Trust also matters because it is a precursor to action, both from individuals – seeking a physician to consult about an issue or following "doctors' orders" – and collectively, trusting others will obey the rules, stay at home if they have an infection for example.

Calnan and colleagues (2020) have explored dimensions of trust in relation to the Covid-19 pandemic and expanded the sorts of trust they consider beyond that linked to competence and intentionality. Other sorts of trust include altruistic, where we curtail our own actions to help minimise damage to the more vulnerable, by wearing facemasks for example. There is also conditional trust, "I will trust you as long as you do this", follow your own rules for example. Deliberative trust sees us weighing up options via discussion and acquiescent trust is where we are ready to accept what someone else wants. These latter two might, for example, be worked out in families with different beliefs about the level of personal risk that is acceptable for each of them.

If government actions call into question their competence and integrity, and this impacts on the trust they enjoy, what happens to conditional, altruistic and deliberative trust? Are these sorts of trust part of the lifeworld and insulated from changes in levels of trust in the system world? The individualism and competitiveness of neoliberalism challenge lifeworld conceptualisations of trust and, over time, these domains can be further weakened by system world shortcomings in the competence and intentionality of government (or in experts). Trust is integral to the social contract and loss of trust is an indicator of that contract's vulnerability.

Some specifics from the Covid-19 pandemic:

- The way government contracts were allocated and the way lock-down rules were flouted by the very government that set them up call integrity and fairness into question.
- First waves of the Covid-19 pandemic disproportionately impacted on members of the black and minority ethnic community. It was also this community that appeared more reluctant to take up the offer of vaccination. This then is an example of failings in competence (and perhaps intentionality) leading to a falling off of conditional, altruistic and deliberative trust.

A generalised loss of trust

The BBC (Radio 4 29 Feb 2020) called the first ten years of this century *The Decade of Distrust*. The key events contributing to this, it was argued, included the sense that the veracity of the reasons given for the Iraq War were doubted, an MP's expenses scandals and the financial crisis of 2008. Underlying these were economic, technological and demographic changes that were challenging established relationships between the public and politicians, and more generally the public's relationship with all elites. By the second decade, this phenomenon had continued, and there was a more generalised loss of faith in institutions, including institutions beyond the government's purview.[19]

Trust is also dependent on our being confident that we are told the truth, and the second decade of the century was also characterised by the idea of a "post-truth" society (see Chapter 2). The creation of false narratives (see Ball 2017) and the confidence that politicians have when they asset the validity of them are not new phenomena but the twenty-first century has provided notably egregious examples including: an aide to President George Bush (in 2004) arguing, in effect, that reality is constructed through the exercise of power, "we create our own reality"; or President Donald Trump feeling able to assert that there are no facts only interpretations (e.g., around climate change). In the UK, the Brexit debate was characterised by a politics of assertion and avoidance. d'Ancona (2017) sees a crash in the value of truth as "comparable to the collapse of a currency or a stock". It's not that politicians have just begun to lie – that is not post-truth – it's the public's reaction to it, when they begin to see lying as the norm. The relationship between President Trump and the public capture much of this shift, it exemplifies the triumph of, "the visceral over the rational, the deceptively simple over the honestly complex".[20]

Examples of breakdowns in trust

I will examine five high-profile areas, chosen because they include key elements that I have already explored in previous sections. These elements are a focus on change in culture (and a concomitant avoidance of blaming individuals); the disproportionate impact of austerity on the already disadvantaged; the collateral damage inflicted by the pursuit of profits; and the inflicting of hurt and harm (including loss of life) on the marginalised. My examples also include the varied aspects of trust introduced above, competence and intentionality, alongside perceptions of integrity, fairness and the manifestation of fellow feeling that can foster a sense of inclusion and its opposite when people are, in effect, cast out beyond the reach of the social contract.

Politicians

Public trust in politicians was damaged by, amongst other things, the "weapons of mass destruction" announcements that preceded the invasion of Iraq in 2003 (the Chilcot Report spoke of Prime Minister Blair deliberately blurring the lines between what he believed and what he knew[21] (The Report of the Iraq Inquiry 2016)); an expenses scandal that came to light in 2009; breaches of Parliamentary rules around MP's consultancies and allied lobbying (the resignation of Owen Paterson MP in 2021 for example); and a series of examples around responses to the Covid-19 pandemic, summarised above. These are issues that address integrity and that undermine a sense of benign intentionality. They also call into question competence – both to deliver what is required and to redress shortcomings when they occur.

Banking

Public money had been used to bail out the banks after the crash of 2008 but banking failures seem to have done nothing to stop the huge salaries and bonuses of a few in the banks.[22] There have been large fines levied on some banks but, in the UK, we have not seen bankers brought before the courts (some have been in the US). The overall response to the misdeeds of the financial sector has been to locate them within a paradigm of breach of principles (the institutions not doing what they should), rather than a rule-based approach. The latter approach would allow the possibility of acting against individuals who break the rules, including prosecuting them. The breach of principal approach is similar to that in hospital and childcare scandals –people have not done the right thing, they have breached the principles of their institutions, so we have to strengthen the culture they have broken free from, rather than individuals have to take the consequences of their actions for breaching rules. (The context of a UK political culture of custom and precedent rather than a written constitution is being played out here.)

The police – Hillsborough

In 2016, an Inquest Jury found that the 96 people who died in the 1989 Hillsborough Football Stadium disaster had been unlawfully killed – the police had made mistakes and had covered these up.[23] The Chair of the National Police Chief's

Council, Sara Thornton, said these events had raised "the gravest concerns about the leadership culture in policing" and that reforms were needed to ensure such events, the events of the day and the subsequent 20 years of covering up, can never happen again (*The Guardian* 14 May 2016). One aspect of police culture she emphasised was a reluctance to admit mistakes (even when there was a considerable weight of evidence to the contrary police would give, and stick to, the most unlikely explanation to justify why they were right all along) and hence no learning from failures was possible. The police, like other public servants should consider the value of a "duty of candour".

Local government - Grenfell Tower

On Tuesday 13 June 2017, in the Royal Borough of Kensington and Chelsea, London seventy-two people died in a fire. A public inquiry was announced on the following day and was opened in September 2017. By February 2020, it had found that cladding on the outside of the building did not meet regulations and was the primary cause of the fire's rapid spread and that several companies involved in refurbishment of the Tower knew the cladding was a fire risk. Eighty-five percent of tower residents who died in the fire were from ethnic minorities. John McDonnell MP speaking at the Glastonbury Festival on 25 June 2017 (reported by the BBC www.bbc.co.uk/news/uk-politics-40401314 (accessed 26/6/2017)) said victims of the Grenfell Tower fire were "murdered by political decisions" – the decisions to view housing as only for financial speculation; to run down social housing, to cut services, to remove regulations. In 2016 the then Business Secretary Sajid Javid had introduced a "one in, three out" rule, for every regulation introduced three had to be cut. In relation to fire safety, this reduced the length of inspections from six hours to 45 minutes. We need to add to this list the pursuit of profit by the company who provided the cladding, they won the contract to wrap the Grenfell Tower in flammable cladding after rigging fire test results.

In addition, previous experience was ignored; in 2009 a fire in another tower block, Lakanal House, in Camberwell south London, killed six people. Findings from a Coroners Court, and calls from the fire service, did not result in a review of building and safety regulations. Former Chief Fire Officer Ronnie King, secretary of the All-party Parliamentary Group on Fire Safety, concluded that,

> They (government) seem to need a disaster to change regulations, rather than evidence and experience. It was the same with the Kings Cross fire and the Bradford City football club fire. They always seem to need a significant loss of life before things are changed.
>
> (*The Observer* 18 June: 1)

Austerity, and the wish to prioritise the interests of the wealthy, also played a part; an anonymous letter to *The Guardian* (17 June 2017) identified austerity policies in the Royal Borough of Kensington and Chelsea that resulted in underspending on revenue budgets so that council tax refunds could be given to the richer residents in the borough. Projected reserves by the end of 2016–17 "had climbed to a staggering £209million - that's £42m surplus to requirements. How many sprinkler systems is that?" The London Mayor Sadiq Khan added,

> residents feel neglected because they are poor… Those who mock health and safety regulations and red tape need to take a hard look at the consequences of cutting these and ask themselves whether Grenfell Tower is a price worth paying.
>
> (*The Observer* 18 June)

A participant on a radio programme titled *Grenfell: dust on our lips* said, "Before Grenfell I had always thought that somehow those in charge would look after us, I don't know if I ever voiced that – it was just what I understood. Now I don't think that" (BBC Radio 4 17 Dec 2017).

The Windrush generation: immigration law and institutional racism

Commonwealth citizens were affected by the government's 'hostile environment' legislation - a policy announced in 2012 by Home Secretary Theresa May which tasked the NHS, landlords, banks, employers and many others with enforcing immigration controls. It aimed to make the UK unliveable for undocumented migrants and ultimately push them to leave. Because many of the Windrush generation arrived as children on their parents' passports, and the Home Office destroyed thousands of landing cards and other records, many lacked the documentation to prove their right to remain in the UK. The Home Office also placed the burden of proof on individuals to prove their residency predated 1973.

In 1941, during the Second World War, George Orwell wrote, the English ruling class, "will rob, mismanage, sabotage, lead us into the muck" but in a crisis it is "morally fairly sound" (quoted in Malik 2020a: 37). The examples I have considered in this section, including banking and police issues, Grenfell, the treatment of the Windrush Generation and responses to Covid-19, as well as the concerns about shortcomings in care for many vulnerable people (explored in earlier sections) might have led Orwell to revisit his "fairly sound" judgement. David Hare did not pull his punches when he said that, taken altogether, there is, "a boneless establishment, which believes that institutional law-breaking is an oxymoron" (Hare 2015: 3).

Conclusions

In this chapter, I have explored aspects of care that may be seen as enactments of culture and that may change as culture changes. The aspects I have considered do not constitute a comprehensive review but they give insights into both the difficult terrain we are exploring and the interface between the individual and the collective that care is enacted across.

Our health service is required to respect the individual needs, and rights, of its patients but it also seeks to maximise social goods, that is to offer the greatest benefit to the greatest number. Reconciling the needs of the collective and of the individual in ways that are satisfactory to both requires trust in decision makers and in the service providers. Just reversing a culture of the primacy of financial targets or a culture that sees individuals rewarded for meeting organisational priorities is not enough. Neoliberalism has seen a hastening demise of the ethical and a shift beyond duty, this allows a disavowal of moral responsibility to be progressed. Bauman (1993) argues that we must return dignity to emotions and legitimacy to the inexplicable.[24] This is the sort of change that would resonate through all the aspects of culture I have been exploring here and would counter a narrow instrumentalism and a harsh utilitarianism.

Notes

1 The way the private is folded into the public in George Eliot in contrast to James Baldwin's sense that something sits outside politics is reminiscent of the anthropologist's sociocultural v's ideational debate – see Chapter 7.

2 They point to how the uncaring and the care-free are rewarded, even envied in the last of these categories in our present society (The Care Collective 2020). (Re uncaring – the way companies can amass profit or get organisational advancement even when poor care is provided. There are many examples – private Children's Homes making considerable profit even when they have gathered critical inspection reports, the way Mid-Staffordshire NHS Trust was awarded Foundation status – see Chapter 2 for the former and Chapter 1 for the latter example).

3 This a distinction explored by Cixous (1986) who sees the gift as a feminine realm and that of possessive, controlling care as discipline belonging to the masculine realm.

4 In Rousseau's *Second Discourse on Inequality*, he presents the history of human needs as tragedy because as man mastered nature he went on to enslave himself in the upward spiral of his own needs (Rousseau 2009, 1st published 1755).

5 David Hume (1739) sought to construct a science of man by which he could appraise the psychological basis of human nature. His argument was that it was passion and not reason that moderates human behaviour, "Sympathy is the chief source of moral distinction".

6 Around the same time as Ledoux was making this point the available literature got richer – Hewison and Sawbridge (2016) and McCaffrey and McConnell (2015) most notably.

7 There are benefits that accrue to the person who is showing compassion. Schopenhauer, for example, says the practice of compassion promises relief from the grasping ego.

8 Ricoeur (2007) said we need to "preserve distance in proximity", a possible aphorism for the caring relationship. Further, if compassion includes respect for vulnerability we should remember that no one is invulnerable.

9 There are moving stories offered by Mukherjee (2018) describing a hospital team working together with quiet precision and Clarke (2021) on the collaboration required by a Covid-19 intensive care team turning a patient. In both examples the efficiency displayed also incorporates a tender concern for the patient that belies Bevan's too simple bifurcation.

10 In Samuel Butlers' *Erehwon* (1872) the ill and the infirm were seen to be morally reprehensible and were punished for their misdeeds. In 1991, in his re-election campaign as US President, George Bush seemed to channel Samuel Butler when he talked about

individual responsibility for health and inferred the culpability of those who fail to stay well (Quillen 1991: 7 quoted in Galvin 2002: 108). In 2020 some of the same tendencies characterised President Trump's response to those who contracted Coronavirus and after his diagnosis and speedy recovery to those who remained ill with it.

11 Measuring choice – GPs to keep a record of how many patients they discussed end of life care with and how may completed paperwork stating their wishes (NEOLCIN 2013). These figures are audited locally and nationally by the NHS and the Office for National Statistics. The comparison between preferred and actual place of death is also recorded (Gomes et al. 2011). These sorts of measures are assumed to indicate the effect of increasing patent choice and the ability of the healthcare system to deliver that choice.

12 http://www.england.nhs.uk/wp-content/uploads/2012/12/compassion-in-practice.pdf.

13 John Berger in *A Fortunate Man* (Berger and Mohr 1967) writes about patients in a GP surgery, describing "their everyday bravery and tenacity" and underlining that "the notion of endurance is fundamentally more important than happiness".

14 There are many tools that are used to assess suffering (Krikorian 2013) and there are studies comparing physician or nurse assessed suffering and patient's self-assessment (Lesho et al. 2009). Relying on formalised assessment is commonplace in medical and nursing care but the complexity and the subjectivity of suffering make such tools of questionable value.

15 Rosen offers the following example: "The worst of what the Nazi state did to the Jews was not the humiliation of herding them into cattle trucks and forcing them to live in conditions of unimaginable squalor; it was to murder them" (Rosen 2012). As I wrote this paragraph I was aware of the dangers of overstating my case, "you should not shout for the mere sake of making a noise" (Shepherd 2011: xii). But I also subscribe to the sentiments of the poem "First They Came" by Pastor Martin Niemoller, it begins; "First they came for the Communists/ And I did not speak out/ Because I was not a Communist…". The poem is about what he saw as the cowardice of German intellectuals as Nazi purges continued (see www.hmd.org.uk).

16 For MacIntyre followers I think this makes Margaret Thatcher the King Kamehameha II of modern times. This was the Polynesian King who told his people to abandon long held taboos in the interests of modernising their society. The ease with which they did this provides MacIntyre with his example of the way ethics have been floating free of any grounding in the character or ends of human life (MacIntyre 2007: 112–113).

17 Are the precursors of post-truth the postmodernists? There is a danger that arguing there are no facts only interpretations (which equates with one, far from accurate, summary of the postmodern position) does lend itself to the triumph of the "reason" of the strongest. But this sort of relativism didn't begin with postmodernism, it's been an ongoing presence since the Enlightenment. It's certainly present in Nietzsche (1873): "What, then is truth? A mobile army of metaphors, metonyms, and anthropomorphisms… Truths are illusions about which one has forgotten that this is what they are" (see Ross 2019: 35). But the small narratives and contingent meanings of postmodernism (or of Heidegger's phenomenology) are not in a spectrum that also includes "fake news". Postmodernists do not deny the existence of truth or humanity – Baudrillard's deconstruction was about demanding that so-called universals be rigorously defined – protecting them from the vulnerability of inherited assumptions (for example that "human nature" defaults to western/white/male nature.)

18 There is a gender dimension to consider – the capacity to express empathy and to sustain affective bonds is often equated with women. It is an assumption that has shaped expectations about the nurses and the doctors' role (see Chapter 4). But assumptions about gender change, a belief that a child could seek aid from a woman, even if she was a stranger, was challenged by the role of Myra Hindley in the "Moors murders" of five children between 1963 and 1965 (Cummins et al. 2019). In 2021 the

conviction of Ghislaine Maxwell for grooming and trafficking children for paedophile Jeffrey Epstein revealed how her presence put the girls she targeted at ease and hence facilitated the abuse.

19 A report in 2017 on the Edelman Trust Barometer reported a global "implosion of trust" – the largest ever drop in trust in governments, businesses, non-governmental organisations, media institutions. (Edelman Trust Barometer – www.edelman.co.uk.) A 2016 Gallup Poll reported that confidence in US institutions was at near record lows – including in those once seen as the pillars of civil society, non-profits organisations, religious organisations etc.

20 Peter Oborne (2005 and 2021) talks about a rise of political lying indicating a new moral barbarism. But these are not new issues, see Hannah Arendt (1972) on the damage deception can do in the political domain – something she described as traumatic "on a towering scale".

21 Tony Blair, in a speech to the Labour Party Conference in 2004, acknowledged that the evidence that Saddam Hussain had "actual biological and chemical weapons" was wrong and further, he said, "I acknowledge and accept it" *Guardian.com* 28 Sept 2004.

22 In discussing the massive manipulation of foreign exchange markets between 2007 and 2011 US Attorney General Loretta Lynch said banks, including many of the largest, were "chasing profits without regard to fairness, to the law or to public welfare" *The Guardian* 21 May 2015.

23 The number of deaths has since gone up to 97.

24 Bauman is not talking about neoliberalism in this work – but rather about the impact of postmodernism on ethics. He sees postmodernism as offering a route to "a re-enchantment of the world" and a re-engagement with the great issues of ethics.

References

Alkema, K., Linton, J.M., Daviers, R. 2008. A study of the relationship between self-care, compassion fatigue, burnout among hospice professionals. *Journal of Social Work in End-of-Life and Palliative Care*, 4(2), 101–119.

van Alphen, E., Bal, M., Smith, C. 2009. *The Rhetoric of Sincerity. Cultural Memory in the Present*. Stanford University Press.

d'Ancona, M. 2017. *Post-Truth: The New War on Truth and How to Fight Back*. Ebury Press.

Arendt, H. 1972. *Crises of the Republic: Lying in Politics; Civil Disobedience; On Violence; Thoughts on Politics and Revolution*. Harvest Books.

Austin, W., Goble, E., Leier, B., Byrne, P. 2009. Compassion fatigue: The experience of nurses. *Ethics and Social Welfare*, 3(2), 195–214.

Baldwin, J. 1963. *The Fire Next Time*. London, Michael Joseph.

Ball, J. 2017. *Post-Truth: How Bullshit Conquered the World*. Biteback Publishing.

Bauman, Z. 1993. *Postmodern Ethics*. Oxford, Blackwell.

Batson, C.D., Eklund, J.H., Chermok, V.L., Hoyt, J.L., Ortiz, B.G. 2007. An additional antecedent of empathic concern: Valuing the welfare of the person in need. *Journal of Personality and Social Psychology*, 93, 65–74.

Beauchamp, T.L., Childress, J.F. 2019 (8th Ed). *Principles of Biomedical Ethics*. Oxford University Press.

Berger, J., Mohr, J. 1967. *A Fortunate Man*. Allen Lane.

Bond, J. 1991. *The Politics of Care Giving: The Professionalisation of Informal Care*. Paper presented at the British Sociological Association Conference, Manchester.

Borgstrom, E. 2015. Planning for an (un)certain future: Choice within English end-of-life care. *Current Sociology Monograph*, 63(5), 700–713.

Borgstrom, E., Walter, T. 2015. Choice and compassion at the end of life: A critical analysis of recent English policy discourse. *Social Science and Medicine*, 136–137, 99–105.

Brody, H. 1987. *Stories of Sickness*. New Haven, CT, Yale University Press.

Buber, M. 1970. [1923] *I and Thou*. T and T Clark, Edinburgh.

Bunting, M. 2020. *Labours of Love. The Crisis of Care*. London, Granta.

Bunting, M. 2020a. Covid shows why care is in crisis: We have crushed the humanity out of it. *The Guardian*, 15 Oct.

Butler, S. 1872. *Erewhon*. London, Trubner and Co.

Calnan, M., Williams, S.J., Gabe, J. 2020. Uncertain times: Trust matters during a pandemic. *Discover Society*, 1 June.

The Care Collective. 2020. *The Care Manifesto: The Politics of Interdependence: The Politics of Compassion*. Verso.

Carnevale, F.A. 2009. A conceptual and moral analysis of suffering. *Nursing Ethics*, 16(2), 174–183.

Chaney, S. 2021. Before compassion: Sympathy, tact and the history of the ideal nurse. *Medical Humanities*, 47, 475–484.

Cixous, H. 1986. Stories. In, Cixous, H., Clement, C. (Eds) *The Newly Born Woman*. Manchester, Manchester University Press.

Clarke, R. 2021. *Breathtaking: Inside the NHS in a Time of Pandemic*. Little Brown.

Coetzee, S.K., Klopper, H.C. 2010. Compassion fatigue within nursing practice: A concept analysis. *Nursing & Health Sciences*, 12, 235–243.

Commissioning Board Chief Nursing Officer and DH Chief Nursing Adviser. 2012. *Compassion in Practice. Nursing, Midwifery and Care Staff: Our Vision and Strategy*. London, NHS Dept of Health.

Cummins, I., Foley, M., King, M. 2019. *Serial Killers and the Media: The Moors Murders Legacy*. Palgrave, Macmillan.

Dept of Health. 2008. *End of Life Care Strategy: Promoting High Quality Care for All Adults at the End of Life*. London, Department of Health.

deSwaan, A. 1990. *The Management of Normality*. London, Routledge.

Dowling, E. 2021. *The Care Crisis: What Caused It and How Can We End It?* Verso.

Figley, C.R. 2002. *Treating Compassion Fatigue*. New York, Routledge.

Flores, R., Brown, P. 2018. The changing place of care and compassion within the English NHS: An Eliasean perspective. *Social Theory and Health*, 16, 168.

Foot, M. 1975. *Aneurin Bevan*, Vol 2 St Albans, Paladin.

Forster, E.M. [1909] 2010. *The Machine Stops*. Lits, Las Vegas.

Foucault, M. 1972. *The Archaeology of Knowledge*. New York, Vintage.

Fox, N. 1995. Postmodern perspectives on care: The vigil and the gift. *Critical Social Policy*, 44/45, Autumn, 107–125.

Frank, A. 2001. Can we research suffering? *Qualitative Health Research*, 11(3), 353–362.

Gadow, S. 1980. Body and self: A dialectic. *Journal of Medicine and Philosophy*, 5(3), 172–185.

Galvin, R. 2002. Disturbing notions of chronic illness and individual responsibility: Towards a genealogy of morals. *Health: An Interdisciplinary Journal for the Social Study and Health, Illness and Medicine*, 6(2), 107–137.

Gawande, A. 2015. *Being Mortal. Illness, Medicine and What Matters in the End*. Profile Books.

Gomes, B., Calanzani, N., Higginson, I.J. 2011. *Local Preferences and Place of Death in Regions within England 2010*. London, Cicely Saunders Institute.

Hare, D. 2015. Justice v Money. *The Guardian Review*, 31 Jan 2014, 2–3.

Hewison, A., Sawbridge, Y. 2016. *Compassion in Nursing. Theory, Evidence and Practice.* London, Palgrave Macmillan.

Hojat, M., Vergare, M.J., Maxwell, K., Brainard, G., et al. 2009. The devil is in the third year: A longitudinal study of empathy erosion in medical school. *Academic Medicine,* 84, 1182–1191.

Hudson Jones, A. 1998. Narrative in medical ethics. In, Greenhalgh, T., Hurwitz, B. (Eds) *Narrative based Medicine* (pp. 217–224). London, BMJ Books.

Hume, D. 1739. (1985) *A Treatise of Human Nature.* Penguin Classics.

Ignatieff, M. 1984. *The Needs of Strangers.* Chatto and Windus, London.

Ignatieff, M. 1993. *Scar Tissue.* Chatto and Windus.

Ignatieff, M. 2017. *The Ordinary Virtues: Moral Order in a Divided World.* Harvard University Press.

Ignatieff, M. 2022. *On Consolation: Finding Solace in Dark Times.* Picador.

Illich, I. 1995. Pathogenesis, immunity, and the quality of public health. *Qualitative Health Research,* 5(1), 7–14 (originally presented as "Against Coping" at the Second International Interdisciplinary Conference, Hershey, PA, June 1994).

James, N. 1989. 'Emotional labour': Skill and work in the social regulation of feeling. *Sociological Review,* 37, 15–42.

James, N., Field, D. 1992. The routinization of hospice: Charisma and bureaucratization. *Social Science and Medicine,* 34, 1363–1375.

Jones, J., Pattison, S. 2016. Compassion as a philosophical and theological concept. In, Hewison, A., Sawbridge, Y., op cit: 43–56.

Kale, E., Finset, A., Eikeland, H.L., Gulbrandsen, P. 2011. Emotional cues and concerns in hospital encounters with non-Western immigrants as compared with Norwegians: An exploratory study. *Patient Education and Counseling,* 84, 325–331.

Kellehear, A. 2013. Compassionate communities: End of life care as everyone's responsibility. *Quarterly Journal Medicine,* 106(12), 1071–1075.

Krikorian, A., Limonero, J.T., Corey, M.T. 2013. Suffering assessment: A review of available instruments for use in palliative care. *Journal of Palliative Medicine,* 16(2), 130–142.

Lawton, J. 2000. *The Dying Process: Patients Experience of Palliative Care.* London, Routledge.

Ledoux, K. 2015. Understanding compassion fatigue: Understanding compassion. *Journal of Advanced Nursing,* 71(9), 20141–2050.

Lesho, E. et al. 2009. The accuracy of the physicians' perception of patients' suffering: Findings from two teaching hospitals. *Academic Medicine,* 84(5), 636–642.

Lindeman Nelson, H. (Ed) 1997. *Stories and Their Limits.* New York, Routledge.

Low, J.T.S., Payne, S. 1996. The good and bad death perceptions of health professionals working in palliative care. *European Journal of Cancer Care,* 5, 237–241.

Malik, K. 2020a. Why do those in power think the rules are for others, not for them? *The Observer,* 22(11), 37.

MacIntyre, A. 1981. *After Virtue.* Notre Dame, University of Notre Dame Press. See also 3rd Edition 2007.

Marx, K., Engels. 1952 [1848]. *The Communist Manifesto.* Moscow, Progress Publishers.

Mukherjee, S. 2018. Bodies at rest and in motion. *The New Yorker,* 8 Jan, 28–35.

McCaffrey, G., McConnell, S. 2015. Compassion: A critical review of peer-reviewed nursing literature. *Journal of Clinical Nursing,* 24, 3008.

McCarthy, J. 2003. Principlism or narrative ethics: Must we choose between them? *Medical Humanities,* 29, 65–71.

McNamara, B., Waddell, C., Colvin, M. 1994. The institutionalisation of the good death. *Social Science and Medicine,* 39, 1501–1508.

Nagel, T. 2021. Types of intuition. *London Review of Books*, 3 June, 3–8.

NEOLCIN. 2013. *End of Life Care Co-ordination: Record Keeping Guidance*. London, National End of Life Care Intelligence Network.

Nietzsche, F. [1873] 2012. *On Truth and Lies in a Nonmoral Sense*. Create Space Independent Publishing.

Nunes, P., Williams, S., Stevenson, K. 2011. A study of empathy decline in students from five health disciplines during their first year of training. *International Journal Medicine Education*, 2, 12–17.

Oborne, P. 2005. *The Rise of Political Lying*. Simon Schuster.

Oborne, P. 2021. *The Assault on Truth: Boris Johnson, Donald Trump and the Emergence of a new Moral Barbarism*. Simon and Schuster.

Paley, J. 2013. Social psychology and the compassion deficit. *Nurse Education Today*, 33(12), 1451–1452.

Pilsworth, T. 1994. Dying is a normal process whether or not resulting from disease. *Journal of Cancer Care*, 3, 2–11.

Rawls, J. 1971. *A Theory of Justice*. Harvard University Press.

Report of the Iraq Inquiry. 2016. *The Chilcot Report*. Report of the Committee of Privy Counsellors. HC 264.

Ricoeur, P. 2007. *Reflections on the Just*. University of Chicago Press.

Riess, H. 2017. The science of empathy. *Journal of Patient Experience*, 4(2), 74–77.

Rosen, M. 2012. *Dignity: Its History and Meaning*. Harvard University Press.

Ross, A. 2019. The eternal return. In, *The New Yorker*, 14 Oct, 34–39.

Rousseau, J-J. 2009 (1st published 1755). *Discourse on Inequalities*. Oxford, Oxford University Press.

Samuelson, S. 2018. *Seven Ways of Looking at Pointless Suffering: What Philosophy Can Tell Us About the Hardest Mystery of All*. University of Chicago Press.

Seale, C. 1989. What happens in hospices: A review of research evidence. *Social Science and Medicine*, 28, 551–559.

Shepherd, N. 2011. *The Living Mountain* (with an introduction by R Macfarlane) Edinburgh, Canongate.

Smajdor, A. 2013. Reification and compassion in medicine: A tale of two systems. *Clinical Ethics*, 8(4), 111–118.

Small, N., Downs, M., Froggatt, K. 2006. Improving end-of-life-care for people with dementia – the benefits of combining UK approaches to palliative care and dementia care. In, Miesen, M.L., Jones, G.M.M. (Eds) *Care Giving in Dementia* (pp. 365–392). Routledge.

Small, N. 2023. *Failures in health and social care. Governance and culture change*. London, Routledge.

Smith, P. 2012. *The Emotional Labour of Nursing Revisited*. Basingstoke, Palgrave Macmillan.

Smith, R. 2000. A good death. *British Medical Journal*, 320, 129.

Tallis, R. 2016. *The Black Mirror: Fragments of an Obituary for Life*. Atlantic Books.

Thomas, C. 1993. Deconstructing concepts of care. *Sociology*, 27, 649–670.

Thompson, N. 2016. Compassion in a materialist world. In, Harris, D.L., Bordere, T.C. (Eds) *Handbook of Social Justice in Loss and Grief*. New York, Routledge, 10–49.

Turkle, S. 2016. *Reclaiming Conversation: The Power of Talk in a Digital Age*. Penguin Books.

Turkle, S. 2017. *Alone Together: Why We Expect More from Technology and Less from Each Other*. Basic Books.

Twigg, J. 2000. *Bathing: The Body and Community Care*. Routledge.

Twigg, J. 2006. *The Body in Health and Social Care*. Palgrave Macmillan.

Vernooij-Dassen, M., Leatherman, S., OldeRikkert, M. 2011. Quality of care in frail older people: The fragile balance between receiving and giving. *British Medical Journal*, 342, d403.

Zuboff, S. 2019. *The Age of Surveillance Capitalism: The Fight for a Human Future at the New Frontier of Power*. Profile Books.

Part IV
Conclusion

9 Conclusion

Introduction

The 1980s saw a paradigm shift in the way the relationship between the state, the economy and the individual was conceived. We now have had this paradigm, neoliberalism, in place for around 40 years. It valorises business and the virtues of the market and carries with it the potential to change the nature of the encounter between the individual and the state, including the welfare state, into a transactional encounter. When we think of transactional encounters in the NHS it's a small step to construe different degrees of worth in the patients being cared for, or to elevate the needs of the institution over the care of the patient. The sort of attitudinal change that accompany a shift like this takes time, new structures and new forms of reward can be introduced quickly, and some people will be enthusiastic embracers of the new market paradigm, but others will continue to practice in a context where they encounter the anomalies between what they have been trained to do, what they are currently being directed to do and what they believe to be right. They have to chart a course within a new scenario and deal with the confusion and anxiety this inevitably creates. As they experience the steady drip-drip of anomalies that they are being asked to incorporate they may find that they withdraw, leave their job or become disillusioned while remaining in it, they may embrace the new way, or they may individually, or with others, actively oppose the new paradigm.

I have examined the antecedents of neoliberalism, its assumptions and the way it is manifest in our economics and in the organisations and professions of the NHS and of the care system more broadly cast. I have considered the candidates to replace it; populism may already be doing that. But I have also argued that there are other influences on our beliefs and on our actions, these are best accessed by using governmentality, a concept linking political power, expertise and the self. According to Nikolas Rose (1999) it is governmentality that "governs the soul".

I have used two main heuristics to advance my argument. The first is a consideration of breakdowns in care. Looking at these allows funding, political priorities and organisational capabilities to be considered alongside the subjectivity of giving and receiving care. The second heuristic is an examination of culture as

DOI: 10.4324/9781003332404-13

diagnosis and as prescription. As I have argued this has become a ubiquitous trope in considering what to do when "things" go wrong. I have sought to interrogate what culture means beyond the too easy invocation of its rhetorical utility. But I have also examined aspects of the care setting and care relationship that might be considered manifestations of enacted culture.

In this concluding chapter, I will critically revisit these central issues and, to avoid the charge that this book is a jeremiad,[1] I will go further – I will suggest alternatives that can help keep the social contract intact: to protect the idea that, if we are able, we contribute and if we are in need we will be cared about and cared for.

Revisiting neoliberalism, the social contract and system world colonisation

Why neoliberalism

There were problems in the provision of care for the vulnerable before neoliberalism, but both the policy and ideological changes that have arisen from a neoliberal ascendancy have amplified previous shortcomings and introduced many new areas of challenge.[2] I have also considered if the neoliberal ascendancy is over – replaced by populist politics perhaps or by an interventionist technocratic hybrid that has arisen out of responses to Covid-19.[3] If the ascendancy is over then this book serves as a critique of its impact and a warning not to return to its orthodoxies. If it continues, populism being just the latest stage of neoliberalism, or if it lies briefly dormant to reawaken when the pandemic recedes, then we are likely to see continuing failures that are similar to the many examples, across a wide range of sectors of society, that I have summarised in this book.

It is also the reach, the resonance, of how we care for the vulnerable into our subjectivities and into our sociality that legitimises using this domain of practice as a route into understanding the impact of neoliberalism. It has been my argument that changes emanating from the economic and political sphere can change personal attitudes and behaviour and thus impact on social interaction and the underpinning social contract. Attributes like compassion and trust need to be exercised regularly; they are habits and can atrophy when not used. Conversely repeatedly being told we are individuals, autonomous agents who need targets, who deliver outputs, who get results, inhibits our seeing and paying attention to what Forster called "The imponderable bloom … the actual essence of intercourse"[4] that we need to engage with when we care for, care with and care about the vulnerable. If neoliberalism has become the heartbeat[5] of the economy and of our politics, its impact has spread into all the capillaries that make up not just the body politic but our ethical positions and the social contract we live within. That spread means that some of its practices and assumptions have become unquestioned, they are accepted as just "the way things are".

The social contract

"It takes and earthquake to make us aware that we had regarded the ground on which we stand everyday as unshakable" (Habermas 1984: 401). The crash of 2008 was something of an earthquake (re-market economics) – as was the 9/11 attack on New York and Washington (re the "end of history" and the "triumph" of liberal democracy thesis).[6] The pandemic of Covid-19 in 2020 is even more of an earthquake (re-globalisation, the capacities of science, a vulnerability as well as a strength in our sociality) and was the epitome of the risk society. Some of us, the comfortable, also underestimate the general tenor of the lives of the more vulnerable in society, people living precarious lives for whatever reason (poverty/social exclusion/oppression/chronic illness and so on) experience many earthquakes (see Popay and Williams 1996; Williams and Popay, 2013).

While we may feel the indignities, pain and deaths experienced in care failures do not constitute an earthquake, in the sense the financial crash, the 9/11 events and Covid-19 might, we should not underestimate how the personal impact of revelations about bad care is an earthquake in the life of the people experiencing it – the ground does not feel safe beneath our feet, what we thought we knew, how we thought we would be treated when we needed care, what we thought our lives would be like, undergo a seismic blow. In addition, the drip-drip of stories of neglect and of bad care and of breaches of trust in institutions in whom we had placed our faith, the NHS, social care, the police, church, politicians, local government, has an impact wider than the more visceral impact on those directly experiencing these things. That impact is on how we see our relationship to the society around us, both to its vertical structures – to those who we see as being in authority over us, or those we feel we have authority over – and to horizontal relationships, to our peers, our colleagues, our neighbours. Our sense of self, our wishes and our fears for our own futures, the futures of those we are close to, and the broader responsibilities for the needy and sick that we have when we are able and well are called into question.

Colonisation of the lifeworld

Much of my consideration of the state of care settings has been informed by the idea that the public world has colonised the private world. This is an argument I have utilised to consider how changes in the economy and in the policy discourse can have an impact on the day-to-day relationships we have with other people. It borrows Habermas's thesis that the system world colonises the lifeworld (an analysis he propounded before the ascendancy of neoliberalism in the 1980s). In presenting this argument, at the time he presented it, he highlights that all was not well before the neoliberal ascendancy. But I have hung a heavy weight of my argument on the thesis that neoliberalism has made a considerable difference to care of vulnerable groups. That difference is, in part, because it has reduced the resources available to care for the vulnerable but, in a far-reaching way, it has also accelerated and extended the inroads of the public/system world into the interactions we have with other people. Marilynne Robinson has identified a primacy of what she calls "cost-benefit analysis" or unthinking "self-interest" as something that undermines the responsibility of "the self as an intelligent moral actor" (Robinson 2017).

But a primacy of this sort of thinking doesn't mean the fight is over. Weintrobe identifies a fight between a caring and an uncaring imagination.[7] The uncaring imagination can be found in politics, in culture, in ourselves. To achieve better care, we need to stop colluding with exceptionalism, people with that mindset believe they are entitled to the lions share. They believe they can rearrange reality whenever reality limits these felt entitlements (Weintrobe 2021).

How system change shapes behaviour change

In this section of my conclusion, I am engaging, once again, with that difficult area of looking at how system change shapes behaviour change, at how economic change and damaging personal interactions in care settings can be linked. In earlier chapters, I have sought to do this by looking at aspects of culture and by utilising governmentality with its consideration of the regulation of the self. Now I want to look at each area in a more granular way.

Contested domains

Medicine and health care[8] can be depicted as the last bastions of Enlightenment thinking, they continue to be informed by a nineteenth-century idea of scientific rationalism, are seen as pursuing an idea of incremental progress and are accompanied by a default assumption that they are personally and socially beneficial (Greaves and Evans 2001). As a "last bastion" they may have enough support to resist the neoliberal assault longer than other areas. But that assault has been going on for a long time, marketisation arrived in health in the early days of neoliberalism,[9] the division between purchaser and provider in the Working for Patients reforms of 1989 was an early example, and its inroads have continued across the tenure of governments of differing political persuasions. But there has also been a rhetorical position that the NHS is sacrosanct and is to be protected (high levels of public support make an alternative stance difficult for politicians to take.) In consequence, we have seen neoliberalism advancing by stealth, austerity for example eroding the quality of care the NHS can provide, private health provision increasing outside the NHS and the growth of private sector involvement within the NHS. In care of the vulnerable, including of older people and end-of-life care, the accumulated pressures of neoliberalism shaping the space where care is provided meets an erosion of that sense of fellow feeling, of empathy, that also accompanies neoliberalism.

As well as scientific rationalism, medicine and health care also engage the ontological issues of birth, disability and death and this means it has an intimate relationship with societal norms, including those beyond rationalism.

If those social norms change so will constituent parts of the relationship, "far from being in a sequestrated compartment it (medicine) actually both reflects societal norms and simultaneously plays an important part in generating them" (Greaves and Evans 2001). Care of older people and end-of-life care then might be particularly vulnerable to the vacillations of the times because they are enacted at a point where the scientific rationalism and optimism of medicine as cure meets the ontological buffers of death and where the economist's rationality of cost-benefit accountancy to determine worth meets the intractability of long illnesses that need much help but are accompanied by deteriorating health, not by health gain.[10]

We approach health, illness, care and cure via a range of both overt and buried assumptions – invoking fate or accepting fatalism, in faith or with recourse to folklore, in the denial that this is happening to me or in a sense that this is what I should expect. We engage in magical thinking and mystical wishes. We hear, but do not always heed, evidence. We know what the advice or guidance is but don't follow it, even if we think others should so do. We think, really, we know better than the experts (and we sometimes do).[11]

The contested domains that care exist within reflect the profusion of meanings of culture and the varied way we can understand risk and compassion – areas explored in Chapters 7 and 8. For example, we might have to balance the competing risks of compromising someone's dignity or hampering our organisation meeting its targets. Table 9.1 illustrates a route whereby neoliberal domains capture contested domains and they, in turn impact on the experience of care. In Chapter 1 I identified the controversy associated with the Liverpool Care Pathway being interpreted by some as meaning that hydration should not be given to the dying. Not giving hydration to a dying patient may be in the care pathway but when this is reframed as not "giving a drink of water" it is a signifier of an older understanding of care and it sees the creation of a contested domain in which the care worker must reconcile different epistemologies. How this sort of contest is understood in the subject of my next section where I will consider the dynamic between understanding passed on through hierarchies and those that engage a different, shared, understanding of right action.

Table 9.1 Contested domains

Neoliberal domains	Contested domains	Not-neoliberal domains
Markets	Culture	Trust
Commodities	Risk	Dignity
Caring for	Compassion	Caring with/caring about
Choice		
The first column encroaches on the second →	*Changes in the second column can seep into and change domains in the third* →	

Rhizomes and molar lines

In previous chapters, I have looked at the colonisation of the lifeworld by the system world and at how considering governmentality can help understand how the self is managed. Using these tools allows us to explain how the personal changes as the political shifts, including how assumptions about proper and acceptable behaviour can change. Looking at the work of Deleuze and Guattari allows us to go into finer detail about the interactions that shape our actions. They use two terms, rhizomes and molar lines. Rhizomes are non-hierarchical and random lines of connection in unregulated relationship (like the roots of a tree). They have "mutual, lateral and circular system of ramification, rather than a dichotomous one" (Deleuze and Guattari 1987: 5). But there are also "molar lines" – these fix and normalise identities within various social institutions and do this via binaries, for example boss/worker. This level of granularity gives an insight into the micropolitics of, for example, a hospital ward. In looking at end of life care for older people Dodd et al. (2020) describe the discomfort or conflict that can result if, "the attitudes, values and needs of the patient's lifeworld [are brought] into a rule-bound and risk averse healthcare system".

In practice we might see a way of interacting that reflects staff responding to this discomfort by exhibiting characteristics that are outside their formal role expectations, they might show risk-taking and flexible practices while at the same time retaining their "insider" paid-worker roles at expert carers. Dodd et al identify this sort of hybrid role as reflecting liminality in action. End-of-life care in this context reflects the "betwixt" and "between" nature of the space between living and dying, a liminal or threshold space (Dodd et al. 2020: 350). Being able to stay in this space is an example of rhizomes in practice, but the molar lines do not disappear – the insider aspects of the staff member's role are still in place. It is possible that the molar lines will strengthen, and staff will be directed to interact in ways that reflect the needs of their employing institution, for example by becoming more rules bound.

Further, rhizomes are susceptible to pressure, Best and Kellner describe how their non-hierarchical and random natures can be changed over time; "They only become organized as unities, foundations and hierarchies by dominant sociolinguistic powers, tyrannical signifiers, political despots, the authorities of the normalizing institutions, or a host of micro practices of everyday life" (Best and Kellner 1991: 101). The changes consequent upon the neoliberal ascendancy do include a shift in the dominant social signifiers, in the tenor of normalising institutions and in the visibility of a new sociolinguistic orthodoxy, and so they are likely to impact on micro-practices, including in care settings. As the rhizome changes the molar lines become more influential in shaping how comfortable the staff member is in staying with the patient in their liminality or in reverting to the insider identity of expert, of definer of needs.

System world and life worlds – the reeling present

Looking at contested domains moves us beyond the reform of institutions and practices in health care and into an engagement with the force of realising how far what goes on is from our sense of what ought to go on. We experience the weight of that force when we hear of neglect and cruelties, and we experience it even more viscerally when we encounter it personally, it can set us reeling in its wake.

This book is set in the UK, in the main in the years 2012–22. It seeks to capture;

> a present that began some time ago. But it suggests that the terms neoliberalism, advanced capitalism, and globalization that index this emergent present, and the five or seven or ten characteristics used to summarize and define it in shorthand, do not, in themselves, begin to describe the situation we find ourselves in. The notion of a totalized system, of which everything is always already somehow a part, is not helpful (to say the least) in the effort to approach a weighted and reeling present. This is not to say that the forces these systems try to name are not real and literally pressing. On the contrary, I am trying to bring them into view as a scene of immanent force, rather than leave them looking like dead effects imposed on an innocent world.
>
> (Stewart 2007: 1)

Stewart wants us to demystify and uncover truths that support a well-known picture of the world but also to speculate, "about the forces that come into view as habit or shock, resonance or impact. Something throws itself together in a moment as an event and a sensation; a something both animated and inhabitable". "The ordinary is a shifting assemblage of practices and practical knowledges, a scene of both liveness and exhaustion…" (Stewart 2007: 1).

These sorts of structures do not work through "meanings", rather,

> they pick up density and texture as they move through bodies, dreams, dramas and social worldings of all kinds. Their significance lies in the intensities they build and in what thoughts and feelings they make possible.[12] The question they beg is…..where they might go and what potential modes of knowing, relating, and attending to things are already somehow present in them in a state of potentiality and resonance.
>
> (Stewart 2007: 3)

To look at ordinary affects is to trace how the potency of forces lies in their immanence to things in our lives that can be fixed or can be unsteady, that can be multiplicious and unpredictable … "arguments about 'bigger' structures and underlying causes obscure the ways in which a reeling present is composed out of heterogeneous and noncoherent singularities" (Stewart 2007: 4). "Someone's ordinary … can shift in the face of events. It can become a vague but compelling sense that something is happening or can harden into little mythic kernels" (Stewart 2007: 4).

If the weighted and reeling present is not part of a totalised system, then culture may not be the best term to capture the context of the forces that are in play. "Structures of feeling" may be a better term, and one not as loaded with complexity or with historical baggage as "culture" (Williams 1958). Raymond Williams described structures of feeling as those distinctive characteristics that define each era and which are less to do with specific objects than general moods they are "social experiences in solution" they "do not have to await definition, classification, or rationalization before they exert palpable pressures" (Williams 1977: 132–133).

I will consider two domains in which structures of feeling and the reeling present are likely to be manifest, one is concerned with the body and the other with how the reeling present is collectively/publicly manifest.

Embodied feeling

Many of the concerns considered in this book are about care of the body. Merleau-Ponty (1945) writes that "knowledge is 'felt': that our bodies think and know in ways that precede cognition". "The body 'incarnates' our subjectivity and we are thus…. 'embedded' in the 'flesh' of the world". The world is

> not the unchanging object presented by the natural sciences, but instead endlessly relational. It is made manifest only by presenting itself to a variety of views, and our perception of it is made possible by our bodies and their sensory-motor functions.

In our hospitals and care homes bodies exist in relationship to place in important ways, "Place and mind may interpenetrate until the nature of both are altered" (Macfarlane in Shepherd 2011: xxix–xxx).

The hyperreal and the spectacle

Our reeling, and relational, present is also engaged with a more collective experience of what we expect from the world around us and how we experience and act with others. When we encounter the health service in our personal lives a public focus on crisis and dramatic error with major consequences, such as that surrounding Mid-Staffordshire, the Liverpool Care Pathway and Shrewsbury and Telford (see Chapter 1), creates a dissonance that enters into our relationship with the institution of the NHS. This dissonance between a public discourse of an institution in crisis and surveys that report high levels of satisfaction with its service suggest that, when we talk about the NHS, we are not only considering its empirical present but are also speaking from a representation of what we think/ wish the NHS is.[13] This wish is anchored in a strong legacy of positivity and a default position that the NHS is wonderful, with just some glaring aberrations. While some of these aberrations are attached to specific clinicians (Dr Shipman most notoriously)[14] they are not generalised to doctors and nurses or to the principles of the institution in general.

But, while these personal dissonances play out, there is a broader public discourse. The press and politicians arguing about the present service provided by

Table 9.2 Dissonance, the hyperreal and spectacle in the Covid-19 pandemic

---
Valorisation of NHS staff as heroes, weekly clapping for example and yet hostility to some staff as potential "virus spreaders"

Expectations about the idea of vaccination "ending" the epidemic but at the same time much anti-vaccination sentiment and conspiracy theories attached to hospitals and treatments.

---

the NHS and about its future create a simulacrum, a representation or imitation of the service that becomes a truth in its own right. Sometimes the dissonance manifests as a bifurcation between a sense that we expect the worst, that is we are pleased if we don't have to wait four hours in Accident and Emergency or if we have an operation scheduled within a few months of referral, sometimes the dissonance is captured in a prevailing construct that "the staff are wonderful", that it's an aberration if our personal experience is that they are not civil or caring.

The Covid-19 epidemic has created a number of representations that are beset by such dissonances, for example hospital as a place of heroic struggle but also as somewhere that needs our protection – this morphs in public perceptions into "don't go even if you have (non-Covid) health concerns because it's dangerous". So, cancers don't get treated and heart attacks don't get reported (Table 9.2).

But Covid-19 has also brought to the fore something best captured by Baudrillard's description of a simulacrum, not a copy of the real but something that becomes a truth in its own right. The simulacrum is approached in stages, through the hyperreal (Baudrillard 1993). The hyperreal is a place characterised by different types of distortions leading up to a simulacrum – a basic reflection of reality, a perversion of reality, a pretence of reality and a simulacrum[15] that bears no resemblance to reality – an image without the substance or qualities of the original.

- On 3rd March 2020, the Prime Minister Boris Johnson told a press briefing that Britain was "extremely well-prepared" for an outbreak of Covid-19.
- The Prime Minister appeared on the ITV's *This Morning* to advocate a "strategy of 'take it on the chin' herd immunity".
- Early in the Covid-19 pandemic Nigel Hunt MP, a former Secretary of State for Health, said that if he had to contract the virus there is no place better to be than in the UK with its NHS.

  Just a few months later the UK (and England in particular) had the highest infection and death rates (per head of the population) in the world – with the possible exception of Belgium).[16]
- On December 3rd, 2020, Gavin Williamson (Secretary of State for Education) told LBC Radio that the UK got a coronavirus vaccine first because it is a "much better country" than France, Belgium and the US.
- A rhetorical presentation of the UK as "world-leading" in, for example, "track and trace" processes evokes echoes of Orwellian "Newspeak" in its ignoring the achievements of, for example, Pacific rim countries.

These are examples of the sorts of hubris and exceptionalism that are often invoked in discussions about the NHS and which stops the sort of useful criticisms of a service that would serve to improve it. When the claims of exceptionalism do not live up to the achievement being claimed we see a break-down in trust.

Further, the proliferation of media attention on hospital faults and on other areas of the breakdown of care, and the febrile atmosphere regarding other transgressions on a previously assumed sense of decency (sexual exploitation of the vulnerable by the powerful for example), produces what Debord (1995) calls "The Society of the Spectacle" in which authentic social life has been replaced with its representation.[17] Thus, he says, "All that once was directly lived has become mere representation". He itemises the changes he believes to have occurred via a series of theses, one and four are most pertinent here: (thesis 1) "passive identification with the spectacle supplants genuine activity"; (thesis 4) – this explains how we can watch but not act even if we pride this service and think it belongs to us. The spectacle obfuscates the past, implodes it with the future into a never-ending present and, in so doing, degrades knowledge and critical thought. For Debord presentation, politicisation and dramatisation of the spectacle insidiously penetrates the psyches of its subjects and exercises an unprecedented sway over public opinion.[18] Saying all is crisis, or the alternative trope that all is wonderful, degrades both intellectual and experienced knowledge. It also makes everything "present" – you can't see how the now links to the past, and you can't see how we can plan for the future. People see the spectacle as real even if it not what they experience.

There is a sense of the now, for example of "pandemic time", being time out of history.[19] This "special time" is one that we will come out of into a return to normal, or a fantasy construction of a new normal. The similarity of the pandemic with events in the past, or the continuity of problems evident before and then through the pandemic disappear from the discourse. There is even very little critical scrutiny of the dropping of existing policies and adoption of new policies, sometimes on a day-by-day schedule, and the retort that policy choice is "led by the science" is ever present, with no space for the deconstruction of a phrase that makes a monolith of certainty out of a complex and contested "science" and leaves the construct of being "led" unproblematised (see Box 9.1).

In Chapter 2, I looked at populism and, as part of that, at distrust of experts and the development of a self-serving cant of categorising what one does not wish to hear in the public domain as "fake news". This is a rhetorical position that can sit aside simulacrum and spectacle. Decrying the objectivity of established media and the truth claims of experts and, as an alternative, simply declaiming a particular belief is a manifestation of power politics not necessarily an example of neoliberalism, nor is it a result of a proliferation of media, nor is it new. The rise of radio as a means of communicating news was decried by newspapers who saw the interloper as irresponsible and needing guidance from its older more established siblings in the print media. Unrestrained radio was portrayed in the print media

---

Box 9.1: Transparency and trust – Covid-19

Nobel Lauriat Prof Paul Nurse, the former president of the Royal Society and a chief scientific advisor to the European Commission, said: "Decisions are too often shrouded in secrecy. They need challenge and we need processes to ensure that happens. If they are going to keep the trust of the nation, they need to make those discussions more public". ….. "It sometimes seems like a 'black box' made up of scientists, civil servants and politicians are coming up with the decisions". Nurse added, "It needs to be more open. We need greater transparency, greater scrutiny and greater challenge to get the best results".

James Wilsdon, Professor of Research Policy at the University of Sheffield, said that: "While it may have been politically and presentationally convenient, the unprecedented public prominence given to Vallance and Whitty was storing up problems, as and when the lines between scientific evidence, advice and decision-making became more blurry and contested", Wilsdon said, "I don't think Vallance should ever have allowed himself and Sage[20] to be used in this way, or for 'the science', as embodied by Sage, to be presented in such a singular, monolithic way" (*The Guardian* 3 August 2020).

---

as one of the most dangerous elements in modern culture and there were many supporting examples as authoritarian leaders and demagogues turned to the radio to, as they saw it, communicate directly with the people. The same arguments are voiced today in relation to social media (Schwartz 2016; Carey 2017). Chen describing how "Trump used Twitter less as a communication device than as a weapon of information warfare" (2017: 78). This argument from Eliot Freidson, made over 50 years ago, reminds us that the process of decrying expertise is not new, even if the specific technology of choice is.

> In our day we seem to be turning away from an uncritical optimism about the role of specialized knowledge in ordering human affairs. We have not yet arrived at a satisfactory new position, however, and in the meantime, we are treated to despairing violence and self-defeating anti-intellectualism on the part of laymen and their champions, self-interested elitism on the part of the intellectual classes, and downright authoritarianism on the part of even those political leaders with humanitarian intentions.
>
> (Freidson 1970: xi)

The hyperreal, the spectacle and the contested domains of our reeling present play out in our relationships with others and our perception of the trust we have in hierarchies. Trust and its concomitant Truth are undermined, and with them the vigour, even the relevance, of our social contract. In the UK, as the centrality of the Covid-19 pandemic disappeared, our politics were dominated by questions of truth and trust, personified in the actions of our then Prime Minister Boris Johnson. His resignation as leader of the Conservative Party in July 2022 was linked to both his rule breaking over social distancing during the Covid-19 pandemic and to issues of trust and truth around the lobbying activities of one of his MPs and his responses to sexual impropriety on the part of another. In Chapter 2, I quoted Donald Rumsfeld on "known knowns, known unknowns and unknown unknowns". But Žižek has added a fourth category, the unknown known, "that which one intentionally refuses to acknowledge that one knows" "the disavowed beliefs, suppositions and obscene practices we pretend not to know about, even though they form the background of our public values". By the summer of 2022, we were experiencing Žižek's fourth category as the everyday in our politics. I will explore this further in my next section.

The many and the one

I have looked at structure and process issues and linked these with changes in economic and political practice and I have asked how the lifeworld can be protected. As part of the protecting the lifeworld, I have looked at governmentality and have argued that we are unable to fully perceive the hidden workings of social practice that we are part of perpetuating. But, throughout, I have been clear that individual agency and hence culpability remains and that is why the more granular analysis of patterns of domination and resistance, described above, become of key importance. While we are, in many cases, not conscious of the subjugation we commit against ourselves and others simply by being what we have been inculcated to be there are also situations where we do make choices and those choices have deleterious effects (or in some cases positive effects) on others. Non-conscious subjugation facilitates symbolic violence that enables the arbitrary domination of some by others (Schubert 2013),[21] but conscious subjugation can manifest actual violence, as we have seen in some of the distressing details reported in Stafford and elsewhere (see Chapter 1).

Deciding what is to be done to address symbolic and actual violence involves considering individual actions, governmentality and the scope for resistance. It means developing means of preserving or enhancing the integrity and independence of the lifeworld so that it can combat encroachments or changing the system world so that these encroachments do not occur, or that they are more benign. System world changes may be needed on a macro scale or they may be best engaged on a smaller scale within institutions or within workplaces. My consideration (Chapters 7 and 8) of more complex readings about culture come into play here, including the potential of considering structures of feeling. In this next section, I will consider individual, system and lifeworld changes. I will look first at some approaches to synthesise a concern with the many and with the one. We need to think sociologically about, "The dynamics between numerated and narrated selves in what are intensified, yet abstracted forces that inform our everyday lives and sense of ourselves and others…" (May 2018). This will lead me into looking at a new ethics and at new politics.

Changing the system world and protecting the lifeworld involves engaging with different assumptions evident in the system world. One is a "breach of principles approach". This locates the focus of concern on institutions not doing what they should. An alternative assumption is a rules-based approach which leans more to seeking change or redress by acting against individuals who break the rules, including by disciplining them or even prosecuting them. I have examined a prevalent idea that when people have not done the right thing they have breached the principles of their institutions, so we have to strengthen the culture they have broken free from. More rarely the approach is that individuals have broken the rules of their organisation and have to take the consequences of their actions.

The breach of principles approach assumes that there is a residual, normative, organisational principal that a person has deviated from and that they can be returned to. But an organisation, including a healthcare organisation, will encompass different organisational principles and an action that is consistent with one, contributing to meeting financial targets for example, may conflict with another, spending more time with a patient or undertaking a broader range of tasks with and for them than your allocated time permits to meet the needs they have that you consider, in the specifics of the moment, to be valid. A rules-based approach has to consider the position of the individual as moral actor within the institution. Just as there are different organisation principles within a single organisation, there may also be different narratives of morality within a life that an individual has to negotiate circumstantially.[22]

MacIntyre would have it that normative morality is invested in a narrative unity of a life; Foucault is clear that there is no such unity (Table 9.3).

In Chapter 8 I discussed the differences between principlist and narrative ethics by asking, "are principles or communication at the heart of moral life?" McCarthy argues that each approach can complement the other – both can be brought to bear on a situation if both are mediated by what he calls a "moral imagination". He also considers if a communicative ethic can unite the two (McCarthy 2003: 70). But if communicative competence is compromised, as Habermas has explored (see Chapter 6), a narrativist approach will not be able to share its access to a moral imagination with a principlist one.[23]

Table 9.3 On narrative unity

MacIntyre 1981	Foucault 1994
The moral acceptability of any choice can be measured in terms of its consistency with the narrative unity of an individuals' life and in terms of its coherence with the conceptions of the morally good life embedded in the community in which the person lives.	The cycle of a human life is characterised by fragmentation, not unity. There is not a single authoritative reading. Nor is there a single tradition within which they live.

But it is not just compromised communicative competence that hinders the narrativist voice it is also the breakdown of the assumption of there being a narrative unity in an individuals' life or an embedded idea of the morally good life in any community. While a principlist position may be reliant on the exercise of a set of skills that can be brought to bear on any situation; conceptual, analytic, deductive, critical and reflective skills, and while these might be timeless the identification of general norms these skills are interrogating is not something embedded in the sense that it is timeless (or even long running), it reflects contemporary power configurations, currently neoliberal configurations.

MacIntyre's observations about narrative unity come from pre-neoliberal days (1981) Bauman has argued that a young person today would not recognise the idea of narrative unity, they are unlikely to see themselves as having a "life project". There is also no coherent conception of the morally good life that includes all sections of a community (Bauman 2000). Precarious job markets, multiple routes to access information, geographic mobility and a politics of identity all contribute, and while these factors haven't been unique to neoliberalism their coming together under neoliberalism contributes to the "liquid modern" that Bauman identifies. There are also fault-lines in society, the resilient ones of class, ethnicity and gender and a heightened awareness of differences according to geography and age. Foucault's picture of a fragmented life, and no single tradition to live within, seems even closer to the contemporary experience of the young than it did to the experience of the baby-boomer generation of young people when he was writing in the 1970s (or even to Bauman's young people of the turn of the twenty-first century).[24]

Neoliberalism might change the moral conceptions of sections of the community, it will certainly privilege some voices in that community over others. Homo oeconomicus is unlikely to exhibit narrative unity with his (sic) predecessors or share conceptions of what is a morally good life with those not signed up to the neoliberal project. The fall of public man and the culture of narcissism (as described by, respectively, Sennett and Lasch and summarised in Chapter 6) further degrades the idea of their being shared narratives as to the nature of the morally good.

Preserving the lifeworld from the system world or trying to reform bad practice by invoking culture (specifically a culture drawn from the lifeworld or from any other system world reading of culture out-with the compromised institutional culture that is the problem) is problematic in neoliberalism. The lifeworld may no longer be the repository of the shared values that we develop over time within our families and communities, the sorts of understandings that are rarely explicitly voiced, that we take them for granted, that are part of what make us who we are. If shared values have changed (or faded away) then the lifeworld might be the problem. If lifeworld conceptions are critical/harsh/marginalising, then you need principlist (or rule-based) underpinnings of moral choice.[25] Narrativists might be bad news in harsh times![26]

Cognitive psychology offers a different view of the same scenarios that I have explored using the lifeworld and system world distinction. We interpret events within frames of reference, but in an organisation like a hospital there may be different frames – a managerial frame might be system focussed and within that, the greatest risk we see is not meeting a system priority – falling down league tables or not achieving foundation trust status for example. The risk of regulatory sanction, or what Newdick and Danbury call "the terror of targets" (2015: 960), heightens organisational concerns and can push out the everyday sense of what should be done, managerial imperatives become more important than patient care. In this situation, clinicians experience a sense of cognitive dissonance, and some resolve that by sacrificing the patient in the interests of the organisation. One clinician told the first Francis inquiry into failures at Mid-Staffordshire Hospital,

> If you are in that environment long enough, what happens is that you become immune to the sound of pain…You cannot feel people's pain, you cannot continue to want to do the best you possibly can when the system says no to you.…
>
> (Francis 2010: 120)

Not all clinicians respond to such dissonance in the same way but when a team who work together to deliver care respond in the same way the result can be disastrous for patients.

The lifeworld/system world scenario also resonates with the debate about consequentialist and deontological positions in identifying the morally desirable and the morally permitted that I referred to in Chapters 1 and 8. I will return to this in my next section.

Ethics, economics and politics

In this section, I will look at ethics, economics and politics and how they can contribute to addressing the deleterious impacts of neoliberalism. George Steiner uses a metaphor of being cast adrift in a small boat in situations of uncertainty and conflict. He says that you really need ballast, it's alright when the sea is flat and the wind is fair but when we are at the mercy of the high seas and the winds, unable to steer and in danger of not keeping afloat, you need a bit of weight to keep you steady and safe (Steiner 1997). Neoliberalism makes the sea stormy and the winds strong and blowing in the face of the poor (although on the backs of the rich)[27] it also takes away many of the certainties of the past, replacing them with a narrow economism and an impoverished sense of one's responsibilities to and for others. My suggestions are designed to add ballast – but also to say that we are not condemned to live perpetually with stormy seas and strong winds.

New ethics (or returning to old ethics)

In this section, I will first return to the consequentialist position I have discussed previously and I will then look more specifically at redressing inequality. Consequentialism is manifest in neoliberalism in part through elevating the instrumental furthering of the market which – it is argued – is to the greatest good of all. It creates wealth which then trickles down, and it maximises the best use of available resources and so benefits more people (the utilitarian position.) These claims may be objectively untrue – trickle down does not happen and markets distort resource use and enhance inequalities – but they still impact on the assumptions of ordinary morality, upsetting what Rawls called "the reflective equilibrium" (Rawls 1971).

When we think about how we value others it is their state as autonomous independent beings that is central. This determines how we should treat a person rather than what we think they should be or do (e.g. that they should be economically independent and that they should be valued for their success in the market economy).

> Treating each of them decently come what may, and demanding such treatment for ourselves, is a vital part of our lives. Most important, it is a distinctive way of thinking about how to relate to one another, the source of our constantly developing interpretations of people's equality of status as the bearer of human rights. Without it the advantages of membership in the moral community would be seriously diminished….
>
> (Nagel 2021: 8)[28]

I have argued that the moral community, and the social contract, is distorted by the primacy of market economics, by the configurations of social power that accompany it and by the impact of these two on the psychological, manifest in the ascendancy of the Foucauldian homo oeconomicus who has incorporated the consequentialist position favoured by the powerful.

The ordinary morality that Nagel explores is manifest in the importance of the human rights of all. As well as defending the moral community a concern with human rights requires us to seek to redress the inequality that spins people off from that part of the social contract that says all will be treated equally. In addressing inequality Rawls proposed an individualist approach while Habermas seeks a solution that starts with the idea of the universal.

- Basic principles of Anglo-American liberalism were re-examined by John Rawls (1971). I have discussed this in Chapter 2 but here want to focus on his argument that freedom and equality can be reconciled in a consensual vision that all members of society can sign up to such that we should all agree to share one another's fate. To do this you have to reconcile political liberalism, with its defence of the rule of law and the protection of formal rights, with social liberalism which is concerned with questions of equality, inclusion and social justice. Rawls offered a thought experiment, the "original position" where people meet to decide the principles of justice for their society. When they meet no one knows anything about themselves in terms of their class position, social status or even their assets and abilities. He believed, in this position, people would want two things; extensive and equal basic liberties and, second, that social and economic inequalities should be managed to the greatest benefit of the disadvantaged.[29] This is essentially an individualistic rational choice approach, a way of achieving consensus through neutrality.

• Habermas, in contrast, sought a route to socialise Kant's individualistic moral theory. His "principle of universalization" holds that every valid norm has to fulfil the following condition: "*all* affected can accept the consequences and the side effects its *general* observance can be anticipated to have for the satisfaction of *everyone's* interests (and these consequences are preferred to those of known alternative possibilities for regulation)" (Habermas 1990: 65 *original emphasis*: see also Scambler 2001: 15).

Sharing one another's individual fate and doing this while adhering to a principle of universalisation would offer us an ethics that could incorporate the needs of the other person and the importance of maintaining the collective via a social contract. Bauman has added to this focus on the individual and the social in his "postmodern ethics" where the starting point shifts to the importance of action: "Being for the Other before being with the Other is the first reality of the self, a starting point rather than a product of society" (Bauman 1993: 13).[30]

Different economics

We need to challenge the foundational assumptions of neoliberalism and we need different models to put in its place.

Against foundational assumptions

The neoliberal order has foundational assumptions (e.g. that you can only do what the market will tolerate) that need to be challenged with questions like "what makes a good society?" These sorts of questions do not assume a legitimacy for the epistemology of neoliberalism (or capitalism). Neoliberalism has reworked the common-sense assumptions of the preceding social democracy – that is what new settlements do, it's what Gramsci (1971) called hegemonic, and others have explored as "the doxa". Doxa is the self-evident, it provides rules of what is and is not possible:

> Every social settlement, in order to establish itself, is crucially founded on embedding as common sense a whole bundle of beliefs – ideas beyond question, assumption so deep that the very idea that they are assumptions is only rarely brought to light. . . . (these have) enrolled whole populations materially and imaginatively into a financialised and marketized view of the world ...
> (Hall et al. 2013: 9).[31]

It is a view of the world that sees its social and political settlement promoting the idea that "The market has become the model of social relations, exchange value the only value" (Hall et al. 2013: 4). One consequence is that "private capital has hollowed-out the welfare state and dismantle(d) the structures of health, welfare and education services" (Hall et al. 2013: 4).

In the 2020 Reith Lectures Mark Carney, recently departed Governor of the Bank of England, specifically links foundational assumptions of neoliberalism (which he calls a "Market society") with an erosion of the social contract. He argues that the expansion of the market is changing the underlying social contract on which it has been based. The emphasis on the individual over the community, on our selfish traits over our altruistic ones, imperils society's values. Carney asks, "In short, in moving from a market economy to a market society, are we consuming the social capital necessary to create economic and human capital?" (Carney 2020 see also Carney 2021) Civic virtue and public spirit atrophy with disuse (and) would grow like muscles with regular exercise. As Aristotle observed, virtue is something we cultivate with practice, we become just by doing just acts, temperate by doing temperate acts, brave by doing brave acts. Do we also become callous by doing callous acts and cruel by doing cruel acts?

Different models

Economic orthodoxies come and go, neoliberalism succeeded a well-established Keynesian orthodoxy,[32] and there have been periods within the neoliberal ascendancy when spending policy has differed significantly, for example in 2001–09 inflation-adjusted spending on health increased by 75% and the huge expansion of UK government spending accompanying the Covid-19 pandemic in 2020/22 constituted a significant shift in economic approach.[33]

"Markets are living institutions embedded in the culture, practice, and tradition and trust of their day" (Carney 2020). They are not some kinds of celestial creation, rather they are a set of rules that can be rewritten (Mazzucato 2020). If you change moral sentiments into market sentiments, which is what neoliberalism does, then society's values become equated with financial value. The subjectivism of neo-classical economics attributes value to consumers views and this implies that price equates to value and anything not priced is not valuable (mental and physical health, human relationships, community, dignity and the general social climate aren't priced). We can critique this idea of value, Mazzucato's argument that value creation needs to be rewarded over value extraction is key here (see Mazzucato 2019), we can look at market economics and its damaging impact on poorer sections of the community (Case and Deaton 2020) and on the way that it has historically provided wealth for some alongside increasing inequality (Deaton 2015), or we can reassert moral sentiments in place of market sentiments. Carney (2020) reminds us that moral sentiments have a long tradition in economics (see Rogan 2018) – from Adam Smith in his second most famous book "The Theory of Moral Sentiments" first published in 1759 (see Mannion and Small 1999) and including Tawney (1920, 1926, 1931) looking at the importance of an economics founded on ethics and, more recently, Karl Polanyi on the limits of markets (1944, see Dale 2010) and Amartya Sen (1970) who would have us evaluate economic policy in terms of its effects on the well-being of the community. Even more recently, and over a sustained period, Hutton has argued for a model where there is more emphasis on social cohesion, citizenship, the mixed-economy and investment rather than the low-tax, low-wage minimal welfare state variant of capitalism. Hutton is proposing (celebrating) "inclusion, commitment, stakeholding, citizenship, the public-good, cooperation" (Hutton 1996: 338–343).

Linking a questioning of foundational assumptions with a different model of how we use resources in an economy Kelton (2020) says that the crucial question is not "how can we afford to pay for the crucial improvements our society needs", but "how do we balance risks against the benefits of a society that is more broadly prosperous, safer, cleaner, and secure?" We need to use the resources we have available to maximise our potential as a society. Everything that we've been led to believe about deficits and the role of money and government spending in the economy is wrong, she argues, especially the fear that deficits will endanger our long-term prosperity. We can think differently about the significance of inflation, about the economic need for austerity and about setting narrow targets that reflect market needs and not social needs. As Raworth has argued (2018) economics is broken, its assumptions about equilibrium, its idea of the rational economic man, its preoccupation with a particular view of growth and its idea that markets need to be left alone all fail in either understanding the present or planning the future. She argues to meet the needs of all and the needs of the planet Economics must be distributive and regenerative.

Mazzucato, in addition to her insights about value, has looked at the role of the state in creating wealth (2014) and, more generally, at how the state can take the lead in engaging with the great challenges of the twenty-first century by taking risks in such a way as to shape markets to emphasise public interest not private gain and to shift from a narrow focus on economic benefit (2020).[34] Hers is a recipe for changing capitalism and, as such, it moves us on from new economics to a new politics. Not all these new politics want to save capitalism from the excess of its economist, atomistic assumptions, they don't want to repair they want to replace.

New politics

Monbiot (2017) says that neoliberalism is best understood as a story – one that was on offer at the moment the previous story of Keynesianism fell to pieces in the mid-1970s. Stories are powerful because they give us, "the means by which we navigate the world. They allow us to interpret its complex and contradictory signals". The particular story of neoliberalism "defines us as competitors, guided above all other impulses by the urge to get ahead of our fellows". Via Thatcher and Reagan, it governed how policies were designed and institutions constructed (or reformed). More diffusely it came "to shape how we understand ourselves, leading us to take on even more responsibility for our own needs, economic security and wellbeing devaluing social bonds and dependency in the process".

One response to this story of neoliberalism is not just to tell a different story but to instigate a social state to protect its members from the morally devastating competitive "war of all against all" (Bauman 2007: 13).[35] Having a state offering collective insurance against individual misfortune

> lifts abstract 'society' to the level of a felt-and-lived community. It replaces the mistrust and suspicion-generating 'order of egoism' (to deploy John Dunn's terms) with the confidence and solidarity-inspiring 'order of equality' (see Dunn 1993). Individuals become citizens, stakeholders as well as stockholders.
>
> (Bauman 2007: 13–14)

That sense of community can protect "against the terrors of falling, or being pushed, overboard from the fast-accelerating vehicle for progress it offers defence against condemnation to 'social redundancy' or consignment to 'human waste'". "Just as the carrying capacity of a bridge is measured by the strength of its weakest support, so the quality of a society should be measured by the quality of life of its weakest members" (Bauman 2007: 9) "If political rights are necessary to set social rights in place, social rights are indispensable to keep political rights in operation" (Bauman 2007: 14).

Identity politics

If we need a left hook to effect a decisive blow for change the capacity to deliver this has been weakened, some argue, by a rise in identity politics. Lilla (2018) sees the malaise of the left as a product of the new social movements of the 1960s and 70s and what, he argues, is a consequent fragmentation of the left. Zamora and Behrent (2015) see the origins of this shift being linked to the impact of Foucault. I do not agree and I have suggested that even though he was not addressing neoliberalism Foucault offers a prescient and trenchant critique via his focus on micro-politics and governmentality (see Chapter 6).[36] For my analysis of institutional and personal impacts of neoliberalism, I argue that both class analysis and a micro-politics that includes identity politics, including one's identity as a health and care worker, are needed. Let's have both, not either/or. It is precisely because neoliberalism fosters intensified individualism and a pervasive sense of competition, each with all, that affirming the relational aspects of our lives and asserting that individuals can act in concert to challenge systems of oppression becomes so important.[37] As to the wanting both sorts of analysis, Foucault's genealogy (see Foucault 1970 and 1972) offers a justification, "Genealogy as critique stands in opposition to the scientific hierarchization of knowledge about human beings and social relations and the effects intrinsic to their associated technologies of power" (Smart 1985: 62).

But the capacity to engage with the relational is not immune to the changes that accompany neoliberalism. Holloway (2010) highlights how an opposition between the capitalist labour we undertake in our jobs and the drive towards doing what we consider necessary or desirable creates a system full of ruptures, cracks in the logic of social cohesion. These cracks create spaces, or moments, in which we live out our dream of being human. Mason (2019) contemplates preserving what makes us human in an age of uncertainty, he tells us we can use language, innovation and cooperation to shape our future. But we can also shape our future through the expression of solidarity and the action of resistance. What binds people together is common struggles for social change. Such struggles enable people to reach out beyond their own identities and give meaning to civic solidarity. It is through such social struggles that we can define what common goals should be, and what we mean by the common good (Malik 2017).

Has neoliberalism gone?

My position on this question, addressed in previous chapters, has been a confident "too early to tell". I return to the question in this section as I contemplate new politics and then (below) specific agendas for change, I want to be clear what the incumbent system, the target for change, is. The case for neoliberalism's demise rests on two main arguments: first, it has been replaced by populism and second, and this specifically links to the responses to the Covid-19 pandemic, it has been replaced by the re-assertion of interventionist states.

I have argued in Chapter 2 that the recent shift to populism is akin to further stage of neoliberalism. We also need to distinguish between different types of populism. In the UK the Conservative Election victory of 2020 was achieved by an appeal to protectionism and exceptionalism, characteristics of populist policies, via the Brexit agenda. But despite pushing that agenda through there remained a caution about the need to keep the alliance of voters that had been assembled under the Brexit rubric together. The arrival of Covid-19 found an insecure populist government that seemed unable to make decisions that would upset people.[38] The resulting hesitancy and delay were instrumental in the very high Covid-19 death rate in the UK. The legacy of neoliberalism was also key to the problems in assembling an effective response – austerity, privatisation, the running down of public health and local government, and the manifestation of Covid-19 as a neoliberal epidemic was evidenced by the differential rates of death in different social groups, replicating long-term inequalities that had, in themselves, been exacerbated by neoliberalism (all of this is considered in earlier sections of this book). An emerging literature on the pandemic, including Horton (2020), MacKenzie (2020) and Calvert and Arbuthnott's (2021) offer damming assessments of the British Government's response to the pandemic, assessments in marked contrast to the populist exceptionalism that characterised the governments highly selective self-serving cheer-leading about their record.

In the US, there was a much more aggressive populism, President Trump may have wished to keep the coalition of support that led to his electoral success together but his stance was to lead the agenda, to tell the people not just what they want but what was "true". The America First / Make America Great Again, agenda of exceptionalism was manifest in denial as to the nature and seriousness of the Covid-19 pandemic. The result was a similar high death rate, albeit behind the UK in deaths per head of the population.

In the UK the same governing party responsible for the shortcomings in the response to Covid will have to manage the recovery. There has been considerable short-term commitment to public spending to support the economy during the pandemic but as yet no clear indication as to the stance that will shape post-pandemic recovery. In contrast in the US a new administration will manage the recovery and here there are clear early signs of a shift in direction.

US President Biden's public spending plans – long-term investment in jobs, education and clean energy and an insistence on the social responsibilities of big business point to this being "a watershed in American economic policy making". He is changing the conversation: "Economically, the essential, leading role of the state has been forcefully reasserted" (Comment: *The Observer* 11/04/2021: 44). There are some similarities with Roosevelt's New Deal in the 1930s – a comparison spurred by a recovery package after Covid-19 of $2.3 trillion to boost the economy. When the proposed Federal Budget for 2022 was outlined it included new Federal spending on healthcare and early years education, together with green technologies and scientific research. President Biden has also proposed a global minimum corporation tax rate, this would prevent big companies shifting profits around the world – so allowing the US (and other countries who support this proposal) to benefit from tax on multinationals. "Washington has turned away from years of economic orthodoxy that stretched back to the early 1980s and prioritised a neoliberal world vision – of free-market competition, government indifference and unblinking advocacy of globalisation." "Neoliberalism's divisive grip is at last being broken; free market dogmas are in retreat. Biden is re-legitimising the power of government and the state to equally serve all its citizens" (Leader: *The Observer* 11/4/2021: 56).

As I write, President Biden's initiatives are in their early stages, they are likely to encounter opposition in the US legislature and elsewhere, the UK may yet return to free-market neoliberal politics and neoliberalism or populism remains dominant in many parts of the world.[39] The Covid-19 pandemic has shifted the debate on the role of the state, including on the extent and nature of public spending. It may have altered our attitudes to the NHS and the Care sector, and it may have a lasting impact on the social contract. Or it may represent an interlude and, when the exigencies of the crisis have retreated, we will return to the market orthodoxies and austerity that preceded its arrival. If there is a permanent (or at least long-term) shift then this book captures a generational, 40-year, cautionary tale about the consequences of an economic and political orthodoxy prevalent across much of the world and its intended and unintended consequences. If Covid is an interlude then the issues the book raises remain urgent, then it is not so much a lament as a call to arms.

If I answered the question "has neoliberalism gone?" with a cautious "too soon to tell" the same goes for populism. It remains widespread across the world and it is clear that populists, in their different guises, are capable of learning from others and making the sorts of changes that allow them to survive, and in some cases thrive. At the same time, the populist approach of reducing "political issues to questions of belonging, and then attack those who are said not to belong" (Müller

2021: 24) can be extended to new groups or used to deflect concerns about governmental performance elsewhere, in 2021 in the UK heightened rhetoric about people seeking to enter the UK by crossing the Channel in small boats can push concerns about governmental performance in the response to Covid-19 from the front pages.[40] (See Box 9.2 on longer-term shifts and Box 9.3 on locating change in historical time.)

Even if neoliberalism' time is up, the residue of its power to structure attitudes and behaviours will last longer than the primacy of its economic manifestation – just as old ways of thinking survived well past the first economic ascendancy of neoliberalism. Market values and reasoning have reached into spheres of life previously governed by non-market norms, including child-rearing, health, education, and civic life. There is considerable evidence that commodification, putting a good or service up for sale, can corrode the value of the activity being priced (see Sandel 2020) and the impact of this commodification's encroachment into health care and the invidious erosion of our lifeworld and social contract that accompanies it will not be reversed overnight. William Faulkner in his novel *Requiem for a Nun* (1951) said, "The past is not dead. In fact, it's not even past".

Box 9.2: The arc of history

Is there an arc of history – a progression in which we can see the future by projecting present trends? The "if present trends continue" teleological view of history, is for some (the Fukuyama of the late 1980s and early 1990s for example), a progression towards a steady state. President Obama has a longer terms view, like Martin Luther King, seeing the arc of history as inclining to justice (see Chapter 2). I have been describing a recent period of history, a generation, in which neoliberalism has been dominant. This may be coming to an end; the rise of populism may indicate this. Or populism may be best seen as a continuing, late stage, of neoliberalism in which some of the priorities of the previous years have been shuffled. But if we look at more recent history, the last few years, this is at best dialectic and at worst chaotic.

> Present trends don't continue they produce backlashes and reshufflings of the social deck. The identities that people embrace today are identities their children will want to escape from tomorrow. History is somersaults all the way to the end. That's why it's so hard to write, and so hard to predict. Unless you're lucky.
>
> (Menand 2018: 68)

In the nineteenth-century Hegel said, "We learn from history that we do not learn from history", and "What experience teaches us is that people and governments have never learned anything from history or acted on principles deduced from it" (1832).

Box 9.3: The end of eras

Fin de siècle phenomenon and Interregnums.

Why did the triumph of neoliberalism, and the drastic change it offered, occur around the early 1980s? Perhaps it's a phenomenon of the end of centuries, a fin de siècle manifestation. The problem with it beginning in the early 1980s is solved if we go along with Eric Hobsbawm (1994) who says, "the short twentieth century finished in 1991". *(In 1991 – fall of Berlin Wall, the break-up of the Soviet Union: 1990 Nelson Mandela released from prison – President of South Africa from 1994.)*

Interregnums and their accompanying problems.

Hermann Hesse, writing in the 1920s, said,

> Every age, every culture, every custom and tradition has its own character, its own weakness and its own strength, its beauties and cruelties; it accepts certain sufferings as matters of course, puts up patiently with certain evils. Human life is reduced to real suffering, to hell, only when two ages, two cultures and religions overlap…. Now there are times when a whole generation is caught in this way between two ages, between two modes of life and thus loses the feeling for itself, for the self-evident, for all morals, for being safe and innocent.
>
> (Hesse 1965: 28)

Antonio Gramsci, whose "Prison Diaries" were written between 1929 and 35, said that "the old world is dying, and the new world struggles to be born: now is the time of monsters". Interregnums are times when a great variety of morbid symptoms appear. (Gramsci 1971).

Hannah Arendt (2018) has talked about shifts in social mood, tipping points. She describes how in Germany in the 1920s and 30s it was fashionable to see how "wicked" you could be, after 1933 nobody joked about being wicked.

Likewise, the hostility to "others" that is the hallmark of authoritarian populists is not restricted to the groups initially targeted, the illegal migrant, the unemployed and the unproductive for example, but spreads to a more generalised attitude towards the "other". Nuance is one casualty. You are either with us or against us, if you have opinions we disagree with you are ipso facto a bad person. Nuance is learned, small children do not have it and once learned it needs to be exercised.[41] If a whole society is being presented with a discourse characterised by haranguing, civilisation is damaged (see Elias 2000). Kate Manne, in the context of discussing misogyny, has described the phenomena of "trickle-down aggression" (Manne 2019; 2021). It fits well here. It infuses our public realm and influences our sociality, and it does not quickly change.

Specific proposals for different systems

I have looked at suggestions about replacing the hegemony of market economies (and neoliberalism) and promoting a new economics and new politics. But, while retaining this big picture focussed on replacing, there are various routes to mitigation that can be considered. Mitigating the impact of finance capitalism, shifting the focus of markets and changing how we value the individual can produce meaningful change that is not a diversion from the more radical needs for replacing, it can offer examples of effective action that can energise further change.

Seeking focussed changes, and then going further, is also a route to the culture change that is the recurring refrain of reports into shortcomings in care. It's an approach that is about praxis, transformation achieved by human action on the social world (Gramsci 1971). Prioritising action over thought allows us to break free of the shackles created by a governmentality that makes us think that what is must be. Sometimes these sorts of actions can be focussed on replicating something that has worked before or worked elsewhere, not everything needs to be new. Sometimes change requires our thinking outside the conventions of our familiar disciplines. Just like a hammer thinks all solutions need a nail we are restricted by overly replicating only what we are used to.[42]

But praxis needs us to act together – change needs to be led by people not done to people (see Ryan 2019). It also needs action to be widespread, for example changing to a paradigm that insists health should be everybody's concern and nobody's business. The approach being contested, neoliberalism/populism, is one that undermines solidarity, both between us as individuals, within states and between states.

Unregulated markets deepen polarisations of human conditions and life prospects, they generate insecurity, alienation and loneliness, and they impact on our subjectivities and weaken the social contract. The imposition of the essentially anti-communal patterns of the consumer market and the characteristic neoliberal withdrawal of the state pushes the task of resolving socially produced problems onto the shoulders of individual men and women while at the same time privileging companies that can use these conditions to make a profit.

The modern nation state can mitigate the impact of markets, including via welfare states. But feral financial capitalism can't be fought by a retreat into, "the supposed sovereignty of long-since hollowed-out nation states…". Globalisation is putting finance and markets beyond the reach of the nation state. What is needed is "a supranational form of co-operation that pursues the goal of shaping a socially acceptable political reconfiguration of economic globalisation" (Habermas 2017: 26).

A shift from conditionality in welfare

The welfare state can be reconfigured by a shift from conditionality in welfare to universal benefits. Conditionality can increase inequalities and it can set one group against another, pitting the young against the old or the migrant against the indigenous for example. Universal benefits foster a sense of collective belonging as opposed to conditional benefits which sees you getting benefits because of some shortcoming on your part that has been so defined by someone else.[43] This would mark a shift in the meaning of the relationship of the individual to each other and to the state. Bauman calls the welfare state the social state, and argues that calling it this, shifts the emphasis from material gains to the principal of their provision (see 1999: 184–185).[44]

Communalities and solidarity

Israeli architect Eyal-Weizman has described, "a politics of verticality - the defeated are being literally overseen and undermined" (see Berger 2007: 63). While he is discussing verticality in the context of the nation state, it is an image resonant of the position of the sick and dying in the hospitals where there have been breakdowns in care and more generally in health and care provision when the needs of the institution (or of the government) are prioritised over the needs of the patients, where care is treated as a business and those receiving care as a second order concern. The alternative is a politics of horizontality, a narrative of communalities built around empathy for the sick and weak.

   We also need to help people feel "grounded in the vertigo of change" by emphasising the strength of plurality. "The People, as a subject, first needs to be constructed before individuals become capable of collective action" (Saxer 2017: 17). One place the people can be constructed is in the agora.[45] Bauman wants us to focus on this rather than on social power or private misery (Bauman 1999: 87). The depredation of Parliament as our public square of politics should not distract us from the potential for meeting, talking and acting together. We are not, for example, welfare customers we are citizens of a social state.

Democratisation of capital (and land/property.)[46]

As wealth is concentrated in capital, there needs to be some form of democratisation of capital holding (Muniz 2017: 13), a state-funded national investment bank for example (see Seymour 2017).[47] Another way of changing economic life is through the promotion of social enterprises – putting people and communities ahead of private profit. There are many thousands of such enterprises in the UK and around the world (see Social Enterprise UK)[48]. Business can be part of the social model, not in opposition to it (Lakey 2016). Local Authorities can also shape economic activity within their catchment areas in ways that can substantially shift the fortunes of many. In the UK, Preston in Lancashire developed a policy of community wealth building (first developed in Cleveland in the US). This involved developing worker co-ops, procuring services from local suppliers, incubating local businesses and paying the "living-wage" (greater than the statutory minimum wage). More wealth was generated in the city and more of that wealth stayed in the city. By 2020 Preston had achieved its highest employment rate and lowest levels of economic inactivity for more than 15 years and, in 2018, it was voted the UK's most improved city to live and work in (Brown and Jones 2021.)

Prioritise something other than economic growth

This is not a new debate, Aristotle engaged with the question about what the best kind of life is and argues that it is one that uses our reason. Human beings are political animals – we need to be able to live with others, eudaimonia (well-being, a flourishing good spirit, happiness and welfare) can only be achieved in relation to life in society – we live together and need to find our happiness by interacting well with those around us in a well-ordered political state. Happiness is not just about how you feel but about a sense of your overall achievement in life, it is a process and not a destination.[49] It is about good social behaviour, about being a solid citizen.

Happiness and pleasure have been recurring features of our philosophy and politics, for example according to Plato, Socrates thought the only way for a human to flourish was to live a morally virtuous life – this includes a concern for others and a concern for the future. At the end of the eighteenth century, Jeremy Bentham presented the felicific calculus – an algorithm for working out just how much pleasure any specific action was likely to bring, and the US Founding Fathers claimed happiness as an inalienable right in the America Declaration of Independence (Robertson 2020).

There are all sorts of characteristics we can associate with seeking the sort of society in which the pursuit of this sort of happiness is possible, we need a sense of community, an opportunity for intimacy, a sense of place and the stability to pursue the sorts of social contract Aristotle and others are describing. Our neoliberal times are not conducive to this – indeed the idea that rootlessness can be a virtue, exemplified by the global citizen as entrepreneur or speculator, that consumption can be an end and that we progress through competition seem to present barriers to the sort of happiness that is located in collective action and in altruism.

Table 9.4 presents some recent examples, from a long list of possible, of prioritising well-being.

Just change one part of the care system

So many aspects of attempts to improve health care are about improving care in hospitals. But many people in hospitals don't need to be there. It is not just that they need to be discharged sooner, but that many do not need to be in hospital in the first place. The development of alternative care settings and innovations in

Table 9.4 Recognising well-being[50]

New Zealand: Well-being Budget, 2019	Bhutan Happiness Index (since 1971).	Welsh Government's Well-being of Future Generations Act, 2015
This would not be dependent on economic metrics like GDP; instead, it used metrics including human health, safety and flourishing to assess the success of policies. It was accompanied by a set of budget responsibility rules and spending limits. The Treasury had 60 criteria represented in a well-being dashboard. The idea is not to dichotomise health and the economy	Bhutan has sought to use Gross National Happiness rather than Gross Domestic Profit – well-being should take precedence over material growth.	This sets up a legal obligation requiring public bodies to improve social, cultural, environmental and economic well-being – to work with people and communities to prevent persistent problems such as poverty, health inequalities and climate change. The Welsh government also has a "Future Generations Commissioner" whose role includes asking how initiatives undertaken in Wales in the present will impact on the future.

the use of the care workforce would reduce pressure on hospital care (see Zaman et al. 2017). Enhanced public health and preventative measures across the whole population would impact on the prevalence of some illnesses (environmental changes and shifts in behaviour in relation to smoking and diet/exercise would impact on major causes of death like cancers and heart disease for example) and would also reduce the complex comorbidities that can make care even more challenging to provide. Social policy changes, improved housing, for example would make care outside hospital more possible (Clark and Whitelaw 2017). Kellehear (1999 and 2005) has developed an influential reimagining of palliative care as public health and as a factor in promoting social change via the idea of Compassionate Cities/Communities (referred to in Chapter 8).

Of course, the things about attitudes to the vulnerable that are important in the shortcomings of hospitals can still be pertinent in other settings, including in the community, and it's also true that the best equipped and best staffed hospitals would still be distressing for some. But the idea of having alternative sites of care and alternative care practitioners connects with a potential historical change, a shift from the industrial being lauded as modern and aspirational towards the bespoke (from Fordist to post-Fordist care) (see Small 2023).

These sorts of changes in care also allow for a change in the dynamic of the relationship between carer and cared for, a shift from compliance to concordance – the former is passive – the latter is active and its implications are collaborative.

Concordance requires shared decision making that respects the wishes and beliefs of the patient, it doesn't come easily it's not just about listening, it's also
about understanding the personal, social and cultural system the other party is
experiencing.

Fordist organisational settings and care focussed on seeking compliance are factors that help shift care into the narrow rationalisation of a system world imperative. The shift is a manifestation of the impact of neoliberalism. But post-Fordism
and care inspired by concordance present us with a domain that can be used to
contest and potentially to negate rationalisation in favour of solidarity, imagination and spontaneity. The expression of those elements of culture that I have
discussed in Chapter 8 – care, dignity, compassion –may be a sort of negation,
they can be examined as places of solidarity, structured around a communicative
experience that is characterised by spontaneity and imagination. They can reassert freedom and expand the scope for meaningful personal action. As such, they
can sustain the lifeworld and support the operation of personal choice.[51]

Change work

Continuing with the potential to effect a change in care by changing work, Jon
Cruddas (2021) advocates for a "good work covenant" – why should we not agree
and support the idea that all labour should be both fulfilling and a source of self-
esteem? He suggests national colleges for skilled work – this could help turn social
care into the respected and well-rewarded vocation it should be. In addition, we
could establish works councils and worker directors (as is done in Germany and
Denmark). Cruddas sees such reforms as a way of renewing a sense of communal
ties and fostering a common ethical life, a reinvigoration of the social contract.
This, he argues, could be part of a post-pandemic restructuring of care.

Is it worth thinking about reclaiming and repairing bits of the care system?

There is a danger that after the long and detailed critique of what is wrong that
makes up much of this book the ideas for what can be done feels thin, a little dis-
appointing even. It is a disappointment I have felt in other books that are strong
on diagnosis and not on prescription.[52] In effect, my long critique will have made
my reader aware that many things would be put right if we abandoned neoliberalism (unless we simply replaced it with the populism that we have seen gain ground
across the world in recent years). My strong preference is to consign neoliberalism
to the dustbin of history rather than send it to the Repair Shop[53] to be patched
up and made to look more presentable. But some problems are attributable to
things that were in place before neoliberalism and, in my next section, I will
look at this. Further, my consideration of ethics, economics, politics and specific
focussed changes in parts of the care system reflects another theme of this book.
I have been concerned with large-scale change but also with small narratives
and contingent meanings, with local action and with change by doing – praxis.

Structural change can shift the parameters of the possible, personal change can follow the realisation that acting to put right wrongs, or to build better, shifts our subjectivities. Putting the two sorts of change together may be a proxy for describing the elusive idea of what culture change is, an idea that threads through all the examples I have considered.

What are the most important changes?

I have talked about the thesis that the mode of production determines the characteristics of our social being and that social being determines consciousness. But I allowed myself the headroom to say, "in the last instance" and so retained the space to explore complexity and uncertainty. Even if a forensic scrutiny can usually unearth the class dimension inherent in social divisions like gender, ethnicity and age these divisions have different sites of operation, different organising categories, they act on bodies differently and govern both our subjectivities and our temporality in different ways. Our attitudes are shaped by an intersection of our economic position and the layering of other social divisions. So too are social attitudes, for example an idea that a person, or group of people, is economic unproductive and a drain on the employed combines a perverse understanding of economic worth with the stereotyping as "of little value or importance" whole categories of people. My examples from Stafford and the LCP in Chapter 1[54] reflects the divisions of age – spinning the old into inferiorised positions – a process of "othering" that makes mistreatment or neglect more possible. Further, the social division of gender is evident in the nature of the elderly patient population, predominantly female, and in the distribution of jobs in hospitals which locates women in many of the more precarious jobs. Deaths in the UK Covid-19 pandemic have disproportionally impacted on people from minority ethnic groups, a pattern replicated in deaths of NHS personnel from Covid-19. This provides a clear example of the clustering of risk, precarious jobs where you are reluctant to take time off even if you feel unwell or if someone in your household is unwell, patient and public facing roles that increase exposure to risk, a home environment which may be more crowded than the average household, more inherent co-morbidities reflecting long-term inequalities in the patterns of ill-health in the population and a higher representation of minority ethnic workers in parts of the country that are economically disadvantaged, that disadvantage being a predictive factor for higher rates of Covid-19.

Having a more complex assessment of what the most important determinates are does not negate my argument that it is neoliberalism that we should look to, in the first instance, to understand both the structural and behavioural dimension of breakdowns in care. But neoliberalism does not determine everything. Any given conjuncture represents, rather, the fusion "into a ruptural unity" of an ensemble of economic, social, political and ideological factors where "dissimilar currents... heterogeneous class interests... contrary political and social strivings fuse" (Althusser 1969: 99: quoted in Hall et al. 2013: 12).

My focus has been on neoliberalism and the rise of a new populism over the last 40 years. But other forces are at play in shaping our public services and need to be considered. Neoliberalism was a further, and particularly marked, example of the paradox of capitalism. Hutton put it this way, "Economic growth parasitic upon growing social disarray and exclusion is ultimately neither sustainable nor worthwhile" (Hutton 1996: 342–343), but the idea that the pursuit of surplus value (profit) is achieved for owners from the labour of workers and that this is *ipso facto* exploitative and alienating has a long history. The factory system of the industrial revolution was parasitic on the social upheaval that saw the growth of the industrial cities and of child labour. "The major force for change in Western capitalist societies is, first the development of capitalism and industrialisation and then the move from industrialism to post-industrialism. Compared to these shifts everything else is just ripples on the surface" (Pettersson 2017: 5). Over a now prolonged period when workers moved from the assembly line to the service sector the way the economy works changed, the capacity for trade unions to organise, the distribution of power in society, self-identity (as a worker) and the nature of our politics changed alongside it.[55]

Alongside the shift from industrial to post-industrial society we see a shift to what Touraine (2001) and others have called a communications society. Zuboff (2019), who I have introduced in Chapter 2), goes further as she depicts a surveillance society. The shift either to communications or surveillance as an organising construct has two main consequences for my argument: first, it further expands power over subjective states; second, it elevates the power of multinational tech companies.[56] These two consequences come together in a marketisation of lived experience. To oppose the deleterious consequences of communication society you need to address not just material power and political power but also the values which have accompanied them, specifically an assumption that improving the reach and speed of communications and human advance go together. Faster and easier ways of spreading around information do not *per se* mean we are communicating with everyone or that we are improving understanding. There is a danger in looking too much to the numerated. In so doing we lose the input of felt experience, we lose the sensible in favour of the (narrowly defined) intelligible.[57]

Over and above the arguments about economic changes and shifts to communication/surveillance societies there is a more general narrative about the importance of locating what is happening with neoliberalism. The accumulation of crises and the shortcomings of attempts to respond to them mean that there is nothing fixed enough to prevent things spinning apart.[58] Is neoliberalism now falling apart beneath the financial crisis which showed the stupidity of deregulation, increasing inequalities, evidence on how unremitting competition produces anxiety, distrust and loneliness, and the need for state intervention in the economy on a massive scale in response to the Covid-19 pandemic.[59] The crisis occurs when social disarray and exclusion increases but economic growth is stalled or reversed. Then it's more pain for the poor and vulnerable and less gain for others (not all – some speculators can still get rich). Crises (like recession) and disasters (like climate change and the Covid-19 pandemic) are illustrations rather than aberrations of prevailing institutional rationalism in practice. They are not an abnormal or perverted digression in the present phase of the unrolling of western rationality; crisis and disaster are the primary and ordinary illustrations of it (see Bauman 1989).

Crises can signal the end of eras, or they can see the regrouping of the existing prevailing hierarchies and a reassertion of their dominance, albeit with some modifications – one of which might be the populist turn that I have described earlier as a further (possibly final) stage of neoliberalism (see Chapter 2).

One manifestation of populism is an upsurge of public nationalism.[60] This reflects the tension between the nation and globalisation if we characterise the latter as something that leads directly to the destruction of tradition and customs (Habermas 1976). The invocation of a nation involves a structuring of consciousness which is capable of colonising and making sense of definitions of what is normal, appropriate or possible (Wright 1985: 142). Populism "demands an ever-deepening source of cultural meaning to legitimate itself" (Wright 1985: 141) and the NHS is a key referent that can be drawn into the cultural meaning populism seeks. Its position as beleaguered but heroic in responding to Covid-19 was accompanied by wartime metaphors and assertions of UK exceptionalism. Invoking the modern past in this way can insert the contemporary NHS, with its market mechanisms, into being part of a new incorporation of national heritage in the interests of contemporary hierarchies.

A book by Patrick Wright's, published in 1985, begins with his reflecting on Margaret Thatcher becoming Prime Minister in 1979 but it is not a book about neoliberalism or the NHS or, of course, about the latest upsurge of populist politics. It is a book about the way history itself has become a powerful source of what it means to be British. Using the past in the interest of the present power structure perpetuates existing political domination. But invoking the aura of a modern past can also be a radical option. If we do not allow the powerful to claim the past we can assert a peoples' history and speak against rationalised experience. We can

> pose the question of an unalienated rationality and of a social experience in which to be human is to be a personality as a whole rather than the subordinate or merely specialised subject of so much modern activity. The modern past may certainly invoke a different relationship between freedom and necessity or between imagination and technical knowledge, just as it may also project a broader circumference of personal action than is available in the manipulating and procuring of so much everyday activity under the modern division of labour.
>
> (Wright 1985: 254)

We don't want wistful invocations of the past – but we do need sufficient respect to extract past intentions and transpose them to the action of the present (Wright 1985: 140). The NHS and the Welfare State are not the neoliberals or populist's property – they are institutions and philosophies with firmer roots that cling on to solidarity and altruism and can do better to mobilise these qualities in the interests of the marginalised now and in the future.

Notes

1 Jeremiah, the weeping prophet, is important in Judaism, Christianity and Islam and his lamentations are the origins of the word "jeremiad" – a long mournful complaint, a list of woes.

2 Robinson's identifying a recent erosion of a sense of personal responsibility sees neoliberalism as different from earlier encouragement of economic activity consequent upon the impact of Protestantism. Max Weber's thesis (Weber 2010, first published 1905) is that Protestantism retained an exacting personal obligation to seek the good of others (Robinson 2017). It may have been small comfort for those working in the satanic mills of the industrial revolution that the mill owner prayed each Sunday for the souls of his workers.

3 I have argued in Chapter 2 that populism is a manifestation of the later stages of neoliberalism, not quite its death throes but a signifier of some of its internal contradictions. We are in territory that has been explored in the analyses of previous hegemonic structures, Lenin seeing imperialism as "the highest (final) stage of capitalism", for example where the dynamics of the economy requires seeking out new markets, secured by conquest, to meet its rapacious need for growth (Lenin [1917] 2010).

4 See Chapter 8.

5 I couldn't resist this metaphor, but I have been arguing that neoliberalism is not characterised by much heart!

6 Slavoj Žižek (2002) called 9/11 "the end of the American holiday from history".

7 Weintrobe is writing about the climate crisis and about neoliberalism.

8 There is a too easy conflation of these terms – the paradigms, assumptions and antecedents of medicine and of health are not the same – they haven't been ever, see the distinction between Hippocrates and Asclepius in ancient Greece (amongst Asclepius's daughters were Hygieia (Goddess of cleanliness), Panacea (Goddess of universal remedies) and Iaso (Goddess of recuperation from illness). Asclepius's daughters figure large in the Covid-19 pandemic, especially through handwashing and hope that a vaccine will be a panacea. Since then, until now, and into the future medicine and health are different.

9 From the establishment of the NHS in 1948 there have been private providers existing in parallel and benefiting from the NHS, consultants trained by the NHS and working in private hospitals for example.

10 An assessment of "Health gain" is something economists incorporate into their formulations of cost/benefit analysis and quality of life measures.

11 There is a considerable literature on this including *The Year of Magical Thinking* (Didion 2006) and *The Spirit Catches You and You Fall Down* (Fadiman 1997). My own research into epilepsy and how people combine folk/faith-based remedies and western pharmaceuticals constitutes a small contribution to this oeuvre (Small et al. 2005).

12 See Barthes (1982) on "the Punctum", "the wounding, personally touching detail which establishes a direct relationship with the object or person within it".

13 Baudrillard (2002) posits there being a "pure" event that concentrates into itself all the events that have never taken place, we might adapt that to the idea of a pure NHS that we carry despite the empirical or subjective reality that we experience.

14 A GP Dr Harold Shipman was convicted in 2000 for the murder of 15 of his patients. The Shipman Inquiry, chaired by Dame Janet Smith, estimated that the total victim count was likely to be 250 (80% of whom were elderly women) (Smith 2005).

15 The simulacrum has been invoked throughout history to help identify the processes by which the representation of someone or something can be distorted – Plato considered this for example (cave walls and moving images). Much more recently Deleuze (1968) saw the possibilities of using simulacrum to challenge or overturn an accepted ideal or privileged position.

16 Writing about a situation that is still ongoing involves the need to be cautious about what are provisional figures – by Spring 2021 Hungary was doing worst in Europe and countries like Germany that had done well in terms of infection and death rates were now experiencing serious challenges.

17 A prevalent trope is that bringing things out into the open facilitates routes to remedy what is wrong. But Debord wants us to think more about such an assumption.

18 Debord also offers a cure – we need collective eruptions of joy or rage. Both are glimpses of unalienated life, they are anticipatory gestures towards utopia. This is a Situationalist manifesto and is the sort of response to contemporary society that infuses much protest, Extinction Rebellion, Occupy Wall Street, Black Lives Matter and many more (see Reynolds 2022.)

19 Other events have been presented as standing aside from history. In so doing they become a spectacle, hyperreal. Baudrillard and Virilio used similar analysis about the 9/11 attacks in New York and Washington in a much misunderstood and gratuitously vilified analysis (see Baudrillard 2002; Virilio 2002.)

20 Prof Chris Whitty, Chief Medical Officer: Sir Patrick Vallance, Chief Scientific Officer: SAGE – Scientific Advisory Group on Epidemics.

21 I am grateful to my colleague Lisa Milne (Bradford District Care NHS Foundation Trust) for making this point known to me.

22 There are some schools of thought that resolve issues about the balance between individual choice and social determinants in a different way. The existentialist position, according to Søren Kierkegaard is that at the moment we are making a decision about how to live (about what to do and how to be with people) that decision can't be made for us by history, society, religion. Any of these causes might emerge when we try to analyse the course of our lives in retrospect, but my future is my responsibility. This explains "the dizziness of freedom", life can only be understood backwards, but it has to be lived forwards (see Carlisle 2020). Viktor Frankl (2020: from talks given in 1946) said that the last of the human freedoms was to choose one's attitude in any given set of circumstances, to choose one's own way.

23 Philosopher Paul Ricoeur (2007) identified a tension between ethics – the quest for a happy and worthy life – and morality – an obligation to obey certain universal standards of good conduct. The challenge of politics is to resolve these two things. We have to develop ways of treating each other without any guide except a fallible sense of "critical solicitude". This is the way to make just decisions, something which involves, "the art of a fair decision in situations of uncertainty and conflict".

24 This does not mean there is not solidarity amongst the young or the absence of an emerging moral tradition – struggles to address racism and climate change offer powerful examples of emerging understandings of a morally good life.

25 The old Bolshevik Rubashov in Arthur Koestler's *Darkness at Noon* (1964) is presented as someone of whom "Ideology and power have rendered (him) incapable of independent moral judgement".

26 The same reservations can be made of public engagement in health care – you can't assume its benign, it may be just another route for the expression of neoliberalist ideology or of right populism.

27 The Covid-19 pandemic generated many homilies – "we are all in the same boat" was one – countered by another, "we are all in the same storm, but we are not all in the same boat".

28 O'Neill (20002) puts the idea of "principled autonomy" at the heart of the way we respond to people we are looking after. This is an autonomy not of individuals but of reason and duty, shared by all human beings, who are all capable of forming such a concept This is the only way to provide a basis for trust not only between individuals but between individuals and institutions.

29 Anyone who has had a discussion with their children around who gets to pick the first slice of cake and resolved this by saying "the cutter doesn't get to choose" has been a bit Rawlsian.

30 This approach is valuable in considering how we care for someone, being "for the other" as a start point would reconcile the need for action with the importance of the primacy of the needs of the person we care for and be with (I have explored this elsewhere in terms of how we care for people with dementia; see Small et al. 2006, 2007).

31 Thrift (2005) discusses how capitalism forms an animate surface to life – there is a "cultural circuit of capitalism" a mechanism for developing new theories of capitalism from within capitalism. The same is the case for its late-life offspring neoliberalism.

32 Jean Fourastié (a French demographer writing in 1979) called the period between the end of the Second World War and the first oil crisis of 1973, "The Golden Age". It was characterised by rising salaries which created demand and led to profit for business, there was organised labour and strong trade unions, Keynesian economics, and voting largely on social class lines – middle-ground parties looked to support social welfare to seek workers votes. But all capitalist economic orthodoxies have winners and losers, workers still sell their labour, owners of capital still take a profit, rentier rewards remain, the labour of the rest of the world was exploited to enrich the masters of capital in the West, this was not a golden age for all.

33 In the UK, the impact of high levels of Government spending in response to the Covid-19 impact on economies have been focussed on supporting workers incomes via furlough schemes and direct support for businesses, for example supporting hospitality via a half-price *Meal Deal* in summer 2020. The *Meal Deal* approach is not really a rekindling of the *New Deal* infrastructure spending that sought to respond to the Depression of the 1920s because it was spending on consumption.

34 See Judt (2007) on the Marshall Plan, implemented at the end of the Second World War, as an example of economic (and international) intervention that had a political agenda, to stop a falling back into totalitarianism.

35 Walter Benjamin said that all truly decisive blows in human history tend to be delivered by "a left hook" (see Bauman 2007: 15). Bauman identified the two defining features of the left in this way: (1) "it is the duty of the community to insure its individual members against individual misfortune" (2) "The left defines a just society as one that is aware that it is not-yet-sufficiently-just…" (2007: 10).

36 Foucault died in 1984 and so was not commenting on the trajectory neoliberalism took. Many significant volumes emerged (or were translated) in the years after his death, for example the volumes arising from his lectures at the College of France, which were delivered in 1978–79, were published in English in 2010, a time span encompassing the neoliberal ascendancy (Foucault 2008, 2010, 2011).

37 Emma Goldman (1869–1940) who, as an anarchist, comes from a different intellectual tradition foregrounds intersubjective relations as the bedrock of and for revolution (see Hemmings 2018.)

38 Was there a tipping point in relation to Covid-19? Initial responses in the UK and in many other neoliberal counties began with either denial or grandiosity (it's not a serious problem and/or we are uniquely able to deal with it) to a sense that there was a danger of being overwhelmed, in the UK this was linked to the demands being made on the NHS.

39 Hall et al. (2013) described three decades of neoliberalism dominating across the world (with a very few exceptions). The banking crisis and credit crunch of 2007–08 and the subsequent economic reverberations of these meant that neoliberalism imploded with toxic debt, credit and interbank lending drying up, declines in output and spending, and rises in unemployment all heralding its demise. Further, when the 2008 crash occurred the predominant response was a bit more neoliberalism, specifically the resort to austerity, a policy which moves the burden of solving the problem to the poorest people. But this obituary was a bit premature, neoliberalism limped on – up to the arrival of the Covid-19 pandemic. It is resilient and may yet re-emerge (or hang on where it is still dominant), perhaps in its hybrid of neoliberalism/populism. There is something of the Jacobean tragedy about this – even after you stab the character (or they stab themselves) they have a lot to say before they finally expire.

40 Numbers attempting to enter the UK illegally were not as high as in many previous years and numbers attempting to enter the UK are lower than numbers entering many other European Union countries.

41 See Oliver Berkman. *The Death of Nuance*. BBC Radio 4 12 Jan 2022.

42 There is a story about the Gallagher brothers, formally of the band Oasis and then very publicly estranged. Noel says of his brother Liam that "he is a man with a fork in a world of soup". This would make an excellent epigram for many of the attempts at changing institutions and individuals described in this book.

43 Alongside this you need negative income taxes/universal basic income/public employment schemes.

44 For example, provide enough financial support to allow people to buy adequate nutritional food and not respond to food poverty by the proliferation of food banks (see Power and Small 2021).

45 The Agora is a gathering place, a place of assembly in Greek City States, it's a place to accommodate the social and political order of the polis. It is not (always) a place of ease – a fear of such spaces manifests in agoraphobia (an open space you can't get out of.) (I have introduced Bauman on the Agora in Chapter 6).

46 In *The Wealth of Nations* (1776), Adam Smith proposed a land value tax as a stabilising force in laissez-faire systems.

47 The Labour Parties' 2017 General Election Manifesto included commitments to renationalise rail, mail, energy and water and to have a social upgrade of Britain's dysfunctional market economy.

48 From 1844 the Rochdale Pioneers used social enterprise to combat the inequities of the industrial revolution using the principles of fairness, equality and community benefit (see Yeo 1988: 28–29). Rochdale in geographically very close to Preston – scene of similar policy intentions in the 2010s and 2020s.

49 See Aristotle's "Nicomachean Ethics" (2009 Edition).

50 There are many other examples including, at a national level (the UAE has a Minister of State for Happiness), organisations with an international reach (The Wellbeing Economy Alliance joins local and global movements that seek to transform the economic system into one that delivers social justice on a healthy planet wellbeingeconomy.com), nationally based organisations (The Equality Trust in the UK seeks to improve quality of life by reducing economic and social inequality-equalitytrust.org.uk: in Denmark there is a Happiness Research Institute, in the UK Oxford University has a Wellbeing Research Centre, the London School of Economics has a Wellbeing Programme that makes the case for measuring national happiness alongside calculations of Gross Domestic Product), many Universities have happiness psychology courses – Bristol, Yale, Berkeley are examples. See the UN's World Happiness Reports – these followed a UN General Assembly resolution in 2011. "Happiness: Towards a Holistic Definition of Development" see www.world.happiness.report.

51 My discussion of care as negation adapts an analysis by Habermas and argues that care may offer the opportunities that he attributed to art. In *Legitimation Crisis* (1976) he discusses bourgeoise art – (for Habermas and the Frankfurt School art is an area of high negation) – only art

> has taken up positions on behalf of the victims of bourgeoise rationalisation. Bourgeoise art has become a refuge for a satisfaction, even if only virtual, of those needs that have become, as it were, illegal in the material life-process of bourgeoise society. I refer her to the desire for a mimetic relation with nature; the need for living together in solidarity outside the group egoism of the immediate family; the longing for the happiness of a communicative experience exempt from imperatives of rationality and giving scope to imagination as well as spontaneity ….
> (Habermas quoted in Wright 1985: 253)

52 There is a section in James Boswell's *The Journal of a Tour to the Hebrides* (1st published in 1786) where he is discussing the approach of his travelling companion Dr Johnson: he

> tells what he observes, and as much as he chooses. If he tells what is not true, you may find fault with him; but though he tells that the land is not well-cultivated, he is not obliged to tell how it may be well cultivated.

He defends his friend against the critics he has, "Here is a man six feet high, and you are angry because he is not seven". But the loyal Boswell has his concerns, "I still think that he had better have given more attention to fewer things, than to have thrown together such a number of imperfect accounts" (Johnson and Boswell 1984: 291).

53 A popular TV series on the BBC sees people bring in much loved heirlooms to be restored by skilled craftspeople. These people are invariably overjoyed with the outcome.

54 The shock of Swift's "Modest Proposal" (1729) has not been surpassed – if society is indifferent to the plight of the poor, if some categories of people are a drain rather than an asset to society, and if there is an obvious route out of this then why not take it? Hence, he arrives at the suggestion that the children of the poor could be sold as food for the rich. Problem solved!

55 There has been a shift from an approach to understanding value from one that sees it linked to a factor of production, specifically labour, to a new approach where it is seen as the value of goods to the consumer, price equates to value. Of note is the capacity of companies to "grow exponentially without creating jobs" (Muniz 2017: 13) (see, e.g., social media and tech companies, Google, Facebook, etc.).

56 In politics the battle for hearts and minds has become a seeking after a mere convergence of opinion. TV ratings have triumphed as politicians' position to first define and then occupy the "centre ground" (a prevalent populist trope) (see Virilio 2002).

57 There is an alternative case made about the benefits of technology. Mason (2016) imagines the collective agency of the technologically empowered and educated populous, allied with a social democratic movement as an alliance to take on the potential for redistributive policy that arises from "technologically efficient" societies. Then a "post-work" society could be characterised by a redistribution of the profits generated by artificial intelligence and algorithms, coupled with an agreed universal basic income. Cruddas (2021) is not convinced, characterising such a view as "techutopianism"

58 I am borrowing from Yeats' *The Second Coming* a poem I have cited in chapter 2. Fintan O'Toole has proposed what he terms the "Yeats Test" – the more quotable Yeats seems to commentators and politicians; the worse things are (referred to in Lynskey 2020: 33.)

59 UK Government borrowing in the first year of the pandemic was at its highest levels since the last year of the Second World War.

60 I have discussed Trump and Brexit – as two manifestations of this in previous sections.

References

Althusser, L. 1969. *For Marx.* Verso.

Arendt, H. 2018. Remembering W H Auden. *The New Yorker*, 3 Dec. (First published 20 Jan 1975), 68–71.

Aristotle. 2009. *Nicomachean Ethics* (Ed Brown, J) Oxford.

Barthes, R. 1982. *Camera Lucida.* Jonathen Cape Ltd.

Baudrillard, J. 1993. *Symbolic Exchange and Death.* London, Sage.

Baudrillard, J. 2002. *The Spirit of Terrorism.* Verso.

Bauman, Z. 1989. *Modernity and the Holocaust.* Cambridge, Polity Press.

Bauman, Z. 1993. *Postmodern Ethics.* Oxford, Blackwell.

Bauman, Z. 1999. *In Search of Politics.* Stanford, CA, Stanford University Press.

Bauman, Z. 2000. *Liquid Modernity.* Polity.

Bauman, Z. 2007. Has the future a left? *Soundings*, 35, Spring 8–15. Berger, J. 2007. *Hold Everything Dear.* London, Verso.

Best, S., Kellner, D. 1991. *Postmodern Theory.* Basingstoke, Macmillan.

Calvert, J., Arbuthnott, G. 2021. *Failures of State: The Inside Story of Britain's Battle with Coronavirus.* Mudlark.

Carey, K. 2017. *Fake News: How Propaganda Influenced the 2016 Election, A Historical Comparison to 1930s Germany.* Marzenhale Publishing.

Carlisle, C. 2020. *Philosopher of the Heart.* Penguin.

Carney, M. 2020. From moral to market sentiments. *The Reith Lectures: Lecture 1.* BBC Radio 4 2/12/20.

Carney, M. 2021. *Value(s): Building a Better World for All.* William Collins.

Case, A., Deaton, A. 2020. *Deaths of Despair and the Future of Capitalism.* Princeton University Press.

Chen, A. 2017. The fake-news fallacy. *The New Yorker*, 4 Sept, 78–83.

Clark, D., Whitelaw, S. 2017. Living well, dying well – the importance of housing. *European Journal of Palliative Care*, 24(5), 199–202.

Cruddas, J. 2021. *The Dignity of Labour.* Polity Press.

Dale, G. 2010. *Karl Polanyi: The Limits of the Market.* Polity.

Deaton, A. 2015. *The Great Escape: Health, Wealth and the Origins of Inequality.* Princeton University Press.

Debord, D. 1995. *The Society of the Spectacle.* New York, Zone Books.

Deleuze, G. 1968. *Difference and Repetition.* Columbia, Columbia University Press.

Deleuze, G., Guattari, F. 1987. *A Thousand Plateau's.* Minneapolis, University of Minnesota Press.

Didion, J. 2006. *The Year of Magical Thinking.* Harper Perennial.

Dodd, S., Preston, N., Payne, S., Walsh, C. 2020. Exploring a new model of end-of-life care for older people that operates in the space between the life world and the healthcare system: a qualitative case study. *International Journal of Health Policy and Management*, 9(8), 344–351.

Dunn, J. 1993. *Western Political Theory in the Face of the Future.* Cambridge University Press.

Elias, N. 2000 2nd Ed. *The Civilising Process.* Wiley Blackwell (originally published in German 1939 and English 1969).

Foucault, M. 1970. *The Order of Things: An Archaeology of the Human Sciences.* New York, Pantheon.

Foucault, M. 1972. *The Archaeology of Knowledge.* New York, Vintage.

Foucault, M. 1994. What is an author? In, Faubion, J.D. (Ed) *Essential Works of Foucault [vol 2]* New York, The New Press.

Foucault, M. 2008. *The Birth of Biopolitics: Lectures at the College de France, 1978–1979.* Palgrave Macmillan.

Foucault, M. 2010. *The Government of Self and Others: Lectures at the College de France 1983–1984.* London, Palgrave Macmillan.

Foucault, M. 2011. *The Courage of Truth (the Government of Self and Others II): Lectures at the College de France 1983–1984.* London, Palgrave Macmillan.

Fadiman, A. 1997. *The Spirit Catches You and You Fall Down.* Farrar, Straus and Giroux, New York.

Faulkner, W. 1951. *Requiem for a Nun.* Random House.

Francis, R. (chair) 2010. Independent Inquiry into Care Provided by Mid Staffordshire NHS Foundation Trust: January 2005 – March 2009: Volume 1. The Stationary Office.

Frankl, V. 2020 (from talks given in 1946) *Yes to Life in Spite of Everything.* Rider.

Freidson, E. 1970. *Professional Dominance: The Social Structure of Medical Care.* Aldine de Gruyter.

Gramsci, A. 1971. *Selections from the Prison Notebooks.* London, Lawrence and Wishart.

Greaves, D., Evans, M. 2001. Medical progress, reason and the imagination. *Journal of Medical Ethics,* 27(2), 57.

Habermas, J. 1976. *Legitimation Crisis.* Heinemann Education.

Habermas, J. 1984. *The Theory of Communicative Action (Vol 1.).* Oxford, Polity Press.

Habermas, J. 1990. *On the Logic of the Social Sciences.* Cambridge Polity Press.

Habermas, J. 2017. For a democratic polarisation: How to pull the ground from under right –wing populism. *Social Europe Journal,* 11, 24–29.

Hall, S., Massey, D., Rustin, M. 2013. *After Neoliberalism? The Kilburn Manifesto.* Soundings.

Hemmings, C. 2018. *Considering Emma Goldman: Feminist Political Ambivalence and the Imaginative Archive.* Duke University Press.

Hegel. 1832. *Lectures on the Philosophy of History. Vol 1* (accessed in the translation by Nisbet H.B. 1975).

Hesse, H. (1965: original in 1927 in Germany) *Steppenwolf.* Penguin, Harmondsworth.

Hobsbawm, E. 1994. *The Age of Extremes: The Short Twentieth Century, 1914–1991.* Abacus.

Holloway, J. 2010. *Crack Capitalism.* Pluto Press.

Horton, R. 2020. *The Covid-19 Catastrophe: What's Gone Wrong and How to Stop It Happening Again.* Polity.

Hutton, W. 1996. *The State We're In.* London, Vintage.

Johnson, S., Boswell, J. 1984. *A Journey to the Western Islands of Scotland and The Journal of a Tour to the Hebrides.* Harmondsworth, Penguin Books. (1st published, separately in 1775 and 1786).

Judt, T. 2007. *Postwar.* London, Pimlico.

Kellehear, A. 1999. *Health Promoting Palliative Care.* Oxford University Press.

Kellehear, A. 2005. *Compassionate Cities.* Routledge.

Kelton, S. 2020. *The Deficit Myth: Modern Monetary Theory and How to Build a Better Economy.* John Murray.

Koestler, A. 1964. *Darkness at Noon.* Penguin Modern Classics.

Lakey, G. 2016. *Viking Economics: How the Scandinavians Got It Right – and How We Can, Too.* Melville House.

Lenin, V.I. [1917] 2010. *Imperialism, the Highest Stage of Capitalism.* Penguin Classics.

Lilla, M. 2018. *The Once and Future Liberal: After Identity Politics.* C. Hurst and Co Publishers.

Lynskey, D. 2020. The apocalyptic appeal of "The Second Coming". *The Guardian*, 30 May, 24–26.

MacIntyre, A. 1981. *After Virtue.* Notre Dame, University of Notre Dame Press. See also 3rd Edition 2007.

MacKenzie, D. 2020. *Covid-19: The Pandemic That Never Should Have Happened and How to Stop the Next One.* Bridge Street Press.

Malik, K. 2017. In a society too short of common goals, identity politics are an imperfect answer. *The Guardian*, 17(09), 36.

Manne, K. 2019. *Down Girl. The Logic of Misogyny.* Penguin.

Mannion, R., Small, N. 2019. On folk devils, moral panics and new wave public health. *International Journal of Health Policy and Management*, 8(12), 678–683.

May, T. 2018. Thinking sociologically in turbulent times. *British Sociological Association News.* https://www.britsoc.co.uk/about/latest-news/2018/september/thinking-sociologically-in-turbulent-times/.

Mazzucato, M. 2014. *The Entrepreneurial State.* Penguin.

Mazzucato, M. 2019 (2nd Ed). *The Value of Everything: Making and Taking in the Global Economy.* Penguin.

Mazzucato, M. 2020. *Mission Economy: A Moonshot Guide to Changing Capitalism.* Allen Lane.

Mason, P. 2016. *Postcapitalism.* Penguin.

Mason, P. 2019. *Clear Bright Future: A Radical Defence of the Human Being.* Allen Lane.

McCarthy, J. 2003. Principlism or narrative ethics: Must we choose between them? *Medical Humanities*, 29, 65–71.

Menand, L. 2018. What identity demands. *The New Yorker*, 3 Sept, 64–68.

Merleau-Ponty, M. [1945] 2002. *The Phenomenology of Perception.* Routledge.

Monbiot, G. 2017. *Out of the Wreckage: A New Politics for an Age of Crisis.* Verso.

Müller, J-W. 2021. Populism in a pandemic. *The Guardian*, 18 Sept, 24–25.

Muniz, M. 2017. Popularism and the need for a new social contract. *Social Europe Journal*, 11, 10–13.

Nagel, T. 2021. Types of intuition. *London Review of Books*, 3 June, 3–8.

Newdick, C., Danbury, C. 2015. Culture, compassion and clinical neglect: Probity in the NHS after Mid Staffordshire. *Journal Medical Ethics*, 41, 956–962.

O'Neill, O. 2002. *Autonomy and Trust in Bioethics.* Cambridge University Press.

Pettersson, K. 2017. Without social democracy, capitalism will eat itself. *Social Europe Journal*, 11, 4–9.

Polanyi, K. [1944] 2002 (2nd Ed). *The Great Transformation.* Farrar and Rinehart (Beacon Press 2nd Ed 2002).

Popay, J., Williams, G. 1996. Public health research and lay knowledge. *Social Science and Medicine*, 42(5), 759–768.

Power, M., Small, N. 2021. Disciplinary and pastoral power, food and poverty in late-modernity. *Critical Social Policy.* Vol 42, Issue 1. https://doi.org/10.1177/0261018321999799.

Rawls, J. 1971. *A Theory of Justice.* Harvard University Press.

Raworth, K. 2018. *Doughnut Economics: Seven Ways to Think Like a 21st Century Economist.* Random House Business.

Reynold, S. 2022. Serious Mayhem. *London Review of Books*, 10 Mar, 19–24.

Ricoeur, P. 2007. *Reflections on the Just.* University of Chicago Press.

Robertson, R. 2020. *The Enlightenment: The Pursuit of Happiness.* Allen Lane.

Robinson, M. 2017. *What Are We Doing Here? Essays*. Virago.

Rogan, T. 2018. *The Moral Economists: R.H. Tawney, Karl Polanyi, E.P. Thompson, and the Critique of Capitalism*. Princeton University Press.

Rose, N. 1999. (2nd Ed) *Governing the Soul: The Shaping of the Private Self*. London, Free Association.

Ryan, F. 2019. *Crippled: Austerity and the Demonisation of Disabled People*. Verso.

Sandel, M.J. 2020. *The Tyranny of Merit*. Allen Lane.

Saxer, M. 2017. Ten theses for the fight against right-wing popularism. *Social Europe Journal*, 11, 14–17.

Scambler, G. 2001. *Introduction to, Habermas, Critical Theory and Health*. London, Routledge.

Schubert, J.D. 2013. Suffering/symbolic violence. In, Grenfell, M. (Ed) *Pierre Bourdieu Key Concepts* (179–194), Routledge.

Schwartz, A.B. 2016. *Broadcast Hysteria: Orson Welles's War of the World and the Art of Fake News*. Hill and Wang.

Sen, A. 1970. *Collective Choice and Social Welfare*. Elsevier Science.

Seymour, R. 2017. *Corbyn: The Strange Rebirth of Radical Politics*. Verso.

Small, N., Downs, M., Froggatt, K. 2006. Improving end-of-life-care for people with dementia – the benefits of combining UK approaches to palliative care and dementia care. In, Miesen, M.L., Jones, G.M.M. (Eds) *Care Giving in Dementia* (pp. 365–392). Routledge.

Small, N., Froggatt, K., Downs, M. 2007. *Living and Dying with Dementia*. Oxford, Oxford University Press.

Small, N., Ismail, H., Rhodes, P., Wright, J. 2005. Evidence of cultural hybridity in responses to epilepsy amongst Pakistani Muslims living in the UK. *Chronic Illness*, 1(2), 165–177.

Smart, B. 1985. *Michel Foucault*. Ellis Horwood.

Smith, A. [1776] 1996. *The Wealth of Nations*. Penguin Classics.

Smith, D.J. 2005. *The Shipman Inquiry: Safeguarding Patients: Lessons from the Past – Proposals for the Future*. The Stationary Office.

Steiner, G. 1997. *Errata: An Examined Life*. London, Weidenfeld and Nicolson.

Stewart, K. 2007. *Ordinary Affects*. Durham, NC, Duke University Press.

Swift, J. [1729]. 2021. *A Modest Proposal*. Independently Published.

Tawney, R.H. [1920]. 2019. *The Acquisitive Society*. Wentworth Press.

Tawney, R.H. [1926]. 2012. *Religion and the Rise of Capitalism*. Aakar Books.

Tawney, R.H. [1931]. 1965. *Equality*. Harper Collins.

Thrift, N. 2005. *Knowing Capitalism*. London, Sage.

Touraine, A. 2001, *Beyond Neoliberalism*. Polity Press.

Virilio, P. 2002. *Ground Zero*. Verso.

Weber, M. (2010: first published 1905) *The Protestant Ethic and the Spirit of Capitalism*. Oxford, Oxford University Press.

Weintrobe, S. 2021. *Psychological Roots of the Climate Crisis*. Bloomsbury Academic.

Welsh Government/ Llywodraeth Cymru, 2015 *Well being of Future Generations Act*. www.gov.wales.

Williams, G., Popay, J. 2013. Lay health knowledge and the concept of the lifeworld. In Scambler, G. (Ed) *Habermas, Critical Theory and Health* (pp. 25–44). Taylor & Francis.

Williams, R. 1958. *Culture and Society 1780–1950*. Penguin, Harmondsworth.

Williams, R. 1977. *Marxism and Literature*. Oxford University Press.

Wright, P. 1985. *On Living in an Old Country*. Verso.

Yeo, S. 1988. *New Views of Co-operation on Working-Class Politics in Britain and Sweden.* Routledge.

Zaman, S., Inbadas, H., Whitelaw, A., Clark, D. 2017. Common or multiple futures for end of life care around the world? Ideas from the 'waiting room of history'. *Social Science and Medicine*, 172, 72–79.

Zamora, D., Behrent, M.C. 2013. *Foucault and Neoliberalism*. Polity Press.

Žižek, S. 2002. *Welcome to the Desert of the Real*. Verso.

Žižek, S. 2004. What Rumsfeld doesn't know that he knows about Abu Ghraib. *Those Times*. 21 May.

Zuboff, S. 2019. *The Age of Surveillance Capitalism: The Fight for. Future at the New Frontier of Power*. Profile Books.

Index

For Product Safety Concerns and Information please contact our EU
representative GPSR@taylorandfrancis.com
Taylor & Francis Verlag GmbH, Kaufingerstraße 24, 80331 München, Germany